LEGACIES

LEGACIES

edited by

Maury Leibovitz
and Linda Solomon

HarperCollins*Publishers*

HarperCollins books may be purchased for educational, business, or sales promotional use. For information, please write: Special Markets Department, HarperCollins Publishers, Inc., 10 East 53rd Street, New York, NY 10022.

FIRST EDITION

Designed by Timothy O'Keeffe

Library of Congress Cataloging-in-Publication Data

Legacies / edited by Maury Leibovitz and Linda Solomon
   p.   cm.
  ISBN 0-06-019045-0 (cloth)
  1. Jewish aged—United States—Literary collections. 2. Jewish aged—United States—Biography. 3. American Literature—Jewish authors. 4. American Literature—20th century. 5. Aged, Writings of the, American. I. Leibovitz, Maury, 1917–1992. II. Solomon, Linda, 1951– .
  PS508. J4L44   1993
  813' . 01089285—dc20   92-56196

93 94 95 96 97 ❖/RRD 10 9 8 7 6 5 4 3 2 1

CONTENTS

Mom and Dad

Grandma and Grandpa

Childhood

Turning Points

War and Remembrance

Heroes and Friends

Passages

EDITOR'S PREFACE

Legacies originated in the mind and heart of the late Dr. Maury Leibovitz, a most extraordinary man. Maury believed that older people have "an undeniable right to live with dignity and joy." Seeking to banish "this feeling of defeat and despair," as he called the common experience of growing old in America, he sponsored a national writing contest for people age sixty and over. Contestants were invited to submit a brief story about their accomplishments, or about pivotal events in their lives, or about the best or funniest thing that ever happened to them, "a story that you would want your grandchildren to know."

We asked for stories, and we got them—more than six thousand of them, from everywhere, about everything. They ranged from the intimate to the epic, from family chatter around the dinner table to the terror of soldiers in battle, from affirmations of the most basic principles of human dignity and justice to the bewildering and painful knowledge that luck, not decency, can determine who lives or dies.

The stories in this book represent just a small sample of the creativity, heart, and style displayed by the writers who entered the Legacies contest. Some of them offer comfort and inspiration. Others challenge us to confront harsh and tragic realities. Still others leave us wiping tears of laughter from our eyes. All of them affirm the dignity of a generation that survived the Depression and two world wars, a generation whose accumulated wisdom is one of our great national resources.

Maury envisioned the Legacies contest as a catalyst for renewed hope and courage among older people and a means of breaking the isolation and silence in which many of them live. Himself seventy-three when he started Legacies, he believed that storytelling is an enduring expression of the human spirit. He also believed strongly in the transformative power not only of telling a story but of *writing* it, crafting it for a reader.

After the contest, Maury sent letters of appreciation to all the participants and asked them what writing their stories had meant to them. To his astonishment, he received more than a thousand replies.

"You ask how the writing of my story affected me," said a Connecticut man. "Is the sky blue? Do the birds sing? Absolutely— it has affected all of my being. I practically wake up smiling, waiting for any challenge to come along." An eighty-one-year-old woman who had tapped "a private place inhabited by remembrance, keepsakes, and dreams" enrolled in a "senior scholar" program in California. A first-time college student, she now walks the campus with "a tenacity that would not have been possible were it not for writing the story of my father." A man from New York was similarly invigorated: "Now that my social status has been elevated from gabby old coot to raconteur, I waddle a little prouder."

After writing her story, one woman had been able "to truly, finally mourn the loss of my late husband." Another called the Legacies office to say that when she wrote about her experiences in a Nazi concentration camp, her wounds finally began to heal. A homeless man who had written a story about his father spoke of searching for "a way to live and die like a man." A woman who had been devastated by the death of her forty-six-year-old daughter found that writing her story helped her "decide to put the past behind and take hold of myself and my tomorrows."

An Arkansas woman's story was "a surprise to my daughters and an eye-opener to my grandchildren. They became aware of me as a person and not just their loving, doting grandmother." An Ohio woman found that writing "helped draw together the strands of my life, which has completely changed," and an Iowa woman "discovered a new depth of life." Also from Iowa came this assessment of Legacies: "Your contest has pulled creativity from us oldsters who sometimes sit around feeling sorry for ourselves and doing nobody any good."

"Your 'Legacy' gave me a new beginning, a new vision, a happier, more constructive life. We went on a weekend writing retreat, all these young people and a no-longer-old me! I feel like kicking up my heels and skipping (at least mentally!)," wrote one New York woman, and another experienced a flood of memories "pounding and hammering away for immediate release, like a crowd of little kids in a small, open doorway, pushing and shoving at the same time—all wanting out first." Perhaps an Arizona woman summed it up best: "If six thousand people feel better because they put something important into writing, we are all winners."

As director of the Legacies project and editor of this book, I have learned a great deal from these writers and their legacy, and I feel honored that they have shared their stories with us. For this invaluable gift of themselves, I thank them all.

I am also grateful to the many other people who helped make this book a reality. Joy Johannessen, our sensational editor at HarperCollins, guided and shaped this collection; without her unfailing enthusiasm and commitment, *Legacies* would never have happened. My teacher and friend Sogyal Rinpoche gave generously of his love and belief in my work, and his guidance sustained me through the making of *Legacies*.

The Legacies project found a gracious home at JASA, the Jewish Association for Services for the Aged. David Stern, Bernard Warach, Roger Meier, Denise George, Gemma Maver, and Carole Baden all made major contributions to the development of Legacies. All profits JASA receives from the sale of this book will be used for programs that support the dignity and autonomy of older people of all religious, racial, and ethnic backgrounds.

There were literally hundreds of volunteers and professionals who lent their time and talents to Legacies. I particularly want to thank Carole Anne McLeod, Frances Goldin, Sydelle Kramer, Kathy Lee, Gerald Siegal, Judy Horne, Peninnah Schram, Mark Kaminsky, Robert Monroe, and Kathleen Teltsch. All these dear people shared Maury's vision and brought their unique richness to the project.

And I thank my family for their constant support. The love and understanding of my husband and our children, of my entire family, has challenged me to extend myself to others, through Legacies.

Finally, I thank Maury Leibovitz, my colleague, my dear friend, for the privilege of watching his vision flower in thousands of stories and thousands of lives, and in this book, which now reaches out to touch a new audience with the art of remembrance.

—LINDA SOLOMON

A Tribute to Maury Leibovitz

Maury Leibovitz loved a good story. Whether he was telling one or listening to one—as he usually was—he loved a good story. His own is one of the best, a fine one, a rare one, a damn good story.

"I believe the essence of life is change," Maury told Betty Friedan when she interviewed him for her new book, *The Fountain of Age*. Change was certainly the essence of Maury's life. He grew up in St. Paul, Minnesota. When he was seven, his father died, and Maury supported his family by working after school. He put himself through the University of Minnesota, graduating at the top of his class, served in World War II as a second lieutenant in the infantry, and then opened an accounting practice in Los Angeles. After a chance restaurant encounter with Armand Hammer, Maury became his consultant and was responsible for some of Hammer's biggest corporate ventures.

At the age of forty-four, Maury closed his hugely successful accounting practice and went to Zurich to study at the Jung Institute. By fifty he had a Ph.D. from the University of Southern California and was teaching psychology. In 1971, after pioneering a number of innovative programs, he persuaded Armand Hammer to invest in the foundering Knoedler Gallery and switched careers again, becoming its president and orchestrating its transformation into one of the world's leading modernist galleries.

This bare outline of Maury's achievements only begins to suggest the passionate intensity that drove this "complex, many-splendored man," as his friend Sam Hunter eulogized him. After his death, Maury's family wrote to friends and colleagues, asking for their remembrances of him. Scores of letters came back, like a chorus of voices singing the song of Maury's life. Over and over the writers spoke of his radiance, his infectious joy, his unstoppable force of will, his warmth and generosity, his profound spirituality, his commitment, in everything he did, "to praise life and the Lord of life." Again and again they described him as "a Renaissance man," someone who lived every minute to the fullest, someone who loved beauty and saw it everywhere—in art, in nature, and most of all in the souls of his fellow human beings.

Maury's insatiable curiosity about people was legendary. He probed with an intensity that left the Grand Inquisitor in the dust, according to Sam Hunter. "He would talk to anyone within ten feet of him," wrote Leonard and Betty Cohn, "and within three sentences would have obtained a complete and accurate psychological profile." Al Vorspan, his cousin, remembers a visit when Maury "took a walk on our country road and passed our taciturn neighboring farmers, who are notorious for their noncommunicativeness. We watched, astonished, as he said, 'Hi there, I'm Maury Leibovitz. How long have you been farming? Where did your parents come from? How can you tell one cow from the other? Do they have names?' They did, and Maury ended up on the side of the road in an engaging conversation with four farmers and seven cows." April and Erol Beker remember the day Maury went for a stroll on a beach in Anguilla; the next time they looked up, he was singing, arms raised to the sky, amidst a circle of dancing children who had materialized around him, seemingly out of nowhere.

Maury died of a heart attack on May 31, 1992. The day before, he supervised the planting of the glorious garden at his Connecticut home, dispensing advice, exuberantly calling out, "More blue! More yellow!" That evening he finished a painting, one he considered his best work. The next morning he looked out at the garden and said, "What a beautiful view! A beautiful day!" I am uncomfortably aware that I may be making Maury sound too good to be true. He wasn't. He was simply as good and as true as they come.

Maury Leibovitz loved a good story. In living his life as he did, he left behind a hell of a story. In sponsoring the Legacies project—perhaps the closest to his heart of all the causes he embraced—he left us thousands more stories, stories that join his and circle it, singing and dancing around him, celebrating the human journey in all its possibility. As Maury told Betty Friedan, "The adventure continues and will continue as long as the energy flows." The energy of Maury's lifework—his endless and manifold encouragement of the gifts of those around him, in projects like Legacies, in his very being—still flows, abundantly, joyously, ceaselessly. The adventure indeed continues.

—CAROLE ANNE MCLEOD
The Leibovitz Foundation

Mom and Dad

Potatoes and Point

Joe Lieberman

It was a perfect potato year. Just enough moisture, nice hot sun, and the potato bug skipped us by. Farmers were singing and loading potatoes high all over the county, everybody full of cheer, adding up the cash money those potatoes would bring.

But when we came to market, the price dropped faster than a hot potato from the palm of your hand. Farmers harvested and marketed quick as they could, but each truckload brought less and less, till the cost of harvesting was more than the price offered. The farmers stopped picking.

Family farms kept on for a while, all the women and children picking as fast as they could to get 'em to market. Even pennies on a bushel was money. But at last the price fell so low it wasn't worth the sweat to pick at all, even with free labor. We picked the best of the nearest field, enough to keep us eating into next year. It looked to be one of those winters we'd live on potatoes and vegetables stored in our root cellar and a year-old lamb we'd butchered our selves. We were lucky at that. How many were not eating regular.

Then farmers everywhere said, "Plow 'em under!"

"Not our potatoes," said Dad. "People hungry everywhere. We ain't goin' to plow good food under. Send out the word, potatoes and point, come one, come all."

Well, we told the town. Soon the county knew. Then we heard people were coming from everywhere in the state and even beyond. Dad didn't care. "Hungry people don't need an ad. Seems word spreads like magic. Let 'em come."

"Dad, what's potatoes and point?"

"You'll see, son."

Dad went and bought fifty herrings just before that weekend. He said, "That ought to do." Soon the people started coming. Families with two, three, half a dozen kids. Guys on the bum, riding the rails. Folks from right here in town on hardest times. Dad gave each group a herring. "Split it down the middle. I'll save t'other half for the next 'uns. There's the fields. Dig and eat."

Campfires and little tents sprang up all over our land. Lots of people just slept under the stars. Sis and me watched, fascinated.

Potatoes baked or chunked and boiled. They all seemed to know what to do without being told. They hung the half-herring above the potato pot. Everybody sat around. They'd fork a potato chunk and take turns rubbing it on the herring to get the flavor and aroma. That's potatoes and point. Nobody ate the herring. It just hung there, never getting used up at all. A herring could last for ten meals or a hundred or until it rotted.

In fact Dad's herrings only lasted the weekend. The potatoes were mostly gone by sundown Sunday, and sometime that night most of the herrings, stiff and dry, disappeared, into whose stomachs nobody knew or cared. Everybody was full for the first time in a long time. One hundred herring halves had gone a long way.

Every one of those people came and thanked Dad before they left to go hungry wherever they went hungry before. Funny thing. I remember going over those fields where they had pitched their tents and sat around eating and just enjoying those two days. There wasn't a scrap of rubbish to be seen. Hunger seems to bring out creativeness. People found ways to make use of everything.

In those days there was almost nothing was rubbish.

IKE THE PIKE

Shirlee Kresh Hecker

It was almost two weeks before Passover, and my father brought home a live fish for my mother to cook for the holidays. He knew this fish would be of the finest quality since it came from his landsman on the East Side. He presented the fish to my mother in a bucket, and she put it in the washtub to fatten up until she was ready to prepare it.

This fish became the family pet and soon had a name. "Look how he knows me," my father said after just one day.

Ike the Pike settled into the washtub in his new home. Each time my father lifted the washtub lid, the fish perked up his head and opened his mouth. My father would feed him little pieces of bread and talk soothingly to him. Poppa was fascinated with Ike's intelligence and would show off his talents to whoever came to the house. "Watch how he greets me."

Although I was very young, I knew that my father had a way with animals, and I believed this fish to be just what my father claimed, "very smart." I knew nothing of the word "conditioned."

One day my father beckoned me over to the tub to look at Ike. "Can you see how much he looks like my friend Levine?" he whispered. "The eyebrows, the one larger eye that held his monocle, the thin lips with the cigar always in place, the high cheekbones?"

Why, he really does look like Mr. Levine, thought I, being as imaginative as any five-year-old should be.

"You know," added my father, "when people die, they can come back as anything or anyone."

"Even a fish?" I asked.

"That's what he came back as," my father said convincingly.

Then the fateful day arrived, and Momma asked Poppa to kill the fish.

"Kill him, are you crazy! That might be Levine, and he stays in the tub forever."

My mother stared at my father and said quietly, "Take that fish out in the yard, and stop telling that child that it's your friend Levine. Levine is dead, and that's how I want that fish."

Poppa left the house, muttering that he would never, as long as he lived, lift a hand to his friend.

For almost two days I stared from one parent to the other, wondering who was going to win the battle. I was counting on my father, but my mother would not relent. "Izzy," she said, "if you make me kill this fish, I will never forgive you."

"Well, Rosie, if you want to see him dead, you be the executioner." And my father sadly left the house again.

Momma walked over to the tub, caught the fish in a big towel, and went out to the backyard with it. "Stop," I yelled. "Don't kill him, please!" My mother raised the hammer and aimed for the fish's head. "Murderer!" I screamed at the top of my lungs. I grabbed her, but she pushed me aside and struck again while the fish kept jumping around. "Die, Levine, *die*!" she pleaded, and with the third blow Ike was still. Momma burst into tears and ran inside with the fish. I had never seen her cry before.

When Poppa came home, he passed by the tub, but he didn't

lift the lid to look inside. He knew just from my mother's face that his friend was really gone.

The first seder was the next night, and after what seemed like endless praying, Momma got ready to serve. By then everyone was on edge. I got yelled at a dozen times for various things I claimed I didn't do to my older sister, and she almost got hit for the things she did do to me. My oldest sister said she wasn't very hungry and left the dining room.

Momma brought out the gefilte fish platter and uncovered it. There on the very top was a fishball with a face. Horseradish for a mouth, carrot for a nose, and raisins for eyes, one of which sported my Charlie McCarthy doll's monocle, just like the one Mr. Levine wore. Between the horseradish lips was a small celery cigar. My sister had done a real good job on the face, but no one appreciated it, no one laughed, and no one ate any gefilte fish. My father left the table, saying he didn't feel good. My mother did nothing but swear under her breath that she was going to kill my sister, who had locked herself in the bathroom. Needless to say, the fish was not eaten, then or the next day. As far as we knew, my mother, who never wasted food, threw it in the garbage. As for my father, he never brought home a live fish again.

PAPA'S MOONLIGHTING

MOONSHINE

Mae Ferris

After dinner, Papa would take his doctor's satchel, in which he kept glass capsules, cotton swabs, and alcohol, and go out to do cupping for ailing friends, neighbors, and relatives. Cupping was a medical procedure meant to relieve congestion, pleurisy, bronchitis, and many other discomforts.

In 1919 the Volstead Act was passed, forbidding the sale of intoxicating liquors, whose principal ingredient of course was alcohol. Without alcohol Papa couldn't continue cupping. But Papa was a sheet-metal worker by trade, so he decided to make his own still of copper, a long coiled tube inside.

The evening he decided that his wooden buckets, filled with fruit and concealed behind a cretonne curtain around the laundry tubs, were properly fermented, he made his first batch.

"Everybody out of the house!" he ordered.

Momma went down to gossip with the neighbors on the stoop, my sister and I went out to play, other family members went their separate ways.

Upstairs Papa closed all the windows, even though it was a humid summer night, taking extra precaution to stuff rags in every crack and under the drafty front door. Then he was ready to cook the fruit, timing exactly when to let a few distilled drops fall on the enamel top of the kitchen table. He lit a match and by the flame knew it was done.

No matter how careful Papa was to conceal his "crime," a strong smell seeped out of the apartment into the hall, down the stairs, and into the street. Any moment I expected to see the police come and take Papa away in a paddy wagon. If no one else noticed, that was because there were too many other noxious stinks in the fetid air, from the gasworks on the next street, from the pickle factory, from the wholesale produce market on the avenue, and more immediately from open garbage cans.

But murder will out, as the saying goes, and eventually my uncle learned what Papa was up to. He brought a bottle of amber liquid, added it to the colorless alcohol, and called it "schnapps."

After that Papa did less and less cupping. Making schnapps had become too lucrative. In 1927, when Lindbergh flew the Atlantic, we moved to a larger apartment on a better street.

In 1933 the unpopular Volstead Act was repealed.

PASSOVER

Frances Feldman

The family was gathered in the large kitchen around the battered old table. Mama as usual sat next to Papa, gazing at him with trust and love. The year was 1930, and we were faced with catastrophe. What to do! The rent hadn't been paid on our small family-run restaurant for the past three months. The landlord had dispossessed us. Our years of plenty were over.

"Well," Papa said, "something we gotta do. The fixtures, dishes, and pots will bring in about a hundred and fifty dollars. That's enough money to go into a new business." Papa's eyes glistened with excitement. He was always ready for new horizons. "It's almost Passover, and for Passover people need fresh eggs. I'll fix up the old Kissel car like a truck by taking out the back seats. Then I'll go to all the farmers around here and buy up all the eggs I can afford. We'll go to New York on the Lower East Side. We'll sell the eggs for thirty cents a dozen. That's a good profit. We'll also sell honey—everyone uses honey for the holidays."

Papa's enthusiasm soon spread to our entire family. In two days we were ready for our new venture. Early Sunday morning, just before dawn, Izzie and Joey helped Papa load the car with large crates of eggs, cans of honey, and secondhand paper bags. Mollie and Jackie, who were good at figures, sat in the front seat with Papa. I was crowded into the back in a semi-reclining position with the eggs, the honey, and the back window, where I could look out at the passing landscape. Mama and the older boys stayed home. The boys could earn a little change by running errands.

We rode along old Route 17 for most of the trip without a mishap. Suddenly the car began to sputter and squeak. Papa said, "I'll have a look." He lifted the hood, examined the motor, and decided that it was either the carburetor, the radiator, the battery, or a loose wire. He proceeded to administer his usual remedy: he poured a large bottle of water into the radiator, then neatly folded an old red blanket across the front of the car to keep it warm.

We resumed our journey, although the car sounded like it had a bad bronchial condition. We passed through Harlem and started downtown. Papa's objective was to get to Avenue C and Third

Street as soon as possible. When we reached Fourteenth Street the wheezing and strangling sounds became even louder. A banging noise joined the other symptoms. Our old Kissel was really in trouble. Then she began to steam and smoke. Papa was shouting in Yiddish, a sure sign that he was under stress: "Oy vey iz mir! Vos vil ich toen?" (Woe is me, what shall I do?)

We were all so spellbound with anxiety that when the car suddenly lurched to a stop a few feet from the Washington Square Arch, we failed to notice the greater danger facing us. The Kissel had stalled dead in her tracks hood to hood with the first official car leading the Fifth Avenue Easter Parade.

A policeman walked over to Papa's window. "What's going on here? Move on, move on," he shouted. Steam was shooting at least two feet into the air. We had painted the car a bright blue, and with the red blanket on the front it was a strange object in the midst of all the splendor. "What's this, a circus?" yelled a fat police captain from his patrol car. Papa, always excitable, for once in his life was struck dumb. Mollie and Jackie sat silently beside him. Nobody said a word.

Peering into the back of the car, the first policeman said, "Young man, you get out here." I had short hair and was wearing my lumber jacket and breeches. Since this was my daily costume when not in school, I wasn't surprised at being called a young man. I struggled out from between the crates of eggs and cans of honey and climbed over the front seat and its occupants to get to the street.

"I'm no boy," I said, "I'm a girl, and it's not our fault. We have to sell our eggs today. Tomorrow night is Passover. We need the money to live on. We've lost our business."

After listening to me for a few minutes, the officer walked over to the fat captain sitting like a Buddha in his regal chariot. Then he got into another police car parked at the curb and pulled over behind us. The official car made room, and the officer began to push our Kissel into a side street heading east. Papa put his foot on the starter, and lo and behold, the car began to purr like a contented kitten. I looked back and saw a smile on the captain's face. With a wave of his hand, he sent us on our way.

We set up our boxes on East Third Street and Avenue C, where all of Papa's relatives and landsmen lived. We sold out all the eggs and honey in two hours, heading for home fortified with fresh kasha kugel, kichlach, and cold tea that one of my aunts had brought down for us. Except for one stop to fill up with gas and oil, our trip home was uneventful. Papa left the blanket on for good luck. Some people carry a rabbit's foot, Papa always took the red blanket on our trips.

The egg business kept us going until times got worse and people didn't have the money to buy eggs at any price. We survived that crisis too. Papa became a bootlegger. But that's a story I'll tell you next time.

THE CARNIVAL

Helen Covell

It was an early afternoon in September 1939. Mama had sent my sister and me on an errand to a friend's house. We were on our way back when we saw two unusual ladies, all dressed up fancy. We had never seen such elegant clothes. Over their blouses were tight red vests covered with jewels. Their skinny knees showed just below full black skirts. They wore black stockings and shiny black shoes laced to the ankles. We stood under a tree watching as they went up to a house and knocked on the door.

Each lady carried a duffel bag that looked bulky and heavy. One of them had red hair, and the other black. Their cheeks were rosy, their lips bright red. Under dark brows their eyes looked like big black olives. Gold bands circled their arms all the way up above the elbow, and shiny earrings dangled from their ears. Strands of beads and chains hung like gold ropes around their necks.

We were taught never to stare, but we couldn't resist. I knew I wanted to dress like them when I grew up—a long time away. For now, Grandmother made our dresses. We heard the woman they were talking to say, "No, I don't have any rooms to rent." As they turned to leave, I saw a fringe of frilly red petticoats.

We hurried to catch up with them. I was looking right into their faces, and I could scarcely talk. "Our mother has a spare bedroom," I said shyly.

They smiled at us. Just to be talking to them was unbelievable.

"We're on our way home. You could come with us," I suggested, glancing at my Saturday dress and wishing I was wearing my Sunday best.

They asked how old we were.

"I'm almost twelve," I said, and my sister announced that she'd soon be ten.

"You're real smart little girls," they said. "Do you like the carnival?"

"We've never been to one," we answered in unison.

"Oh, you'll love it!"

When we got home, Mama was on the porch watering plants, wearing a pretty afternoon apron.

"Mama, will you rent your spare room to these ladies?" we said right out.

"I'm Stell," said one of the ladies.

"I'm Daisy," said the other. "We're with the carnival."

"Rent the spare bedroom?" Mama asked in amazement. "Yes, we always have room."

TZEDAKAH

Sam Fishman

When Pa was about sixteen, his family fled the Russian pogroms and settled in Brooklyn. As a boy in the shtetl, he had studied all day memorizing the Torah and the Talmud. Here in America, Pa had to earn a few dollars working in a sweatshop.

Ma's family had come to Brooklyn from Romania. When she met Pa, she was seventeen and working as a seamstress. Ma was a beauty. Pa loved her, and she loved the gentle scholar. They were married in 1912. I was born in 1913.

Together Ma and Pa worked and scrimped, and saved enough money to buy a knitting machine and start up a business making sweaters. For a few years they were moderately prosperous, lived a bit easier, and along the way had another child, my sister Shirley.

Intent on expansion, Pa went into debt and didn't put aside any reserve funds. Of course the Depression wiped us out. Pa's spirit broke. I still remember the terrible crying jags. Ma was a constant source of comfort, hope, and love unlimited. Her repeated "It will be all right" kept us intact and gradually healed Pa.

Eventually Pa managed to borrow two hundred dollars to buy a little candy store. For the rest of their working years, Ma and Pa spent eighteen-hour days, seven days a week, fifty-two weeks a year (excluding Rosh Hashanah and Yom Kippur) in candy stores, sustained only by their hopes for their children's future.

From behind his soda fountain, Pa explored the universe. "Ah," he would say, "God created such wonders—the skies, the mountains, the oceans. Such beauty, if only people wouldn't spoil it." And yet to him a human being was the most marvelous creation of all. "I'll never understand how even God could make us."

One morning Pa was at the soda fountain as usual, waiting for the rare customer. I was off in a corner reading a magazine. About ten o'clock a short, thin, middle-aged man came in out of the scorching sun and walked very slowly to the soda fountain. He was neatly dressed in a well-worn blue suit and tie. He asked Pa if he might have a drink of water, apologizing because he didn't have the two cents to pay for a glass of seltzer.

"Here, take the seltzer," said Pa. "You'll owe me two cents."

Sipping slowly, the man began to tell Pa in a low, halting voice how he had walked here all the way from the Bronx, hoping to find work in a tailor shop down the street. It was a temporary job, but it paid a full ten dollars a week. He'd read the advertisement in the evening edition of the paper and had left his home long before dawn. Our store was in a section of Brooklyn close to Coney Island—miles and miles from the Bronx. By the time he got to the tailor shop, the job had been taken. Now he had to walk all the way home to tell his family.

"When will I ever get a job?" he sobbed.

I'll never forget Pa's face as he cried silently with his fellow man. He went to the register, took out two dollars and change— the whole morning's receipts—and gave it all away. Afterward, he never said a word about it, never spoke of it at all. It was done. It was gone. To Pa, nothing rare or unusual. It was just Pa....

Now long gone, but still with me today, in all I do.

THE VISIT OF THE FAIRY GODMOTHER

Mabel B. Herring

It is early fall in the middle of Texas, and the cotton harvest is in full swing. I walk home along the dirt road where the school bus has deposited me. Today my thoughts weigh heavily on my mind, and the subject is clothes—or rather, the lack of them. I am a sophomore in high school, and this is the second year my father has permitted me to attend school in town. My mother makes clothes for me on the old treadle sewing machine whenever she can, but she has little money for material, and little time because of the burdens of farm work and the rearing of five children. She does our laundry in a big black pot over a wood fire in the backyard, which makes what clothes we do have old and shabby before their time. Besides, the clothes I crave are store-bought clothes like the town kids wear.

My envy and longing are so great that in a rare leap of courage I approached my father yesterday, despite my fear of incurring his wrath. We were in the cotton fields, where I joined my family after school, dragging heavy sacks along seemingly endless rows. I stopped by my father and hurriedly delivered my carefully re-hearsed request.

"Daddy, I really need clothes for school. I know the crop has been better this year. I've worked hard in the fields this summer and after school and on Saturdays. When you sell the cotton, you keep all the money. I think some of that money belongs to me."

"Well," he said. "You belong to me, so anything you make belongs to me too, so you won't be getting any money."

On occasion Daddy whips me with his belt or the razor strop, but nothing has prepared me for the pain of this declaration of my status as a slave, an object of ownership without any separate existence or rights of my own. I immediately surrendered and resumed work, suffering my hurt in silence. That night I asked my mother, "Why is Daddy so hard on me? He doesn't want me to have any-

14

thing, be anybody, go anywhere, or do anything but work on this old farm all the time."

"I don't know," she replied with bitter resignation. "That's just the way he is, and you'll have to put up with it same as the rest of us do."

Now I am dejected and morose as I head for home and another session of field work until dark. What's the use? I think. I'm a good student and I love school, but overcoming the roadblocks my father throws in my way is sometimes too heavy to bear. Still, I know that if I don't graduate I'll never be able to get a job in town and I'll always be stuck on this sharecropper's farm. At least he hasn't stopped me from attending school. I'll just have to go on with the same old clothes and try to be less self-conscious about my countrified appearance.

Arriving at home, I enter the room my little sister and I share. On our bed I see a large bag from Heidenheimer's, a small department store in a small town some miles distant. I open the bag in speechless wonder. There, in my size, are five sets of clothes— beautiful, wonderful, glorious clothes, bright, sparkling, precious clothes. Clothes like the other kids wear. I sense my mother's presence at the doorway and turn to her. "Did Daddy let you get these for me after all?"

"He didn't have nothing to do with it," she says. "He's mad and he won't pay the bill, but Mr. Heidenheimer said I could charge it, and I'll find some way to pay. You got to have clothes for school, and that's all there is to it."

We are a family lacking in any demonstration or word of affection, and I do not know how to tell my mother how much I appreciate this marvelous gift she has given me. It is not just the physical fact of the clothes that overcomes me with feeling. It is the unspoken but eloquently conveyed assurance that I have her support in my determination to finish school. I do not know how to say these things to her. I do know that on this day I have been the beneficiary of a deed of great goodness. Although she may never appear again, I know that today my Fairy Godmother has come to life in the person of this careworn, brave farm woman, and that the sheer beauty of her compassionate and generous act will stay with me all the days of my life.

MUSIC

Myor Rosen

My mother came to this country as a young Russian immigrant, married, and bore three sons in five years. We lived in various sections of the Bronx, always in walk-up tenements, sometimes on the top floor and sometimes a bit lower, depending on the fluctuations of my father's meager income as an embroidery salesman. Harsh though conditions were in the twenties and during the Great Depression, my mother dreamed of raising a family of artists and musicians.

As a native of czarist Russia, my mother knew how strictly proscribed higher education and the professions were for Jews living there. She also knew that the only exceptions were in the area of music. Apparently the Russian predilection for anti-Semitism was exceeded only by an innate love of music, so that a young boy (forget the poor little girls) found to be unusually talented—even if he was Jewish—might be admitted to a Russian conservatory and permitted to become a musician. Like so many other displaced persons who come from oppression to a land of comparative freedom, my mother brought some of her fears with her and believed that music would be the guarantor of her sons' lives.

Music was part of our lives from the time we could begin to recognize sounds. Mother used to save her nickels and dimes, and once each month we made a pilgrimage to the local record shop for the thrilling adventure of selecting a Victor Red Seal 78 for our tiny but growing collection. At home, the three brothers scuffled to be first to wind up the Victrola, listening eagerly to the ballet music from *Faust,* or arias from *The Pearl Fishers,* or a Caruso record.

I remember my mother taking us by subway in the bitter cold of winter to the eight free Saturday night concerts at the Metropolitan Museum of Art, to hear David Mannes and a symphony orchestra performing the classics. When I hear the Dvorak *New World* Symphony or Brahms' Third or Beethoven's *Eroica* today, my mind conjures up the vision of the pharaohs' tombs and the rich tapestries under which we sat on our coats on the floor of the Great Hall of the Museum, absorbing the glorious sounds.

In my ninth year, despite very limited funds, my mother rented a piano and engaged a fine piano teacher to begin our musical education. My uncles and aunts thought she was daffy, throwing good money away on music lessons and a piano, instead of having us learn a trade or some commercial skills. My father concurred, and their combined criticism and derision was unrelenting. My mother was undeterred.

By the time I was ten, I had skipped several grades and soon found myself attending Paul Hoffman Junior High School in the east Bronx, near the old campus of Fordham University, along with my older brother. One day it was announced that our school had been singled out for a pilot program in the study of the harp. Students were invited to register for a course of twenty free lessons, at the end of which a competition was to be held and the winner awarded a scholarship. The sponsors of the program were the patrons of the New York Philharmonic.

When my brother and I came home that day, it didn't take much coaxing to persuade my mother that we should change from the piano to the harp. The piano was fine, but the harp was exotic, unusual, and *free*. At least the lessons were free; for we soon found that practicing at school was far from satisfactory. We needed more practice time and missed the instrument on weekends. More important, how was our six-year-old kid brother to learn the instrument? So the piano was exchanged for a harp, and the three brothers took turns plucking the guts of that poor instrument, several hours daily.

For our lessons we were brought to the home of a young woman who was then one of the harpists in the New York Philharmonic. Her name was Steffy Goldner Ormandy, and her husband was the concertmaster and conductor of the Capitol Theater in New York—Eugene Ormandy! Steffy couldn't have been more than twenty-one at the time, but to us she became the Queen Mother. The Ormandys had no children of their own, and in a short time her affection and our idolatry expanded considerably. She showed a keen interest in our family life and soon discovered that we had a third brother at home whom we were teaching as well. When she learned he was barely six and was keeping up with our progress, her amazement was apparent.

"But how does he reach the pedals?" she asked.

"We attach some small blocks of wood to make it easier for him."

"Bring him to a lesson," she said.

So the next time we came with our little brother, Max, and her heart swooned when she saw this cherubic child sit down and play note for note the music we had been assigned.

When the lessons ended and the competition was held, the jury couldn't decide between me and my brother, and awarded us both full scholarships. Within a month, Mrs. Ormandy obtained a third scholarship for Max, and the three of us were launched on what became a seven-year scholarship with the New York Philharmonic, and a subsequent full scholarship at the Juilliard School of Music. Our careers as successful musicians seemed assured.

But those years of study were far from unalloyed bliss. My father's financial status seesawed more violently than the stock exchange, and the arguments between him and our mother became increasingly bitter. As a concession to his insistence that his sons should learn commercial skills, my older brother and I switched from an academic to a commercial program in high school. This proved to be a lifesaver for our family, since my parents' rocky marriage foundered totally by the time I was fourteen, and they parted for good. We were reduced to welfare, and my mother took in sewing and tried to help us survive by selling women's stockings and corsets.

Our golden harp remained in our living room in the midst of all this frantic activity, and our practice sessions continued daily. The only interruptions occurred when a customer arrived to try on my mother's merchandise. I remember one day when two very stout women came in and I had to leave the room. While one of them was struggling to get into the largest corset my mother produced, her companion was looking at the harp quizzically. Finally she turned to my mother and asked, "What is it, a sewing machine or a loom?"

After school hours I delivered orders for a local grocer and tailor shop, and in the summer I hawked ice cream all day on the blistering Coney Island beaches. Soon after my graduation from high school I landed a job with a film company that distributed documentary and educational films to colleges and other organizations. At fifteen I was given the important title of director of distribution, for the munificent weekly salary of eleven dollars. This sum went into the family kitty, and I was quite content to receive my subway round-trip fare of ten cents, plus my lunch brought from home.

Like my older brother, I got my first real break as a harpist through the Works Progress Administration, playing with one of the WPA symphony orchestras. From there I went to the New York Philharmonic as second harpist and then began a series of engagements as principal harpist with major orchestras.

The zenith of my career occurred in 1960, when I was invited to join the New York Philharmonic Symphony Orchestra as principal harpist under Leonard Bernstein. It was my pleasure and honor to hold this post for twenty-eight years, collaborating with Maestro Bernstein, Pierre Boulez, Zubin Mehta, and dozens of celebrated music directors who came to us as guest conductors each year. My two brothers have also had successful careers, as harpists, arrangers, and composers. Abraham, the eldest, was principal harpist under Dimitri Mitropoulos, with the Minneapolis Symphony Orchestra. Little Max, better known as Robert Maxwell, is the composer of world-famous hits such as "Ebb Tide" and "Shangri-La."

In retrospect, I can truly say that my musical life has been a blessed one in which I had the doubly good fortune of loving my chosen profession and making a very good living at it. I can also say that I owe an eternal debt of gratitude to the Society of the New York Philharmonic. But my greatest thanks goes to my mother, who not only gave me life, but whose single-minded perseverance and inspiration helped make me what I became.

They Don't Make Jewish Mothers Like They Used To!

Sybil Wyner

I was a Great Depression baby, born in the early 1930s, when times were hard. My sweet, gentle father was a shoemaker who had his own small store. We lived in a town in the South where we were the only Jewish family in a population of ten thousand.

While the men of the town would gather around the potbelly stove in my father's shoe store to discuss the troubles of the world and whatever men discuss, Mama rarely socialized with the town ladies, whom she considered worthless "with their fancy hairdos and painted nails." Country women were more to her liking. Her steady companion was a .22 pistol for scaring off chicken thieves or killing opossums in the henhouse. The goyim of the town, many of them Ku Klux Klan members, loved my father and respected my mother.

Mama led me and my two sisters and brother to believe that the reputation of the entire Jewish people rested on our actions. If we misbehaved in school, our entire family would have to move out of town in disgrace—a reflection on all the Jews of the world.

During the Depression, when there was little or no business and people were starving, our family ate well because of my mother. She had a cow and sold cheese and milk. She raised chickens and sold the eggs. She grew fodder for the animals since there was no money to buy regular food, much less animal food. In a small backyard, she raised enough fruits and vegetables to feed our family all year. During berry season, we would go on picnics in the woods and pick buckets of wild blackberries to preserve for the winter. In the fall, we would gather bags of wild hickories, walnuts, and pecans to crack on the hearth as we listened to the radio in the cold.

Mama detested the "goyish white bread" in the stores. She baked bread every other day, mostly whole wheat. Every couple of weeks she would go directly to the mill, buy a bushel of whole grain, and have the miller grind it into flour for her. She baked and cooked on a wood stove that had no thermostat or dial indicators. The aroma of fresh bread would permeate the neighborhood, bringing endless numbers of hungry people to our door. As poor as we were, Mama's hand was always open to the less fortunate. No one was ever turned away without food.

Multitudes of flowers decorated every corner and nook of the yard and garden, from seeds and cuttings Mama got by swapping her garden produce or eggs. She was constantly sending bouquets to the hospital a couple of blocks away, behind our backyard, with instructions that they be given to people who didn't have any flowers in their rooms.

Nothing daunted my mother. Once, when she was going at least sixty miles an hour in a forty-five zone, she was stopped by a highway patrolman who didn't know her. Before he could ask for her license, she began to cry. "Please help me, officer. My husband"—Papa, who didn't drive, was with her—"is very ill. I have to get him to the hospital quick! Please help me!" The officer immediately escorted her to the hospital with siren screaming. Mama took Papa into the emergency room and then out through the back door to go home.

Papa bottled boot oil and sold it in his shoe store. A tavern owner in a nearby town saved empty whiskey bottles for him, and Mama picked them up. One day she was zooming down the highway, greatly exceeding the speed limit, and was stopped by a patrolman who discovered the whiskey bottles in her car. Thinking that she might be connected with a bootlegging operation, he arrested her and brought her back to town. When her trial date arrived, she stood before the judge in front of a packed courtroom. "Why, Joe Montgomery," she declared, "I used to change your diapers, wash your backside, and powder it dry when you were just a baby. You know good and well my husband uses these bottles to sell shoe oil—you buy it from him yourself for your hunting boots. Now, let me out of here. I have to go feed my chickens! How's your mother? Are you still driving her crazy like you did when you were a kid?" Case dismissed.

Mama is now in her late eighties. Aides from the health-care service come in once a day to bathe her, help her exercise, and take her vital signs. My sister, who lives with her, leaves the front door open for them every day when she goes to work. A couple of weeks ago, there was a knock at the door around the time the aides usually come. Thinking it must be a new girl, Mama shouted out, "Come on in, honey. I'm in bed waiting for you!" After a few moments' silence, a male voice answered, "Sorry, lady, United Parcel only delivers packages." For the first time in her life, Mama was speechless.

Nope, they don't make mothers like they used to anymore!

A PENNY'S WORTH
OF CRUMBS

Herbert Jaediker

Manhattan's East Sixty-third Street, where I was born in 1894, would seem foreign, hardly recognizable, to anyone living today in that neighborhood of luxury apartments now separated from the East River by traffic on Franklin Roosevelt Drive. I once saw a cow grazing there. The people were mostly poor Irish immigrants, some Italians and Germans, and we lived—we kids especially—in the street.

Ma and Pa arrived in the U.S.A., unknown to each other, from Germany around 1870. Ma was seventeen and got a job as the upstairs maid for the yeast millionaire, Fleischmann, in one of the midtown brownstone mansions. She was small, plump, rosy-cheeked, with a smiling, trusting nature. The Irish girls who worked there taught her some English. Pa was two years younger, sturdily built, large-boned. He had twinkly blue eyes and a strong face and trimmed his mustache like Kaiser Wilhelm, his namesake, whose obsessive militarism he came here to escape. Around 1875, when he was working in a hat factory blocking caps, he met Ma in a German boardinghouse and fell in love. There was one obstacle:

Pa came from a very strict Lutheran family, and Ma's mother wanted him to embrace Judaism. Pa took instruction from a rabbi and got circumcised.

Even though Pa converted to Judaism, they never talked about religion, as far as I know. But Pa taught me a simple prayer in German to say at bedtime. The English translation was something like "Dear God in heaven, my eyes are closing. As I lie in my bed I place myself in your care." It rhymed in German. I think the religion they really shared was caring for others.

Our flat, on the first floor, had a large kitchen/dining room, a parlor, and three small bedrooms connected by a sky shaft. A toilet in the hall was shared by the tenants on each floor. We used newspaper cut to size for toilet paper. Our rent started at nine dollars a month, raised many years later to twelve.

Ma and Pa had four boys when they moved to East Sixty-third Street in 1885: George, Max, Louis, and Henry (another, Adolph, had died of meningitis). The only girl, Lydia, was born during the blizzard of 1888, Theodore in 1891, and I at last in 1894. It was the worst time for Ma, the eighth time she labored, always at home with the help of a midwife. It meant another mouth to feed. My oldest brother, George, who was seventeen, gave Pa hell, even though I was born with a caul—the membrane that's part of the amniotic sac and was supposed to be a lucky omen. Sailors wouldn't work on a ship that didn't have one, but Ma refused to sell it because she thought that might be harmful to me and my luck.

The kitchen was the heart of the house, the warmest place. Every morning when it was still dark and nobody else was up, Ma started the fire in the coal stove and prepared oatmeal and cocoa and sugar buns or cinnamon toast for all. On cold mornings the family gathered there to dress. The temptation to spit on the stove lid and watch the glob bubble and skid like quicksilver was too great not to risk a scolding.

Ma was always busy. She made root beer, rice and tapioca puddings, cakes, and cookies that filled the washtub. By Saturday the washtub was empty and we took our baths. By Monday Ma had filled it with cookies again.

As if that wasn't enough, there was a Viennese bakery on First Avenue and Sixty-second, where through the window I could see coffee cake on the counter in a large black iron tray with crumbs all over. Whenever Lydia gave me a penny, I went to the bakery. The saleslady treated it like an important sale and always asked me what I wanted, as if she didn't know. Maybe she liked to hear me say, "A penny's worth of crumbs."

As cold weather approached, the coal wagons rumbled up Sixty-third Street loaded for delivery to the rich. The older boys climbed on the back and pushed coals off with a stick, and we were ready with our pails to pick them up. We were warm all winter. My brother Ted was partly run over by a coal wagon, but the damage wasn't permanent. He lived to ninety-six.

Ma was the one everyone called in emergencies. Only once did her strength waver. She had gone to Flower Hospital to be operated on for gallstones, and while they were preparing the bed, she went into a panic about what would happen to the children. She rushed out, and only the thought of the family kept her from ending it all in the river. She came home in pain and misery to a turbulent scene, George hitting Max over the head with his student violin and Max yelling, "I'm dead, I'm dead!" He lived to ninety-three.

One year the hat workers were locked out for forming a union, and Pa hadn't worked for months. He didn't want to be a scab. He and a partner invested two hundred dollars in a horse and wagon to go into the junk business, but the horse had different ideas. He ran away the very first day, dragging a broken wagon after him. Pa read a want ad in *Die Staats Zeitung* for a boy to learn wood engraving, and he apprenticed my brother Max, barely fourteen, at sixty cents a week. And when the strike ended, Pa worked again.

We weren't aware of the stresses Pa suffered except for a nervous habit he developed of falling out of bed from the sudden shock of waking up. Ma tried to calm him, but once when he complained of poor appetite she said, "Du ess wie ein sparrow und sheiss wie ein elephant."

As December 31, 1899, approached, there was a lot of talk about what changes the new century would bring. The war with Spain was over, and people looked forward to better times. For weeks we kids collected pieces of wood for the New Year's Eve celebration. And what a celebration it was!

Bonfires were lit in the middle of the streets, and everyone was out throwing on more wood, even old furniture, to keep them going. The rich people held fancy balls, but the rest of us blew horns in the streets. At twelve o'clock the boats on the river all tooted their foghorns, and people banged pots and pans. It was the twentieth century!

The next morning everything went back to being the same again.

NAFTALE

Gertrude Reiss

"Papa, I want to know about your life."

"So come, I'll tell you."

My father was a man of medium height, on the heavy side. He had always had a mustache. I think he must have been born with it. Day and night his head was covered by a skullcap; he never took it off, not even when he slept, in deference to his God. His pants never stayed up, and his shirttails never stayed tucked in. My mother took care of him like he was a child, inspecting him carefully before he stepped out of the house, constantly scolding him about his appearance. "Look at him, a grown man walking around with his pants falling down." He didn't seem to mind her nagging. It was an amusing game they both played.

My father was born, he told me, about November 4, 1880. He was not sure of the date, since no records were kept, but he knew he was born after the High Holy Days and before Hanukkah, so for him November 4 is his birthday.

He was the first of seven children. His mother, Leah, and his father, Hershel, were bakers. They lived in two rooms in Mahden, a shtetl in Galicia, then Austrian Poland. It was a poverty-stricken town; all the Jews, about three hundred families, lived from hand to mouth. Leah and Hershel baked bagels, zeml, and bread in their two little rooms. "Good bakers they were, too." My father bent his head back and closed his eyes. "What good smells! I can remember them still."

My father had more education than most of the children of his village. His schooling stopped after his bar mitzvah, at the age of thirteen, when he was sent to a neighboring town as an apprentice baker. "There I remained until I was eighteen. My father died of double pneumonia. He was forty-seven years old. Since I was the oldest, I had to leave my job and come home to help my mother support my brothers and sisters." Here he paused, took a deep breath, and went on.

"Now I come to the second and most important part of my story. I was betrothed to the most beloved and true girl, who is now my wife."

My mother, who was listening, blushed. "Go on, go on. You don't have to write that," she told me.

"I must say everything, just the way it was. Put it down. Just like that," said my father. "I was betrothed to the most beloved girl. I was twenty years old, and it was time I had a wife, so the shadchan ran around and tried to match me with this one and that one. None of the girls pleased me. I had my eye on your mother. Her father and my father were second cousins. My father, may his soul rest in peace, was very fond of your mother. She was a strong, industrious girl, with rosy cheeks and merry brown eyes. 'Hear now, Shmul,' my father said one day to your mother's father when we were both very young, 'my Naftale will be your Frumit's intended.'

"I loved your mother, and she was crazy about me." His eyes twinkled. My mother laughed. "After all, you mustn't forget, I was quite a catch. I was charming, handsome, and learned too! Your mother was an excellent cook. Everybody praised her. She was a virtuous girl, worked for a rabbi. So we fell in love and saw each other every day. What a scandal in the village! We weren't supposed to see each other until the wedding, but your mother couldn't stay away from me. Nu, we became engaged and exchanged presents. I gave your mother three rings."

"What kind of three rings!" exclaimed my mother. "You gave me a ring."

"Don't interfere. Who is telling the story? It's my life! Write exactly what I tell you. I gave her three rings, and she gave me fourteen gulden. It was supposed to be twenty-four gulden according to the agreement. You know, your mother still owes me ten gulden." He looked at my mother slyly.

"What are you talking about?" she said. "Didn't your son pay it back to you at our golden wedding? I don't owe you anymore."

"So we were married," my father continued. "We got a room for twenty gulden a year. We started with no money and no furniture, but we got flour and yeast on credit, so I baked bread and your mother baked cake. Little by little we were able to buy a few things. One child came and another. We managed to scratch a living for a few years. Then times got bad. What to do? Your mother and I put our heads together and made up our minds that I would go to America."

The crossing was rough, four weeks of traveling third-class. He could not eat the ship's food because his religion would not permit it. All the immigrants shared whatever food they had. "We lived on herring, challah, and cake."

In New York, a great-aunt who owned a little grocery store on the Lower East Side took him into her home. She had found him a job in a bakery for four dollars a week.

"Oy, was that a job. The boss wasn't of the best. Just because I was a greenhorn he thought he could pull the wool over my eyes. A greenhorn I was, but not a fool. Besides baking, he tried to make me lift heavy baskets of bread. 'Reb,' I complained, 'I'm a baker, not a donkey.' Nu, so what does that schlimazel do? He gave me such a smack in my face that I thought the heavens would open up. But I was clever. I raised such a cry that all the people came running. The entire block heard me. What a commotion! My boss got scared. After all, we were all greenhorns, and they took my part.

"'Naftale,' said the boss, 'why should we fight? Jews shouldn't fight with each other. So I lost my head for a moment. Come, take twenty-five dollars and let's call the whole thing settled.' I took the money, but I swore I wouldn't work for him anymore. Besides, I was tired of being a baker. I wanted to learn a different trade. The money I sent home to my wife.

"My great-aunt lived on Ritt Street. On Saturdays men would congregate on the street outside the shul. I became friendly with one of them who was a garment worker. 'If you want to get into the garment trade, I can take you to a shop where they need a pants presser,' he told me. When I got there the boss said I was to work for three weeks without pay and on the fourth week he would give me two dollars. I agreed. What was my joy to see a landsman of mine in the shop! He worked there as a pants presser too. I could see everything was going to turn out well.

"During the week we were supposed to sleep in the shop. We

made our beds on the worktables, using piles of pants as a mattress. That first night I didn't sleep so well. In the dark I heard someone moving near me, so I jumped off the table, and who do you think it was? My landsman! Imagine, he was going through my pants, trying to rob me. What a nerve! All I had to my name, four dollars, was in my pocket. I gave him such a laying-to that he would never lift his head up again.

"I climbed back on the table and had finally managed to close my eyes when someone shook me. 'Get up, Naftale. It's time to go to work.' All the men were stretching their tired bones, scratching their uncombed hair. A fire was started in the stove. We worked from three-thirty in the morning until seven, when we stopped, got out our phylacteries, and said our prayers. Then it was time to eat. 'Let Naftale go buy the food,' everyone agreed. 'The grocer will have pity on him and give him more because he's just off the boat a few days.'

"That's the way it was. I came back so laden with food and beer that the men let out a cheer. We dug into that tztzl bread, onions, and beer. The men urged me to go again, and without too much coaxing, off I went. Three times they sent me out for more beer. Before I knew it, I felt very merry and started to sing. I sang all the songs I knew in a good loud voice, and pretty soon everyone was singing with me. There was no more work that day."

Until I asked my father to tell me about his life, I never knew he was a happy man.

A LEGACY OF SOUL

Letha S. Marshall

It was a day in mid-December the year I was twenty. My mother and I went Christmas shopping together. Snow-covered ice crunched beneath our rubber galoshes as we stepped gingerly from store to store, and our breath lingered in the air as we spoke. Store windows were tantalizingly dressed with gift items ranging from very useful to frivolous, and the recorded sounds of Christmas carols wafted to the street each time a door opened. On every street corner, behind a hanging iron kettle, stood the surest of all signs of the approaching celebration of love and giving: a shivering, red-cheeked young woman in the blue uniform of the Salvation Army, ringing the familiar small brass bell to remind shoppers of the opportunity to share with needier citizens.

As we walked, Mom and I spoke wistfully of how much fun Christmas could be if we were able, just once, to select and purchase our gifts without looking at the price tags. On this particular occasion, however, we were optimistic. I was earning my own money, and Mom had taken a part-time job. My father had had half a dozen years of steady employment. Because he had been working a great deal of overtime, was moonlighting a second job, and could make improvements on our old house himself, our wood-burning stove had been replaced with a forced-air furnace that maintained even warmth. An electric refrigerator had supplanted our ancient icebox. Most exciting of all to the three children, we no longer had to high-step a distance of fifty feet through the snow to an outhouse. We had a gleaming white flush toilet upstairs. Dad had installed a shower in the basement, and a sink in the kitchen as well.

As we neared our favorite department store, our attention was arrested by a pregnant young woman whose wide eyes were fixed, trancelike, on some object we could not yet see. Her nose was so close to the store window that her breathing steamed a small circle on the glass. There was an expression of such raw yearning on her face that I felt as though my heart was turning to liquid in my chest.

"I wonder what it is that poor girl longs for so very much and can't have," my mother said softly.

I suggested that perhaps we would be able to tell what she was looking at when we arrived at the entrance to the store.

Suddenly Mom said, "I wish I had a million dollars."

I laughed at that pretty forty-year-old woman who was enjoying ownership of a flush toilet for the first time in her life and asked teasingly, "Why, Mom, what on earth would *you* do with a million dollars?"

The earnestness of her response jolted me as though I had sustained an electric shock.

"I would hang on to it," she said matter-of-factly, "and each time I saw someone pining for something as much as that young woman is, I would buy it for them."

In that moment I saw my mother's soul, and it was beautiful.

JUST ONE BITE

Betty Tarbell Barten

The Great Depression touched the lives of most everyone who is over sixty years old today. It led to lost fortunes, shattered relationships, and suicides—among other things.

My sister Jane and I loved to go grocery shopping with our mother, though there was never enough money for a treat, not even a five-cent candy bar. There were no supermarkets in those days. The storekeeper knew most of his customers by name, and he'd talk to them about family and current events as he went from shelves to counter filling their orders.

We lived next door to an abandoned button factory, where we were forbidden to go. But go we did, running around back to a concrete slab hidden by tall grass. We'd pretend the slab was a stage and we'd put on plays.

We had a playmate across the street, a scrawny, wily little girl named Philomena Caprio who looked like her mother. She had two younger brothers who looked like their big, burly father. He was one of the lucky ones. He had a job on the railroad. Mrs. Caprio *drove* on Saturdays to do *her* grocery shopping, and when she came home she'd put *two* candy bars in the hands of each of her children. How we envied them! They never gave us any, but that didn't stop my sister from asking.

"Oh, please, Philomena," Jane would say, "won't you give me just one bite?"

Well, one day Philomena said, "Oh, all right, here's a bite," and she took a piece of chocolate out of her mouth, all saliva-covered. As Jane reached for it, I could feel red sparks flashing through my brain. With no thought of consequences, I batted the gooey mess out of Jane's hand and grabbed the rest of the candy bar out of Philomena's, shouting, "Come on, Jane! Run! Quick!" We ran in back of the abandoned factory and sat down on the slab, divided the chocolate, and silently savored every mouthful.

Philomena and her mother stormed across the street to our house and demanded that our mother punish us for stealing Philomena's candy bar and buy her another. We could hear our mother laugh as she replied, "I saw what they did, and lady, I can't buy *my* kids candy, but if I could, I'd teach them to share. Now go home and let me handle this." Mrs. Caprio left with Philomena in tow, and we sheepishly came home, expecting the worst.

All my mother said was, "Make sure, Betty, that you always take care of Jane as you did just now," and I always have.

My sister died of Alzheimer's last year at the age of seventy-three. I cared for her the last fifteen years of her life, and I made sure she had all the chocolate candy she wanted.

GREAT JONES STREET REVISITED

Neil Quinn

East Third Street in New York City, between the Bowery and Broadway, is called Great Jones Street. I never found out why, or who Jones is. It's an ordinary downtown side street, except that a short way off the Bowery there's a firehouse. Though one of the oldest, it remains an impressive building of red brick and sandstone, with wide doors and ample room for two awesome fire trucks, sundry apparatus, and a large company of men. The metal plaque outside proudly displays the legend: Engine Company 33.

I saw it for the first time, through astonished eyes, in the summer of 1926, when I was five years old. My father was a New York

City fireman, a battalion chief stationed there. One day, that great day, he took me to work with him. It was my day of glory: sitting up on the enormous hook and ladder ringing the bell, sliding down the pole, riding in the chief's car, eating with the men, taking in the sights of the neighborhood. I remember the old tenements across the street, the fire escapes, the shabby stores, the el tracks on the Bowery, the roar of passing trains.

There is a touch of irony here, even humor. The first time I saw it, I was a happy kid who wanted to be a fireman when he grew up. The second time was over fifty years later, when I was a decrepit skid row bum who never grew up to be anything.

It was in the spring of 1979. The el tracks were gone, the stores looked different, the fire trucks were bigger and handsomer, but everything else seemed to be the same. I stood across the street by the curb, a pint of Sneaky Pete on the hip, staring. I'd just walked up from the flophouse I was staying in. I had to see it again— Engine Company 33. It was a wet, foggy morning, and a murky drizzle soaked my tattered clothes. I was filled with a sense of inner loneliness, a feeling of emptiness. I knew I had let the old man down. I had to fight a compulsion to run across the street and peer inside, talk to one of the men, talk about anything, then casually say, "You know, my father was a fireman. He was stationed here once."

I remembered the day he took me to see the parade for Colonel Lindbergh. On the way home he said to me, "Whatever you do, son, make a plan. Make a good plan and stick to it. Don't wait for someone to show you the way. Nobody will. There's never a way until you make one." I tried hard to make one. Whatever it amounted to was blown to hell by the war and a craving for French cognac. "The best laid plans of mice and men ..."

I remembered the day my sister called to tell me Dad had passed away and I realized I hadn't seen him for years. I was ashamed to go near him. But I hated myself for not having been home before he died, not having seen him, talked to him, if only to say I was sorry.

I remembered the last meaningful words he said to me, the day he saw me off to college. It was September 1939. Hitler's army had invaded Poland. We didn't talk about that, but we both knew what it meant. Just before I boarded the train, he shook my hand and gave me a slap on the shoulder. "You have one life to live, kiddo, and one death to die. Be sure and do both like a man." We said goodbye.

I walked slowly back toward the Bowery, my mind a muddle of vagaries. Can a man ever really know himself, rich man, poor man? The guys in the black hats don't always lose, the guys in the white hats don't always win. But I felt sure of one thing. I still do. Come what may, I know I will end as a man.

Before then, I might even know why they call it Great Jones Street.

ONCE IN A LIFETIME

Bernice Davis

As a child I fantasized about having an American father like the ones I saw in the movies. An American father would tell me I was pretty and smart and could be president of the United States if I wanted. Most of all he would tell me that he loved me.

My European father never told me any of these things I longed so to hear. He told me that if I didn't get all A's on my report card I would be a garbage collector when I grew up. When I saw the neighborhood garbage truck with the collectors standing on the running board, I would freeze in fear and fascination, wondering if someday I would occupy that position. As the years passed, my child's mind gave up these fantasies, but whenever I saw a movie with a loving, tender scene between father and daughter, there was a slight ache always in my heart.

At the age of one hundred and two and a half my father was still alive, and though he was frail in body his mind was keen. Yet as I sat with him during my visits he seemed to withdraw, and I found myself groping for topics of conversation.

"Pa, tell me, what was the happiest day of your life?"

There was a moment of silence and then the astounding reply. "The day you were born."

Had I heard correctly, or was my mind putting words in his

mouth, the words I had always ached to hear? Oh, how sweet they sounded to me! Over and over and over again I played them in my head, a song I never tired of.

A week later, sitting with my father, I found that repeating his words to myself began to pall. No, it simply wasn't the real thing. As though a net had been thrown over me and I could not resist, my mouth formed the same question.

"Pa, what was the happiest day of your life?" I had to savor his answer again, and no self-humiliation could stop me.

The narrow eyes glinted in disapproval, and the long finger pointed to my mouth. "Bernice, never ever ask the same question twice!"

Once in a lifetime of one hundred two and a half years could my European father say those precious words. It was enough.

My Fifty-Cent Father

Edward Justin

When I was a little boy, my father ran a saloon in a corner store in the building next to the no-bath, shared-toilet-in-the-hallway tenement in which we occupied a three-room "apartment." The iron washtub in the kitchen served a dual purpose: laundering and bathing.

It was my father's custom to take time off at the end of the day and come up to have his evening meal with my mother. Even when I was very young, he insisted that I sit next to him at the table so he could feed me small bits of his food over my mother's anxious protestations. As soon as I was old enough, he began to tell me bedtime stories in Yiddish before returning to the saloon. My best recollection is that many were simple tales of his adventures, or imagined adventures, as a young boy.

At the time, my father's command of spoken English was very limited, and he couldn't read more than a few words. He didn't own any English or even Yiddish storybooks, so he made up the stories as he went along. Some were short, some were "to be continued tomorrow night if you're a good boy," and some were of the "let this be a lesson when you grow up" variety. I learned later that he was studying English in an exchange program at the saloon: whiskey for lessons, his tutor a lovable, somewhat eccentric character known to me as "Tommy the Irishman."

One of my favorite stories was about a young soldier in the Hungarian army (my father was very sentimental about "the old country") who effected the surrender of a seemingly impregnable Russian fortress with his wallet. A helluva story to tell a little kid. With it came two or three maxims—"Never beat your head against a stone wall," "All is not lost when you've got something to offer"—but I was far too young to think of it as anything but a pure adventure tale.

Years later, with five months to go to my fifteenth birthday, I was registering for my last semester in high school. Having completed all but two or three required courses, I was free to choose two elective subjects. Among those available was commercial law, which sounded as if it might have some practical use in the future. I enrolled.

The teacher was a nervous, obviously unhappy lawyer who practiced his profession after school hours and made no secret of the fact that he regarded teaching commercial law to a bunch of kids as a demeaning waste of his time and talent. He was a terrible teacher, rambling on for most of each period, discouraging questions or discussion, and almost never calling on anyone. Note taking was the major student activity in that class—note taking and daydreaming. But what I found absolutely fascinating about that man was that he had a five o'clock shadow at nine in the morning, probably less than an hour after shaving, and that he had to shave almost to his lower eyelids. I had never before, and have never since, seen a man whose beard grew so close to his eyes.

The course was a snap, and on the rare occasion that a student was called upon, it was never me. I took some notes, but mostly I spent the term watching the teacher's facial hair grow.

The night before the last day of the school term, my father, a western movie buff, said to me at the supper table, "There's a good western playing tonight at the Odeon, and I'm taking some time off. If you've finished your homework, you can come with me. Mama wants to do some ironing, so we can catch the seven o'clock show and you can be home and in bed by half past ten."

Without a moment's hesitation I said, "Thanks, Pop, I'm all finished." Actually, I had done all my homework except for the commercial law assignment. However, since I had never been called on during the entire term and the next day's class was the last, and since I didn't intend to bother with that assignment even if I stayed home, it didn't occur to me that I was lying.

The movie was a William Farnum western, and we loved it. I went to bed with a fast pulse and a clear conscience.

Of course I was called to read from my homework the next morning. I tried to fake it, but the teacher could tell that I was improvising. When he asked to see my notebook, all was lost!

"Sit down and remain after class," he said to me in the tone that I imagined a hanging judge would use when sentencing a hardened criminal to life.

The after-class exchange was brief and to the point. "You haven't done a stitch of work all term," said Mr. District Attorney. "You've just been sitting there, half asleep. Bring your father to see me on Monday. If you don't, you don't take the Regents exam and you fail the course!" With that he turned and left the room.

I was in a dilemma. Obviously, I would rather fail the course than tell my father that I had lied to him, if innocently. Besides, I didn't need credit for that course in order to graduate. But I had suffered through a term of boring sessions, and I knew I'd have no trouble with the exam. More important, I didn't want to give that creep an excuse to hand me my first failing grade in four years of high school. There had to be way out!

Surely I wasn't thinking of my father's Hungarian soldier at that very moment, but he and my father's aphorisms must have been lurking in my subconscious. Instead of going directly home after school, I crossed the street into Seward Park.

It was a pleasant afternoon in June, and along with many women and baby carriages and small children, there were a goodly number of middle-aged men, obviously out of work, relaxing and sunning themselves on park benches. Most of the conversations in the park were in Yiddish or Italian. It was that kind of a neighborhood.

I strolled through the park and furtively scrutinized the occupants of the benches. The second time around, I stopped at a bench where several men were sharing a *Jewish Daily Forward,* a widely circulated Yiddish-language newspaper.

36

"Gentlemen," I said in fluent Yiddish, "please excuse me for disturbing you. I'm in trouble and I need a bit of help." They looked apprehensive, probably expecting that I would ask for "carfare home to Newark" or something like that.

"And I'm willing to pay for it," I added. At that they relaxed and got interested.

"He speaks a fine Yiddish," one of them said. "Perfect," agreed another. I knew that things were going my way.

"Today was my last day in high school," I said, "except for the Regents examinations we have to take next week. And today, for the first time in four years, a teacher got mad at me and told me that unless I bring my father to school on Monday, he won't let me take the exam and he'll give me a failing mark."

"So bring your father," said one of the three.

"I can't," I said, almost in tears by now.

"Why?" he asked.

"Because my father is a sick man with a weak heart and I'm afraid that the aggravation might give him a heart attack."

"A good son," he said.

"So what do you want from us?" asked another. "We should kill the teacher, maybe?"

"I want one of you to come to school with me for ten or fifteen minutes on Monday and make believe you're my father."

"We don't speak good English," he said.

"All the better. I'll tell the teacher, 'This is my father. He understands English but he doesn't speak it.' Then all you need to do is stand there and let him tell you what a loafer I am. If you just look unhappy, he'll be satisfied."

"How much?" asked the first fellow.

"A quarter," I suggested. It was 1927, and a quarter was not to be sneezed at.

"Not enough," he said.

"Do you have a suit jacket?" I asked.

"For fifty cents I wear a suit jacket and I do the job."

"It's a deal," I said, extending my hand. We shook.

"When do I get paid?"

"A good question," I replied. "You meet me in front of the main entrance at ten o'clock on Monday, wearing your jacket. I'll give you a quarter when we go in and another quarter when we leave, if you don't do anything to spoil my story."

"A pleasure to do business with you, young man," he said. "What's my name, my son?"

"Max Josowitz. J-o-s-o-w-i-t-z. See you Monday at ten sharp." Wishing them all a good Sabbath, I said goodbye and left.

Monday morning at ten my fifty-cent father was waiting at the main entrance to the school. He was dressed as if for a bar mitzvah: not only a suit jacket but a clean white shirt and a carefully knotted tie. I gave him a quarter and we entered. After I introduced him and explained his problem with speaking English, my teacher let him have it, both barrels. He made me out to be a totally disinterested lout who was wasting his time in school. "He'll wind up a bum unless you put your foot down and see that he gets a job, Mr. Josowitz."

My man was a born actor. He shook his head sadly and glowered at me. For a moment I thought he might get carried away and strike me. Toward the end, he had tears in his eyes. When it was time to leave, he gripped my arm and led me toward the door, still shaking his head.

As my teacher opened the door to let us out, my wonderful fifty-cent father grabbed his hand and pumped it warmly as he muttered, "Tank you."

At the school exit I handed him the second quarter, complimented him on his performance, and thanked him profusely in Yiddish.

"A pleasure," he said in better-than-average-sounding English. "That man is a lunatic! And," he added with a chuckle, "I'll bet fifty cents that your father's not sick!"

PRETTY MAMMA

H. Darcy Abbott

According to news reports of the time, I was one of three children found abandoned in a house in a slum on Chicago's South Side. It was 1919. I was three years old. Since no parents or relatives claimed us, we became wards of the court.

For all I knew, I'd always lived at St. Mary's along with hundreds of other orphans of all ages. Ever since I could remember, I'd wanted a pretty mamma, but my remembering began at about age seven. I had only the vaguest recollections of life before then....

As in a dream I am sitting on a bench. I have peed my pants. I am clutching a sticky box of Cracker Jacks. Even now, in my seventies, the smell of urine-soaked wool comes back, along with a terrifying fear of the unknown thing behind closed doors. There is a large person—a man?—holding me in strong arms. I am smothered against rough cloth with shiny metal buttons hurting my cheek. We are locked inside a box that moves. Shiny doors clang shut. Everything turns dark....

The strict routine of orphanage life was governed by tinkling bells. The bells told you when to get up, when to say grace, when to eat, and when to march out into the courtyard, the only place where you were allowed to run and scream.

I was standing there in the courtyard one day when a girl grabbed me by the arm and pulled me along with her as she ran. "Hey, Darcy!" she yelled. "Your brother wants to see you." I stumbled along, trying to make sense of what was happening. The word "brother" made a picture in my head. A boy feeding me food from a bucket, a boy named Joey. A great swelling filled my body as I approached the forbidden gate that separated the girls from the boys. I noticed sunshine! I felt vibrations in the air.

Through a peephole in the metal gate I met my brother. I saw how blue his eyes were, how shiny with tears. I saw gold freckles on his face and very short reddish hair. A girl behind me hissed, "Jiggers! Here comes Martin!" Sounds of feet scampering.

My head was yanked from the peephole by the hair. I was hustled along to the billowing and rasping of black veils and skirts. All the time I fought, dragging my feet, flailing at the smothering cloth, until at last some of it came free in my hands and I lay crouched on the floor of a small room at the feet of Sister Mary Martin.

She knelt before me, this nun, this Bride of Christ. "Oh, forgive me!" She had her hands folded in prayer. I looked to see if God was in the room, but He wasn't. "Forgive me, child," she said. "I have sinned against you." I can't remember what else she said, but I left there feeling saintly, or maybe like a person, from that day on coming into reality. First my brother and now this, being prayed to by a nun.

I also became a celebrity. Outside, in the courtyard, girls crowded around me with eager curiosity. "What did she do to you?" I described the frightening journey to the nun's room. Gasps of horror. "What did she do then? Did she beat you with whips? Did she put the Crown of Thorns on your head? Was she bald when you pulled off her veil?"

I remember only two girls by name: Susie Dischario, my best friend from my earliest to my last days at St. Mary's, and Mary Noonan, one of the older girls, a monitor. It was Mary who told me about mothers. Mothers were not nuns like Mother Superior. Mothers lived in houses outside the walls of St. Mary's. They had children like Susie and me. They wore flowered dresses and had hair that showed. Their legs showed too. They were pretty and held their children and kissed them. Susie and I said we wanted mothers. Mary said she did too, but the only way was to wish hard.

So we did. Every day we sat in the laundry room window with our wish lists, long, skinny pieces of paper. Susie holds my rolled-up list. I close my eyes, hold my breath, and pull, hoping it stops at my favorite wish: "Pretty mamma." We take turns. Susie's wish list says, "A mother." For some reason, I had to have a pretty mamma.

We never saw the people who came to look us over, people who wanted to adopt children. We knew they were there somewhere, hiding. The courtyard buzzed and hissed with hope. We tried to act like angels. By the time I was eight I'd given up hope. People only wanted little kids. I quit trying to be an angel and ran around screaming like the other big kids.

Then one day Sister Mary Cecilia summoned me for a talk. She put her hand on my shoulder. She reminded me that I must never give up my faith, no matter what happened. This meant that something was going to happen. I must have done something bad. "My dear child," she said, "you will be leaving us. Your mother is coming tomorrow to take you back to your home in Chicago."

I was ten years old. I went first to the encyclopedia, even though I have no memory of learning to read or even of attending school. There I found a picture titled "In Old Chicago." It showed a little girl in a long skirt herding geese up a muddy lane with a switch. That was me! And that was where I was going to live!

That's what Sister Mary Cecilia told me. Mother. Home. Chicago.

Susie wept. But I had cooked up a plan. All she had to do was to hide in the laundry cart that was taken outside the big gates and left there till morning. I would come back and get her.

I was summoned to Mother Superior's office and told to wait on the bench outside. I sat there shivering, once again facing a closed door with the unknown behind it. I could hear voices, high and low, a soft voice. A voice that made my heart hurt. I knew that voice. Mother Superior opened the door and crooked her finger for me to enter. Inside sat Joey, looking white, his freckles standing bright like golden spots. A woman leaned against a chair. She had on a flowered dress, and her red hair lay in puffs against her pink cheeks. I looked at her legs, and they showed too. "Child," said Mother Superior, "this lady is your mother."

She didn't have to tell me. I already knew. My pretty mamma.

GROWING UP—FAST

John Woodward

I was an old nine at the time. Eighteen days before ten. It was 1933.

The day was slightly overcast. It was late in October. I was scuffing down the sidewalk on northwest Fourteenth Street in Washington, D.C., coming home from grammar school. Sacred Heart.

We met at the corner, Fourteenth Street and Parkwood Place. It didn't often happen that we hit home at the same time, George and I. George was my older brother. We turned the corner and walked down Parkwood toward our home, midway down the block on the left. I remember the neighborhood well. Row house upon row house. Quiet middle-class housing, presentable even after four years of deep Depression.

I cannot remember what George and I were talking about as we climbed the steps of number 1361. The front door looked the same as always. No hidden secrets. Full paneled glass, top to bottom. Don't know which of us tried the knob first, but the door was locked.

We took turns pounding on the door and ringing the bell. We knew Dad was supposed to be home. Mom and my older sister, Marge, had told us this morning that they were going downtown to look for jobs. Our family had lost all in 1929.

No matter how loud we yelled or how hard we pounded, the door remained closed. George, invoking his four-year seniority, sent me back up the street, through the cross alley, and down the brick pavement behind our row of houses. Out of breath, chest heaving, I climbed the concrete steps, ran across the backyard, and stumbled up the four wooden porch steps.

I quickly tried the back door—also locked. I tried the dining room window—wouldn't budge. Frustrated, I returned to the door, cupped my hands to either side of my face, and pressed my nose against the lowest pane. It was then that I made out my father's form, stretched peacefully on the kitchen floor.

"Hey, Dad! It's me, Red. Open the door." No response. "Dad," I shouted, "get up." His features were serene, and he never blinked an eyelash. The racket I was making should have awakened the dead. He was lying there on the kitchen floor, a pillow under his head. I felt a surge of relief. He hadn't fallen! He was just taking a nap.

On the kitchen floor?

I turned and ran like mad through the backyard, down the steps to the alley, and around to the front of the house. Even before I reached the porch, I was yelling at George that something was wrong with Dad.

George bounded down the front steps and soon outdistanced me. Even if my stubby legs could have kept the pace, my shortness of breath slowed me to a stumbling trot. By the time I gained the back porch again, cramps almost doubling me over, George had broken one of the glass panes and had reached through and unlocked the door.

A strange, strong smell came funneling out. Momentarily, I couldn't place it. Then I remembered turning on the gas stove once when the pilot light wasn't lit.

George yelled, "Quick, open the doors and windows." All the

time he was shutting off the stove burners and the oven. "Hurry," he screamed. "Help me lift Dad." I grabbed two ankles but was in no condition to help.

My brother, tugging hard, tried to drag Dad to the living room. The burden was too much. "Red, go up to the Pauls and have Edith come help me. Then ask Mrs. Paul to call the rescue squad."

I ran out the front door, up two houses, and told Mrs. Paul what had happened. From then on, events are blurred. I remember sitting on the Pauls' front steps, watching the red fire truck careen around the corner and pull up in front of our house, facing the wrong way. They'll get a ticket, I thought. I don't even remember seeing them put my father in the ambulance.

My next concrete memory places me in my aunt and uncle's upstairs bedroom in Silver Spring, Maryland. My cousin Bob was hovering over me, adjusting the headset from his shortwave radio on my ears and telling me to listen to the music from New York City. I remember saying, "With these on, nothing goes in one ear and out the other."

At home the following day, Aunt Flora told me that my father had a weak heart and no matter how hard the doctors tried they couldn't save him. Later I overheard my mother telling my younger sister, Virginia, that we must find someone to take care of the cat. "Why?" Virginia asked. "Cats," my mother replied. "Cats have been known to scratch a dead person's face." I wondered how a cat could get into the funeral parlor.

The next morning, when I came downstairs, I was totally unprepared for the scene facing me. There, on the far side of the living room, I saw my father laid out in his coffin. I paled, my face screwed up in confusion and fear as I scurried down the back hall to the kitchen.

"Why is Dad here?"

"We can't afford a funeral parlor," Mom answered.

Dark thoughts welled up in my childish mind. I could envision coming downstairs in the shadowy night and seeing my father's face marred by deep claw marks. It was with overwhelming relief that I learned he was to be buried the next day—and yes, a neighbor was keeping our cat.

The day I returned to school, the uninhibited, innocent malignity of children showed its ugly face. I had just reached my seat, after slinking into class, when the girl in front of me turned during a moment of deathly stillness and said in a distinct voice, "Your father committed suicide." What could I do but hang my head in deep, agonizing Catholic shame? I wanted to disappear.

Never should it fall to a nine-year-old child to be the one to discover that his dad has killed himself. I know he didn't mean it to happen that way—but it did.

MOTHER'S NIGHT

Marian McHale

The little girl wearing only a thin flour sack walked quickly down the dark graveled road, following the staggering figure ahead. It seemed that she had been walking for hours, and she was very tired. Her feet were bleeding, and though they pained her she did not pause, for she was terrified of losing the figure.

In reality, it had been at most an hour since the two left home. The little girl had been lying in bed under a ragged quilt, warmed by the heat from the bodies of her brother and sister, when she heard the voices. Her breath came shorter and shallower as the slurred words grew louder and obscenities spewed into the night. They were drunk again, fighting again. Daddy might hurt Mother again. His voice rose in a threatening rumble, and hers, shrill with hate and cheap wine, screamed out, "You can't hit me, you bastard. I'll get the cops to throw you in the can. See how you like that!"

The child slipped from bed in time to see her mother dash out, fright and rage hurrying her unsteady feet. Love and fear drove the child after the woman. "Mother, Mother, where are you going?" she called softly. The woman turned, picked up a rock, and threw it viciously at the child. "Get back to the house and go to bed. Who do you think you're spying on?" The child ducked and stood in the shadows till the woman moved on, intent on her senseless goal. Then she followed—her mother was in no condition to take care of herself; she must see that no harm came to her.

And now she had been following for so long, and her feet were cut and bleeding, and fatigue made her hopeless grief seem a savage thing that would go on forever. She would never know rest again. She stumbled endlessly through a black world full of dense wavering shadows and knew that her life would always be this way—meaningless and filled with terror.

A round brightness appeared on the jagged horizon as a full moon rose calmly and quickly in the sky. But it was not the flat circle of light the child had always seen before; it was a ball, a world, a planet thick with mountains and plains and reality—a world there in the darkness, lighting up that darkness with its serenity and beauty. The girl stood still. In her joy, she forgot her fears. She forgot her bruised feet and the unloving mother who was stumbling more now, exhausted by her drunken frenzy. She forgot all that and saw grandeur, saw love that would come. Love with grandeur that would come and be hers.

She stood for a moment more, then with pity ran to the lost, bewildered figure ahead of her and turned her mother toward home.

My Parents

Frances Schmadeke

My father didn't come home for dinner often. My mother managed with no comment or complaint. When he was around, my brother and sister and I had dinner early and were sent upstairs to be quiet.

My mother would fix a special dinner, one she knew he'd enjoy, and would even put lit candles and flowers on the table. The three of us would keep looking over the railing and whispering, which must have upset her. I learned five years or so later that my mother knew he had a mistress and wanted to please him when he did come home.

She must have loved him very much.

LOVE IS LOVE

Beatrice Kalver

My mother and her sister were crazy about their handsome cousin Mushkatt. That's what everybody called him. He called himself Mushkatt-Blatt with a hyphen. Very elegant, or so he thought. Not *elegant* like what the scientists called Einstein's theory. *Elegant* like holding your teacup with your little finger sticking out.

The two sisters loved Mushkatt's Old World courtly manners, bowing and clicking his heels as he kissed their hands. And the way he dressed! In the winter he wore a black cape with a red lining, and he tossed one end over his shoulder like a Spanish grandee.

When he wasn't hanging around in the Café Royale downtown with the intelligentsia, as he called them—actors and writers and artists—he was hanging around our house, whispering secrets and compliments to the giggling sisters over Russian tea served in glasses, into which they stirred heaping teaspoons of raspberry jam instead of sugar.

Even I had a crush on him and couldn't wait for his visits. He always had a candy bar or something in his pocket for me, as well as flowers for the ladies. And he would bow and kiss my hand too and make me feel grown up and glamorous, even though at age eight I was so skinny and pale they called me the Green Lily.

Mushkatt lived to have fun with the ladies and to gossip. "He has never worked a day in his life!" the two sisters would say admiringly. They looked down on my father for working so hard and falling asleep at the opera and never having time for them. Mushkatt had plenty of time, and knew just what to do with it.

How did he support himself? He always managed to have a wife in the background who was willing to slave for him and leave him free to go visiting or to the café.

The wife I remember was named Manya, a big redheaded woman. She ran a ladies' hat shop, and when business was bad she told fortunes in the back of the store to supplement their income. She was very successful at the fortune-telling, with customers who came regularly for her predictions and advice, even on the stock market.

On Sundays Mushkatt would permit Manya to accompany him to our house, and after dinner the two sisters would beg her to tell their fortunes. Manya would produce a pack of cards and lay them out on the dining room table. She even told my fortune once. She said she saw me grown and beautiful. In the cards I was plump and rosy-cheeked, and a prince would fall in love with me and marry me and we would have five children. Three boys and two girls.

"But I don't want to get married," I cried. "I want to be an artist."

She looked harder at the cards and said, "Yes, I see that too. You will also be a great artist!"

No wonder her customers came back again and again and paid good money for her fortunes.

One day Manya came to my father for help. It seemed that while hanging around the Café Royale one day, showing off by reading the French newspaper (they had newspapers from all over the world there, rolled up on sticks), Mushkatt had come across a story about a Russian émigré princess who was working as a waitress in a restaurant in Paris. It showed a picture of her too, and he liked her looks. So he wrote her a letter telling her how sympathetic he felt for the sorry state of affairs in which she found herself. A princess having to work as a waitress! A disgrace to the world!

Apparently Mushkatt could make himself as charming and gallant on paper as he could in person, because the princess answered, and a correspondence ensued that grew warmer and warmer over the months, until now they were so madly in love that if they couldn't meet soon, they would both die!

"So what's the trouble?" Papa asked impatiently.

The trouble was, Manya told him, that Mushkatt had to get to Paris, and he had figured out that it would take a minimum of three thousand dollars for the trip across the ocean and for cutting a *bella figura*, as the Italians put it. He couldn't go like a pauper to a real princess. A member of the nobility had to be wined and dined in proper style or he would die of shame.

God only knows what lies he must have told the princess about his financial status.

Manya said all she had in the savings bank was about five hundred dollars, which she was afraid to part with in case she should get a cancer or something from all her troubles. But Mushkatt was driving her crazy begging her to arrange somehow for him to go to Paris. If she would do this one thing for him, he promised, it would be his last romantic adventure, and he swore he would return and be a good husband to her for the rest of his life.

Where could she turn, she asked Papa, except to him, their best friend, who was known for his kind heart and his charities and his generosity to everyone.

You won't believe it, but I saw it with my own eyes. Papa took out his checkbook, and saying, "What can you do? Love is love," he wrote out a check for three thousand dollars so Mushkatt could go to his princess in style and not disgrace the family.

The two sisters looked at my father with new respect after that. They had never suspected he could be so romantic. They had thought of him only as a dull businessman who fell asleep at the opera. Now they both got a crush on him and plied him with the same attentions they used to shower on Mushkatt.

Mushkatt stayed in Paris three months and wrote glowing letters home about how he and the princess were eating dinner every night at the Chalet des Iles, where you picked out your duck from the pond in which it was swimming and they cooked it for you crispy and delicious. The whole family was thrilled.

Finally the money was gone and Mushkatt returned. He was honorable, and he kept his promise to be a good husband to Manya. He even helped in the hat shop, and the customers adored him, and the business flourished. On Sundays the two of them came to our house for dinner, and Manya told everybody's fortune for free.

A Spirit
That Would Not Let Go

Michael Caracappa

For the first time in her seventy-eight years, Mama had to go to the hospital. She had never been sick. She never showed signs of fragility. One day she was strong, and the next her arms and legs went limp. "Hardening of the arteries," the doctors said.

Mama was given little or no chance of survival, but she did survive. She had no fear of being discarded in a nursing home. She took good care of us all those years. How could we not take care of her now? The ultimate sacrifice was made by my sister Betty and her husband, Phil, who lived in Minnesota and took Mama in. Together they did everything they could possibly do for her, with love and devotion.

Mama and I talked often on the phone. She always gave me her standard greeting: "Did you get married yet? Marry Lena and be happy like your brothers." But I had a different destiny. No mortgage payments for me. No crabgrass. No lawn to cut and mouths to feed. Growing up in the Depression years, I had no image of prosperity. I never dreamed of luxuries because they were always unattainable. I believed that to undertake marriage and a house and children before you could afford it would perpetuate poverty. Still, I knew Mama felt her work was not finished upon this earth until she saw the last of her sons married and her job passed on to another woman. Such was her passion.

Mama was hospitalized two more times. Each was supposed to be her last. As I was standing at her bedside the second time, she whispered, as always, "Did you get married?"

"No, Ma, not yet. We're waiting for you to get well."

Her gaunt face wore a strange expression. She could not speak, but her soulful eyes seemed to say, "I cannot wait much longer." At that moment I had an inspiration. I knew what I had to do.

There was nothing more the doctors could do for Mama. They thought it best that she die at home in a loving environment. She went back to the room where Phil and Betty provided for her. One day she asked for me, so Lena and I made the long motor trip from New York. When we arrived she asked me the eternal question. Lena showed her the ring on her finger. Mama held Lena's hand and smiled. I had never lied to her before, and I knew she would never suspect that I was lying now. That evening she wanted me to feed her, and Betty said she had not eaten like that in some time.

We spent five days with Mama and planned to leave on the next. In the early morning hours of the sixth day I woke suddenly and went to Mama. Her room was totally silent—no sound of traffic, not even the ticking of the clock. There was so much suffering on her face. I stood watching her for some time. A splash of heavy rain against the window drew my attention, and when I turned back to Mama her eyes were open. She looked confused, almost angry. Her face showed the grotesque shapes of pain and despair. Did I wake her? Then her eyes softened and some strength came to her face. She tried to smile. I told her I was leaving today but I'd be back. Then I lied again. "I'm in good hands now, Mama. Lena will take care of me." She looked at me through misty eyes. A mysterious peace suffused her face. She smiled and lifted her shoulders as if in a silent sob. She squeezed my hand and closed her eyes. In an instant she was gone.

A MOTHER'S LOVE
IS FOREVER

Nat I. Kornhaber

"There isn't much we can do for your mother," the doctor had told me. "It's a matter of time."

I had come very early to see her. It was a dark, rainy day, unusually cold for May. I sat by her bed, my eyes on the gaunt face. She was all of seventy pounds now, barely made a ripple under the covers. She was sleeping, so I got up and looked out the big window. When I heard a small movement, I returned to the bed.

It upset me to see her hands tied down. The nurse had told me that she'd pulled at the IV tubes connected to her body. She opened her eyes, and when she saw me a faint smile creased the corners of her mouth.

"Hello, Ma," I said softly, leaning over.

"Hello," she whispered. She moved her head slightly, and her eyes looked toward the window. "It's...so...dark." She spoke the words in Yiddish.

"I know, Momma. It's raining."

Her lips moved, but I couldn't hear anything. I bent very close to her. "What is it, Momma?"

It was almost inaudible, but I heard my mother say, "Raining.... You take...your rubbers?"

WINGS

Mollie Zucker

The grill is full of hamburgers. It is one o'clock. I have an eerie feeling, sort of disembodied, as if I am neither here nor anywhere else.

"What's the matter with you," my husband, Abe, is saying angrily, but he seems so far away.

What is real is a big rush of wind, as if a flock of birds were whizzing by overhead. My head feels light.

"Mollie, what on earth is the matter with you?" says Reggie, my friend who works with us. "You're as pale as a ghost."

"I don't know, Reggie."

I turn to a customer waiting at the counter. "What do you get on your hamburger?"

"You know, Mollie, the usual."

What is the usual? I wonder. "Will lettuce, tomatoes, and mayonnaise do it?"

"Mollie, I get mustard, ketchup, relish, tomatoes, and lettuce. You know that."

"And you?" I ask another customer.

He looks at me, surprised, but tells me he wants mustard, ketchup, relish, pickles, and tomatoes.

Eventually, with Reggie's and Abe's help, I fill all the orders and go outside to sit on the patio. Will this day never come to an end? I can't wait to go home. Finally it is 2:30 and the lunch-hour rush has subsided. "Mollie, you don't look well," says Abe. "Why don't you go home?"

I go across the street from our hamburger stand on Sweetzer Avenue and Santa Monica Boulevard to wait for the bus. I feel like I'm going to faint, and there is no bench to sit on. I sit down on the curb. People must think I'm drunk, but I don't care.

I'm glad to get home and immediately go to bed. Just as I'm dozing off, the phone jerks me awake.

"Mollie, it's Harry," says my brother-in-law in New York. "Your mother passed away today."

"Oh, Harry. What time did she die?"

"Four o'clock. She looked very peaceful. The funeral will be tomorrow afternoon."

I lie on the bed, still suspended in a netherworld, unable to comprehend what has been happening to me this day. Then I hear my mother's voice close by my bed.

"When my *nishuma* left my body, you heard me going and said goodbye. That was me overhead, my spirit, not the flapping of birds' wings."

THE AMBER GLASS BUTTONS

Elizabeth Thomson

I never see buttons on anything to this day without counting them.

Mother called me from play to open a package from Aunt Minnie. Inside were four amber glass buttons, dome-shaped and

52

hollow, sewed to a white card through two small holes in the top of the dome. They looked like four little glass bowls from a toy tea set.

"She sent them for your new winter coat. We're going downtown to buy the material this afternoon. We'll use three buttons and have a spare," my mother said.

"I want four buttons on my coat. I won't lose any." I was six years old with ideas of my own.

"No, dear. An odd number of buttons is more stylish. Always remember that."

We did not go downtown. At lunchtime my mother got a severe headache, passed out, and died in a few hours.

After the funeral, Aunt Minnie took the amber buttons home with her. When she sent my coat a week later, the buttons looked beautiful against the dark-brown corduroy. I cried, but no one knew why. My new coat was double-breasted. It had four buttons.

Sunday I wore it. While Miss Bell, my Sunday school teacher, talked about the shepherds, I twisted and twisted one amber button. Aunt Minnie had sewed it on to stay, but by the time the shepherds reached the manger that button was lost forever, pushed through a hole in the floor-furnace grille of Centenary Methodist Church.

Walking proudly home, I looked heavenward and whispered, "God, please tell my mother she'd like my coat now. It's much more stylish with three buttons."

WHERE IS MY EVERYTHING?

Elizabeth B. Cowles

I was the little nine-year-old in a long summer nightie standing at the upper windows of my grandmother's old Victorian house. I was watching a small group of my mother's friends walk up Grandmother's street. What were they doing here in Stillwater so early in the morning? They belonged in Winona, where we lived, in the rectory next to the church.

I thought of my father, who was across the ocean visiting old friends in London. It frightened me that he was so far away. *He* would know why these people were here.

I turned from the window and went down the hall to my mother's room. She was asleep. I tugged at her arm. "Mother," I asked anxiously, "what are those people from Winona doing here?" She was instantly awake. Flinging off her covers, she stood listening to the low voices on the porch below, the voices of her friends, who were ringing the bell hesitantly.

"I'll let them in," I said, and dashed down the stairway, happy to see them. But they did not speak to me or even smile as they crowded inside. Aunt Jennie started up the stairs to Mother's room, and I followed closely. Mother was just standing there. I heard Aunt Jennie say, "Eva, there's been an...an accident. Edward..." I watched my mother sink slowly to the floor.

Frightened, I ran into my older brothers' room, shaking them awake. "Father's had an accident!" I cried. I sat on their bed. Alice, twelve, joined us. We all talked of accidents—broken arms, broken legs. It might take Father weeks to return by boat, but by then he'd be all right. My brothers pushed me out so they could get dressed, and I went back to question Mother. But now she would not let me in. When I pulled on the door, Aunt Jennie opened it a peep. "Run along," she whispered. "You mustn't disturb your mother!"

Quickly I dressed and went downstairs. Everything was confusing. I heard whispered words. "So sudden...heart...dead." The words infuriated me. They couldn't be talking about my father. *He'd* had an *accident!* In the kitchen I stared at Annie, our cook, who had come with us from Winona. Her face was red and blotched with tears. She raised mournful blue eyes to me. "The poor dear," she said softly. "Right in the middle of his sermon he was...he just slipped away to God." Who was she talking about? Angrily I grabbed a raisin muffin from the oven pan. Annie did not snap at me to "put it back!"

I wandered through rooms. What was the matter with everyone? No one was explaining about the accident. Upstairs, in my little sisters' room, someone was hastily packing their clothes. Why? Then there was a taxi at the door taking the two little ones and Aunt Jennie away. Why didn't Aunt Jennie take me too?

Alice was lying on the big double bed where she and I slept, her face in the pillow, crying in great gulps. Pressing against the bed, I whispered, "Alice, did Father break his arm? Was it his leg? What happened to him?"

"He's dead," she sobbed.

"Alice! You're lying! I heard Aunt Jennie tell Mother he'd had an *accident!*"

There was no answer.

I remember sitting on the top step of the stairway. I could hear muffled voices in Mother's room. Then the door opened, and there was Mother, all strangely dressed in black, a short black veil over her face. As she passed me, starting down the steps, I clung to her long black skirt, crying, "Mother…where are you going?" Someone released the material from my tight fingers. From the stairs I saw the front door open. I saw another taxi, saw friends help Mother in, and then they were gone.

The house was so quiet. Were they all going to go and leave me? I did not want to stay here alone with my grandmother.

It was many weeks before I got back to Winona, and then I wasn't allowed to go home or see my mother. I stayed with a maiden aunt two blocks from the rectory. I was told Mother was ill and I was not to disturb her. The rest of the children were scattered among friends. I didn't see them either.

One day Aunt Nellie came out on the front porch, where I was playing jacks. "I have to run over to the rectory for a few minutes," she said. "I'll be right back." When I begged to go with her, she hesitated, then said, "All right." Did she know I was beginning to be afraid to be alone anywhere?

We walked down the tree-shaded street. As we drew near, I could see that our big house was newly painted. "Father will like that," I thought happily as I hurried up our sidewalk. Aunt Nellie opened the front door and dashed down the hall to intercept a departing painter. I stood in the doorway frozen with terror.

Everything was gone! The large, empty rooms and halls glistened with fresh paint. The windows were curtainless, the waxed floors bare.

Where was my mother! Where did I live? Where was our *everything?*

Aunt Nellie returned, smiling, and took my hand. "Doesn't

everything look nice and fresh?" she said. "The new minister and his family are moving in tomorrow."

For many days I pretended it wasn't true, but when we children were together again in a small, strange house, still tiptoeing around so we wouldn't disturb Mother, I knew that Father would never come back. ... I would never see my father again.

ELEGY

Jim Barwick

The grave was near the gate. The coffin was surrounded by flowers and wreaths, and this was the first time he had seen it from ground level. His mother was seated with several other ladies, and the Tall Men stood behind them. He looked at his mother's red eyes and wanted to crawl into her lap. There wasn't room. The minister was holding up his hand now, and the low voices and whispers that drifted among the Tall People subsided.

Suddenly he had to pee. He backed away from the seated group and blended into the forest of Tall People legs. This was the world of the four-year-old boy. Tall Women had surrounded him as far back as he could remember. He could identify some of his mother's friends by their legs, from broomsticks to pine stumps. The Tall Men's legs were all covered by trousers and all alike. There weren't many of these in his life, but there were always the Tall Women, except at night when he and his mother held each other and she rubbed his back as he went to sleep.

He ran behind a large car parked by the gate and quickly pulled aside the leg of his short pants to relieve himself. He didn't want to go back. The Tall People were too many, and nobody spoke to him. He sat down on the running board, facing away from the cemetery. He had never seen a car this large. It was long and black and had lots of silver trim. He wished now that he hadn't peed on the tire. Maybe no one would notice.

As the preacher's voice droned on, he sensed that a part of his recent life was coming to a close, all the trips to the hospital in D'lo where his daddy had stayed for a long time. The last time he'd seen his daddy in the hospital room, his face was red and swollen and rubber tubes were running from his back. He'd only gotten a glimpse before the nurse, Miss Hughes, took his hand and led him outside to the large swing on the grass. It had a floor that moved, and two facing seats suspended from a small roof. He had long since decided that Miss Hughes was the best part of the hospital visits. She spoke softly and had a beautiful face, like the women in his fairy tale book. Sometimes she held him close, and he could feel her body shake briefly as if she were trying not to cry. But when he looked at her she was always smiling, asking questions about the things he liked and the things that made him happy. There were always easy answers. He loved her.

For the next two days, he had spent as much time as he could in the backyard or looking at his books on the cistern porch. There was now a coffin sitting on a high wheeled stand in the living room, and the Tall Women were always there. The leg sizes changed, but the house crawled with them. There was always the smell of powder and perfume and occasionally soap. More and more flowers accumulated around the coffin, their scent blending with the smell of the Tall Women.

This morning he had sat beside his mother in the Methodist church. Her eyes were red. He had never seen her cry. The Tall Women gathered close around her, and if a tear ever fell, it couldn't have fallen far. The congregation sang "In the Garden," and the Masons came filing in carrying what looked like pool sticks and wearing small aprons that hung over their crotches. He tried to ask his mama why they dressed that way, but she quickly shushed him. They sang "Abide with Me," and then one of them spoke a few words. After more singing and the preacher talking, he rode in a car with his mother to the cemetery.

Now, as he sat on the running board of the large black car, he looked up at the tall oaks outside the fence. They appeared to touch the summer sky. He saw squirrels playing in the topmost branches, undisturbed by the activity far below. His best memory of his daddy was the walks in the woods. They would hunt tiny beechnuts, mayhaws, and chinquapins. When nothing was in season, his daddy would sprinkle Tom's Toasted Peanuts over the leaf floor under a large tree and call him to see the discovery.

Only the squirrels and the tall oaks saw the large figure of a man in a dark suit walk by the boy and disappear into the trees. They didn't hear him say, "Goodbye, son." They saw the child look up quickly and follow the fading figure with his eyes. They saw no tears. They saw his lips move.

"Goodbye, Daddy."

LEGACY OF LAUGHTER

Lillian Garfinkle Rhodes

I had never seen a dead person. I guess I was lucky, never losing anyone really close to me before. But it had to happen sooner or later. Parents just didn't last forever. I stood there in the funeral home, greeting the distant relatives who came to pay their respects, dreading the moment when it would no longer be possible to avoid looking at him in the coffin.

"Come on, don't you want to say goodbye to Pop? They're going to close the casket soon." It was my older brother, Arthur, taking my elbow and trying to steer me to where our father lay.

"I don't think so, Arthur. I'm afraid if I look at him now I'll never be able to get it out of my mind."

"Oh, come on, Lil. There's nothing to be scared of. He really looks very peaceful."

And firmly but gently, my eyes tightly shut, I was guided to the coffin. It was a simple wooden one, in keeping with Jewish tradition. I summoned all my courage and opened my eyes.

"My God—he looks like he's smiling. I can't believe it! Now I know what they mean when they say, 'He looked very natural.'" All my tension drained.

"See, Lil? Aren't you glad you're facing his death? It's not such a terrible thing when a sweet, kindly, eighty-three-year-old man dies suddenly, without suffering. It's a nice thing—it's like the kiss of God!"

"You're right, Arthur," I said to my beloved brother, who had sustained me through so many crises, both as a child and as an adult. "Remember what Pop always used to say?

> " 'When I die
>   Don't bury me at all
>   Just pickle my bones
>   In alcohol.' "

"Remember what else he used to say, Lil?

> " 'It ain't the cough
>   That carries you off;
>   It's the coffin
>   They carry you off in.' "

And as we stood there smiling down at Pop, our two brothers, Howard and Eddie, and our sister, Irene, joined us. Softly joking about Pop and how he used to kid about death, our smiles turned to laughter.

An impeccably dressed funeral attendant approached us, saying in hushed tones, "Won't you please take your seats inside the chapel? The service for the departed is about to begin." Like rebuked children, we stole softly into the quiet room where the assembly awaited the rabbi in silent anticipation.

Mother sat in the front row all alone, an elderly, stoical woman who looked as if she had dealt with life and come out the winner many times. We joined her in the front pew and tried to shift from levity to somberness. It was always like this when we met, no matter that we were now grown, with children of our own—when we got together, something clicked and we were like kids again. Pop used to encourage us; he was proud when his family was the loudest group at every wedding, bar mitzvah, and party. He would look around at us and say with a twinkle, "You know, you can all drink and you can all dance." And he was the best drinker and dancer of us all. If he ever had worries or troubles, he certainly never let his children know about them.

Mother took care of all the worrying in the family. Her favorite spot for it was at the kitchen window, where she would sit with her elbow on her lap, her hand propping up her chin. When she was asked what she was worrying about, she said, "And who needs a subject to worry about? I just worry!" And here she was at Pop's funeral, finally with something to worry about, although what probably concerned her more than anything was how she would get through the service. A bladder problem had plagued her for many years, and one of Pop's standing jokes on all their trips was how many gas stations he had to stop at.

Rabbi Gabelman began his eulogy. He had never known Pop very well, which told a lot about both of them. Pop was not very religious. He went to the synagogue only on the holiest days. He summed up his religion in a few words: "Just because you eat ham doesn't mean you have to murder someone." The rabbi spoke of Pop in the most glowing terms. His resonant, singsong voice went on and on, describing all Pop's virtues, how hard he worked to support his family...

At this Howard whispered, "Remember how he wanted to retire when he was forty-five and you wouldn't let him, Mom?"

"Yes, he said to me, 'I've worked hard all these years to support you, now it's your turn to support me.'"

And Howard and Mom smiled, and the smile passed down the row. The rabbi, meanwhile, was extolling Pop's love for all things great and small, his kindness to children.

Arthur whispered to Irene, "Remember that time we were standing on the subway platform and that troop of Boy Scouts filed into the train and Pop took out his false teeth and held them up to the window, clicking them in time to 'Yankee Doodle'?"

Irene giggled softly until I shushed her. But when she gasped to me, "Boy Scouts...false teeth...subway," I felt my face turning red with suppressed laughter. The whole family was caught up in the tide of restraining their emotions. When I breathed to Eddie, "I hope everyone thinks we're crying," the jig was up. Our faces flushed, our shoulders heaved, our hands covered our mouths— and fortunately our eyes teared. I heard old Tante Lena, in back of us, remark, "Vot a loving femily!"

"Oy, I have to go to the bathroom, I'll never last," Mother panted, unable to contain herself any longer.

At that moment came deliverance. The rabbi was saying, "The immediate family will rise and leave first." Arthur took Mother's arm, and with bowed heads we walked down the aisle through the gauntlet of eyes, some concerned, some merely curious to see who was taking death the hardest.

In the privacy of the antechamber, we finally exploded into poorly muffled laughter.

"Do you think Rabbi Gabelman realized what was going on?" I asked.

"Never. He's so entranced with the sound of his own voice that he's oblivious to everything else," said Arthur.

"Well, you'd all better behave yourselves from now on," Mother called from the ladies' room, "or the gossips in this town will have a field day."

We left the funeral home, the ushers helping us solicitously into the lead limousine. As we settled in for a nice reminiscent chat about Pop, Rabbi Gabelman got into the car.

"The funeral director is of the opinion that I should ride with the immediate family," he proclaimed in his booming Shakespearean voice. "Ah, yes, your father was truly a man of God. How I will miss seeing him at services every Friday night."

"But Rabbi, Pop didn't go to—" Arthur felt my elbow digging into his ribs. "Pop didn't give up easily, but he was getting too old to be out so late at night."

"Yes, yes, wonderful man, too bad he had to leave us."

The rabbi's voice droned on, barely penetrating my subconscious. He was a very self-possessed man. A beautiful white mane of hair framed his bold features and his penetrating dark eyes. His bearing was regal, seeming to proclaim, "I am doing God's work and I am what God should look like!"

Mother had begun to fidget in her seat as the funeral cortege swept off the bridge and started to wind its way through the streets of Staten Island. She leaned forward. "Pardon me, driver. Are you sure you have enough gas? Maybe you should find a station. Soon you'll be out in the country and there'll be no place to stop."

"No problem, ma'am. We always travel with a full tank."

"Oy, so do I, so do I," she muttered to herself, the only one to hear her being Irene, whose face started to redden again. Why had they put the rabbi in the family car? Maybe it was a lesson for us, we should learn there were times when we had to be serious. Irene regained her composure, but she knew it was only temporary. One more remark like that last one of Mom's...

Arthur, the family spokesman, took his responsibilities very much to heart. If the conversation lagged—and it was lagging—he considered it his duty to keep it going.

"It was just the other day I drove out to see Pop. He was sitting around looking bored, and I asked him if he'd like to go for a drive. We were rolling along when he said, 'Let's go over the bridge to Staten Island. There's a little restaurant there that serves the best ham sandwiches—'"

Arthur suddenly realized he was revealing to this godlike creature that his very own dear father, who was hopefully on his way to heaven right now, had broken the Jewish law. Why was he talking about ham, of all things, to a rabbi? He felt like he was snitching. If he kept Pop out of Jewish heaven, he would never forgive himself.

"Of course, Pop had never tasted the ham sandwiches," Arthur continued, "but he'd heard about them from a friend—he had many friends, not all Jewish, nothing wrong with that—and he figured that if they had such good ham sandwiches there, surely they would have a good vegetable soup or maybe even a superb cup of coffee and a piece of cheesecake—that's kosher, isn't it?"

With each word Arthur spoke, he got himself into deeper and deeper trouble. We could think of no way to extricate him, because we were too busy dissolving into helpless stifled laughter. Rabbi Gabelman, his eyes ever gazing toward heaven, appeared to be above it all.

"Well, anyhow, we were driving along looking for this place. The name was Sam's, and he said the slogan was 'Go to Sam for the Best Damn Ham'—you should pardon the expression. Pop never swore, of course, he was just repeating what his friend told him. But we never found the place. It started to rain, and I could see he was getting tired, so I turned around and drove him home. And that was the last time I saw him. What a guy! He really knew how to enjoy life."

Mother was still in trouble. As she tapped the driver on the shoulder, this time to *command* him to make a rest stop, the cemetery came mercifully into view. We were turning in when Rabbi Gabelman's hand rose dramatically, the outstretched holy finger pointing across the road to a sign over a building. Theatrically he read, "You have come to Sam for the Best Damn Ham." The whole family, as if on cue, broke into torrential laughter, and joining us in our knee-slapping mirth was none other than red-faced, bellowing Rabbi Gabelman.

After a hurried stop at the ladies' room, we stood on the bank of the yawning, welcoming fresh earth. Now we waited—serenely, respectfully—for our friend, the rabbi, to begin the graveside service.

> "Yiskadal
> Yiskadal
> When I die
> Don't bury me at all...."

Grandma and Grandpa

LEGACY OF A KIDNAPPING

Carrie E. Stewart-Haynes

Ellen Rivers, age thirteen, was a very skillful hand in the cotton fields of Gil Lender's plantation. She had immensely round blue-black eyes, ebony skin, and thick, silky braids. Her nimble fingers added extra bales of cotton to her parents' daily count. Her younger sister and brothers worshiped her as she supervised them in the art of cotton picking.

Ellen and her family yearned to be free from slavery's shackles, to till their own land, to learn to read without hiding under the bed with a lighted candle. They hoped and prayed that rumors of a North-South shooting war would materialize, with the North victorious and slavery outlawed.

One Saturday evening, at a birthday celebration for Ellen's sister, three young men played violins. One violinist, Benjamin Washington, liked Ellen's shy, dignified style, and fell in love with the swaying rhythm of her statuesque body on the dance floor. Ben stood erect at six feet four inches. He was nineteen years old, with a handsomely broad face and a strong, muscular body tuned by laborious work in the cotton fields and on the plantation.

They met again the following Monday morning in the fields and worked side by side every day. In 1855, after two years of courting, their parents approved their marriage. In full African tradition, with the eldest male family member presiding, Ellen and Ben, in flowing, colorful robes, exchanged vows and were blessed with spring water. The ceremony ended with a spirited dance. After the wedding, Ellen and Ben lived with Ellen's parents for three months while their fellow plantation hands built them a new home.

The newlyweds made sure that their marriage was properly entered in the family Bible by the family recorder. Since whites did not recognize Africans as humans, such statistics were not kept in the county records. The family Bible was a revered historical record of births, deaths, weddings, and all other notable events.

Gil Lender was dirt-poor, forever making deals to sell off his slaves to other plantation owners. One of them, Durek Legree, known as a ferocious slave beater, wanted to buy Ellen, but Lender refused to negotiate because he had transferred Ellen from the field to his house to take care of his six little children.

One day, four years after the marriage, Ellen was hanging clothes in Lender's backyard when Legree rode up on his horse, snatched her, flung her across the horse's backside, and sped with her to his plantation in North Carolina, many miles away. Lender was too poor to spare a horse to pursue the kidnapper.

Ben swore that he would track Legree down and rescue his wife. For days, nights, months, Ben sorted through the gossip he heard among the white slave overseers on the plantation and at the country store. Three years later, after the Civil War erupted, Ben made his plans. He had finally found out the location of Legree's plantation. In late November 1863, when Northern troops had begun to ravage the Southern plantations, Ben escaped from Lender's cotton fields and joined the Union Army, which welcomed slave recruits.

Wearing his uniform, Ben was assigned to deliver a message to the commanding officer at the headquarters barracks in the southern tip of North Carolina. His mission completed, he galloped at top speed to Legree's plantation. As he rode through the grounds, he had to guide his horse carefully among the many dead bodies. Suddenly Ben dismounted.

Durek Legree was lying face up in the dirt, dead. Ben stared down at this monstrous thief who had caused him and his wife so much grief. With the full strength of his two hundred and ten pounds and all his untold anguish and rage, he stood on Legree's dead body in his heavy army boots, and stomped, and stomped, and stomped, as if Legree were still alive and Ben had to crush the last breath out of him.

Ben searched the grounds until he found Ellen. She was unharmed and attending to the sick and wounded, victims of the Union raid on the plantation.

Ellen and Ben settled on Saint Helena, a beautiful sea island off the Atlantic coast of South Carolina. They farmed their own land, and by 1895 they had over three hundred acres. They raised nine sons and three daughters, one of them my mother. They are my family legacy.

MY GRANDFATHER'S FACE

Miriam Salpeter

As I stood looking out the hotel window at the gray city of Riga, I knew that I had been there before. All my life I had carried vivid images of my native Latvia. Mainly I remembered miles and miles of white beaches nestled between a blue sea and forests of birch and pine. In my memory the sun was always shining, making the sand glisten with the promise of amber. Every summer my friends and I spent hours sifting through the sand, soft as white flour, searching for the small splinters washed ashore from what seemed to be an inexhaustible supply. I did not know then that the Baltic Sea was famous for its amber, and I assumed that this was what all children did on any beach—hunt for amber when not building castles or bicycling on the edge of an endless sea.

The beach of my memories was not always the same. Sometimes it was a beach near Riga, chosen so my father would have an easy commute from his work in the city. Sometimes it was in the port city of Liepaja, five hours by train, where my grandparents, uncles, and cousins lived, and where my paternal grandfather had his amber workshop. When the summer was over and we were back at school, my friends and I would compare our prize finds. I felt a little guilty showing off what I collected by dipping into the box of waste pieces in the back room of my grandfather's workshop, but he did have beautiful big chunks, to which none on the beach could compare.

What I saw now was not those sunny beaches but a gray sky over gray buildings exactly as I remembered them. Even the pigeons looked familiar. "That's the opera house," I heard myself say to my husband, who was standing beside me. And pointing out this landmark, the center of long-ago Sunday outings, I knew that I had truly come home. For years I had resisted going back to the city I left just ahead of the war, the Nazis, and calamity. Everything and everybody associated with joy and love in this city was gone. Many had been brutally murdered by the Germans and their collaborators in this place where anti-Semitism was no stranger. Yet now I was back, and the sense of excitement was overwhelming, almost dizzying.

"Let's go down and have breakfast," my husband urged. "Then we'll walk through the city and you'll lead."

It was not easy to sit still and wait for service from inattentive waiters. Memories crowded in upon each other. I looked around, and my gaze rested on the image of a face crowned with gray hair at the other end of the large dining room. I tried to ignore it, occupying myself with the menu, but the face did not let me go. It could not be, but I knew that face. More than forty years ago, leaning out the train window, I had seen it on the receding figure of my grandfather, come from Liepaja to say goodbye—his form fading and only the face staring at me through time.

I groped for an explanation. I had to speak to that face. Who was this man, this double of my dead grandfather? Casting shyness aside, I crossed the dining room. I was almost running, but it seemed to take forever to reach him in my dream state.

"Excuse me, sir, what is your name?"

"My name?" the astounded man said, rising slowly with such familiar gestures.

Before he answered I knew who he must be, yet I needed to hear it spoken. I held my breath.

"My name is Mark."

"So is mine. I am Mendel Mark's daughter, and you must be his brother, my uncle Moishe from Berlin."

Uncle Moishe had survived the war and was now living in East Berlin. He was visiting Riga on business and had to leave the next day. And I had chanced on him, looking for my grandfather's face. Suddenly the crowded room disappeared and I was in his arms, held in a tight embrace. And in that embrace I felt the embraces of my other uncles, murdered here so long ago. They had often come to Riga on business, selling amber. Those visits, the highlights of my childhood, had been accompanied by trips to the circus, by laughter, by games of chess and gifts of amber. How could I have left them behind so carelessly?

"Have you had breakfast? Do you want to eat?"

My uncle's questions brought me back to reality. The commonplaces that followed—the hugs, the small talk, the arrangement to meet that night in our hotel room—did not diminish the heightened tension. I knew that this would be a special day!

That night my uncle visited our hotel. It was a warm meeting. I was touched by his gift of an amber necklace in memory of my grandfather, the amber merchant, whose remembered face had brought us together. We talked about my father's death, my mother's health, our own lives. Most of the time he sat staring at me, taking in every feature. I knew he was a silent man, and the silence was not disturbing. The joy of having met was real and sufficient. Each of us knew that this might be our only meeting, our lives worlds apart. But that did not matter. I was at peace and was able to return home, leaving Riga and my ghosts behind.

GRANDPA SPEAKS

Naomi Russo

At a very early age, I learned to love words, the motion of hands depicting them, the shape hands assumed forming letters of the alphabet. My grandfather was hearing impaired, and he taught me sign language when other youngsters were just learning to hold crayons.

Grandpa was a powerful man in his youth. Working on a tugboat with his father, he shoveled coal that produced steam to run the engine. A pulley and rope were used to lower containers of coal and lift out ashes. One day the rope broke. The worker on deck shouted a warning, but the deaf man in the hold didn't hear it. The container slammed down on him, smashing his pelvic bone near the hip. From that day the deaf man limped.

No longer able to perform heavy labor, Grandpa hired on as a city street cleaner. It was the era of horse-drawn vehicles. Street cleaners wore—of all things—white uniforms and pushed carts with brushes and shovels slung on the side. Eight hours a day they walked, picking up trash and manure.

Grandpa lived in a silent world. All through my childhood I heard people describe him as "deef" and call him a dummy. I would become very angry and shout, "My grandpa is *not* a dummy."

On Sundays and holidays, weather permitting, Grandpa and I went for long walks. Sometimes my legs felt worn off right up to my knees, I would be so tired. Because he was accustomed to walking all day, I don't think Grandpa realized how far he took me. How well I remember the little bags of confections he always carried to give me as we went along.

One day I discovered that my grandfather was not born deaf. When he was a small boy, he was stricken with spinal meningitis. His hearing diminished until there was none, not even the memory of sound. I was young and naive, and my love for that dear man led me to believe that if I tried, I might get him to make sounds. If so, he might learn to speak.

I explained my plan to Grandpa. He shook his head that it wouldn't work, but to please me he did as I asked. I began with animal sounds, shaping my lips to form "moo" and "baa." "Oink" was too difficult.

Perhaps Grandpa was amused by my performance. Not wanting to disappoint me, he forced grunts and strange noises. It wasn't long before he was able to discipline the sounds to come out "moo" and "baa." That was a start. As he exercised his vocal cords, he went from "ma" and "pa" to "bread," "coffee," "donut." No toy or gift could have made me happier than hearing the sounds slip out between Grandpa's lips. He learned to say "Rover." Can you imagine the pleasure he felt when the dog bounded up to us, his tail going a mile a minute?

Pleased with his success, Grandpa began trying to string words together. He hugged me, telling me it made him feel good, proud of his accomplishments. One warm, sunny day we walked to a park. My hands told Grandpa I wanted to rest. We found an empty bench and sat, letting the sunshine refuel our energy.

In a tree overhead a mother bird was teaching a fledgling to fly. Grandpa studied them for a while. Suddenly he looked at me, his eyes brimming with tears.

"No-mi, I love you," he said. "Ma teach ba-by." He pointed to the birds. "You teach me."

What elation! I had experienced a miracle. What joy!

FORTY MILES ON A ROSARY

Mildred Bunk

Great-grandma Bunk was a devotee of the rosary. If the beads were not in her hands, they were sure to be in her pocket. At home she prayed to the rhythm of her rocking chair, on vacation with us she prayed to the purr of our motorcar.

One trip found us driving through dark, dense forest where the trees were so tall and grew so close together that sunlight never reached the ground; we had to stand in the middle of the road and look straight up in order to see a glimpse of blue sky. The road was only dirt, little more than a path that the highway department had recently cut through the woods. There were no rest areas, no homes or stores, and plenty of wild animals. When we stopped for lunch, which we carried with us, we simply parked in the middle of the road and walked around eating our sandwiches and fruit. It didn't matter that we were blocking the way; there were no other cars.

The road wrapped around the mountain like ribbon around a surprise package. There were no signboards, and we had no way of knowing whether we were going in the right direction except that there was never a crossroad, so we couldn't have gone any other way. It was late in the afternoon when Paw stopped the car and announced to us and the spooky shadows hiding behind the trees, "See that bull moose standing in the road? Well, we'll have to spend the night with him if we don't get to a gas station soon. The gauge is on Empty, though that usually means there's a quart left, more or less, maybe enough to take us four or five miles."

The afternoon wore into twilight, and Grandma began to pray aloud. "Hail Mary, pray for us now and ... "

Just then we saw some men cleaning a bulldozer where they had cleared a pile of brush off the road.

"How far is it to the campgrounds?" Paw asked.

"Oh, a skip and a hopper. Forty miles or so," one of them said.

"How far to the next filling station?"

"Same."

"But we're out of gas," Paw almost cried.

"'Peers you'll have to do some coastin'," came the unsympa-

72

thetic answer. Then, as if he was feeling a little sorry for us after all, the man added, "But it's mostly downhill."

From Grandma in the back seat: "Hail Mary, give us gas in the tank."

After that Paw put the car in neutral and coasted wherever the grade was down. We drove on and on and joined Grandma in her devotions. She sat on the edge of the seat and leaned forward and held her rosary out in front as if she thought she could propel the car by prayer power.

Our rosary roundelay was frequently interrupted.

> Holy Mary... was that a bear?
> Pray for us and ... don't hit that skunk!
> Hail Mary... was that scream an owl?
> Now and at the hour... Look! Sunshine!

Sure enough, after an hour of twisting and turning among the trees in the dark forest, grotesque shapes leaping in the glare of our headlights, we had reached the end of the forest. We looked down into a beautiful valley filled with flowers reflecting a golden sunset. The first building was a gas station. Paw coasted right up to the pump and ordered, "Fill it up!" just as though he had known all the time that we could go forty miles on a rosary.

THE DIRECTION OF THE SPOON

Matilda Friedman

Grandfather Isaac said it was the beginning of how he learned to think for himself.

He lived, at the time of this story, in a thatched-roof house in a shtetl in Poland, with his parents and his aunt Fanny. They are poor, naturally, but they have food. For Isaac it was never enough.

Growing rapidly when he was was eleven years old, he was always hungry. During the week the food was very plain, but on Friday his mother usually managed a little something extra. On this particular Friday, she was preparing a cholent with a good piece of meat. The aroma filled the house, making him restless. He couldn't concentrate on his studies, his chores. He was intoxicated by the cooking smells.

Walking around outside, tossing stones in a bucket, he hears his mother scream. He rushes into the house. Mother is wringing her hands, asking God to forgive her. Aunt Fanny looks stunned. She had been cooking rice and milk. Mother had accidentally taken the milk spoon to stir the cholent.

Isaac was afraid his mother, a pious woman, would throw away the cholent because mixing milk and meat was a violation of kosher laws. He begged his mother to wait. He will go to the rabbi and ask for advice. Although not agile, he ran two miles in record time, blurted out the story to the rabbi's wife. She listened respectfully but said he would have to ask the rabbi, as this was too important for her to handle.

It seemed forever until the rabbi arrived, buttoning his trousers. Isaac retold the story. The rabbi asked such questions as: In what direction was the spoon facing? What time of day did it happen? And so forth.

Impatient as he was, Isaac answered to the best of his ability. Finally the rabbi asked him how old he was. When Isaac told him, the rabbi said he was too young, not yet a man, to deal with a matter of such importance. "Go home and tell your mother or father to see me about this," he instructed Isaac.

Isaac arrived home half dead from exhaustion and anxiety. His mother was waiting. "What did the rabbi say?" she asked.

"The rabbi said, 'Throw away the spoon and eat the cholent.'"

A BIRTHDAY PARTY

Marie Elizabeth Dodson

           In the summer of 1934 the Depression's gloom still hovered over the small rural community in South Carolina where I grew up. When it was decided one day that I would be sent to my grandmother's for the summer, I was overjoyed. Not only would I escape the suffocating confines of a small town and the tense economic climate of my family, but most important, once away from the rivalries of five sisters, I would be an individual! I knew my parents were hoping that a summer's diversion would help their capricious, unruly ten-year-old daughter to grow up.

On a hot day in June I was deposited at my grandmother's home in a college town in North Carolina. She received me with the stoic reserve she had adopted to meet life's challenges. She had raised her nine children with little help from her husband, whose poetic Irish temperament and love for the bottle kept him from earning bread for his family, and the Depression years had only intensified her struggles. Although she was scarcely sixty years old, my grandmother's hard life had etched deep lines in her face, and her tired eyes reflected the miseries she had known. Her plump little hands belied her personality. Their determination and deftness kneaded dough into lively, buoyant loaves, tended the flower and vegetable gardens, preserved and canned fruit from the orchard. Those same capable hands fashioned unique and beautiful garments for the town's society ladies.

During that memorable summer, my grandmother's garden became an earthly paradise for me and the neighborhood children who gathered there each day. We frolicked among the cherry, apple, pear, fig, and plum trees, hid among the twisted scuppernong vines, and ran barefoot over the lush carpet of grass, squealing with delight as our suntanned bodies dodged the pelting spray of the water hose. We tried hard to avoid trampling the flower beds where my grandmother's bright zinnias, marigolds, larkspurs, snapdragons, and roses reigned supreme. To quench our thirst on sweltering days, we chased the bell-clanging ice wagon down the street, catching the chips of ice that escaped. Our favorite spot in the garden was a far corner where the chinaberry tree stood. It offered refuge from the heat, provided low, sturdy branches for climbing, and yielded its gold-bronze berries as ammunition against enemies. On cool evenings, after supper, we huddled under the tree telling ghost stories. We captured lightning bugs in mason jars for our lanterns, and sometimes, at dusk, we strolled along the tree-lined walkways on the college campus, ending up at the ice cream store.

One night at the end of August I lay awake agonizing over some way to hold on to this happiness, to seal in my heart forever the magic of this summer. In black darkness I devised a plot, one in which I would star. I would pretend it was my birthday and host a farewell party for myself. I visualized myself surrounded by adoring friends and heaps of presents, and of course we would play our favorite games, perhaps for the last time. Unbeknownst to my grandmother, I made the rounds of the neighborhood the next day, inviting fifteen playmates to my "birthday party" at four o'clock the next afternoon.

At her sewing machine by the window, my grandmother caught a glimpse of the procession of children heading to her yard, little boys in short linen suits, little girls in pastel organdy dresses, with ribbons in their hair, all carrying boxes wrapped in tissue paper and colorful bows. Putting her sewing aside, she came to the front door, where I stood in a clean cotton dress, face freshly scrubbed and hair combed. By now she was getting accustomed to the bizarre, unpredictable behavior of her grandchild, and she intuitively sized up the situation. A model of grace under pressure, she suppressed her vexation and began making plans.

She greeted the guests and received their gifts, piling them on a hall table. Then she sent us to the garden to play and hurried to the kitchen, where she brought out a fresh loaf of bread from the cupboard, filled little glass dishes with strawberry and blackberry jams, and made lemonade in the brown crockery pitcher. In a shady spot under the chinaberry tree, she covered a table with a crisp white linen cloth and set out the china and silverware and damask napkins. We were called from play and ushered to the tea table, where my grandmother presided with quiet dignity. The late afternoon air, heavy with perfume from the clematis, rang with the excited chatter and laughter of the children. After tea was over, we were allowed a few more games, and then my grandmother bade the guests goodbye, tucking into the arm of each the birthday gift he or she had brought.

As we watched my playmates skip homeward, the afternoon sun sank, and with it my heart. Long before the party was over the excitement had faded for me. I looked into the tired, worn face of my grandmother, reflecting on her goodness in turning my act of ugliness into one of beauty and joy. The realization of the pain I had caused her made me break into uncontrollable sobs. I felt her warm, tender arms embrace me, the peace of her presence, and I knew I had been forgiven.

That was the last time I saw my grandmother. Some months after I returned home, we received news that she had died of a massive heart attack. She carried our secret of the birthday party to her grave, and I have carried its memory in my heart through many years. It is my hope that somewhere, in some paradise of her own, my grandmother smiles at the knowledge that a wayward grandchild's exit from the garden marked the end of innocence and the beginning of her determination finally to grow up.

GRANDMA BROOK

Martha Kezer Merideth

Grandma Brook was a little short dumpling of a lady. She had the sweetest face, the most loving arms, and the most understanding nature of anybody I knew, except my own mama, her oldest child.

And like Mama, she had pride and a stubborn streak. When she was a little girl, Grandma was sent to Dwight Mission, a church school in Indian territory. At mealtime, the children waited on tables, then washed the dishes and cleaned up the dining room and kitchen. One day, when Grandma was about nine years old, one of the diners made some disparaging remarks about "little half-breeds." Well, Grandma was one-half Creek Indian, and she didn't like the way the man talked. He made a particularly offensive remark as she brought coffee after the meal, so without a word she served him his coffee in his lap. She was punished, but she had her revenge!

Grandma and Grandpa Brook lived on a farm northeast of Okemah, Oklahoma. They had to be self-sufficient. She had lots of folk remedies stored away in her memory, and they were always effective. If someone cut himself—even a very bad cut—she would go to the tack room and gather spider webs from the dark corners. These she wadded together and placed on the cut, which always stopped the bleeding. The cure for a cold or cough was "pot likker," made from a mixture of cabbage, tomatoes, onions, salt, and pepper. When it was boiling, she put it on the table and bent you over the pot, placing a towel over your head like a tent. You inhaled the steam and sipped spoonfuls of the liquid. That really cleared the head!

I once had a puppy named Poodle. Like all puppies, Poodle was inquisitive. Grandma always had cats around to catch mice and rats, and Poodle had never seen a cat. One day he got too close to the old mama cat behind Grandma's big kitchen stove, and she took a vicious swipe and clawed right across his eyeball. He yelped pretty good! Without a second's hesitation, Grandma poured out a handful of salt and threw it in Poodle's eye. He didn't like that either, but his eye healed perfectly.

When new chicks were hatched, they were put in big boxes lined with paper and hay, covered with "cup towels," and kept warm behind the stove. I have been told that one day I went to Grandma and said, "This little chick won't cheep anymore!" No wonder. I was holding it by the neck.

The best thing about the stove was the warming oven. It was the first place we grandchildren checked upon arrival. There were always leftovers of some kind there, and *we* could *eat* them! Best of all was a biscuit. Grandma's biscuits were as big as our hands. She didn't cut them, she pinched off a handful of dough and patted and shaped it like a small loaf. Nobody's biscuits tasted like Grandma's. Sometimes there would be leftover bacon, thick and tasty, or home-cured ham. *So good!* And I never went home from Grandma's that she didn't send me with a quart jar of her home-canned pickled peaches, dill pickles, kraut, or a jar of wild plum jelly. Those were my favorites, and I felt she made them just for me.

One day when I was about thirteen, Grandma had been out

feeding the chickens. She was coming home, carrying the empty feed bucket, when she noticed a cow bawling in the meadow just south of the house. She went to investigate and found that the cow was caught in some wire. Grandma managed to untangle the wire, but instead of trotting off the other way, the cow charged her. Grandma swung at the cow with the empty bucket, all the time running toward the house. She was sixty-two years old then, and it was pretty hard for her to run. When she got to the yard fence, she had to climb over it to reach safety.

A couple of days later, Grandma went to Oklahoma City on the bus, planning to spend the weekend with Aunt Nettie and family. She didn't feel well but insisted on going anyway. Soon Aunt Nettie called Mama and told her that Grandma was in the hospital and very sick. She had ruptured a vessel in her intestine while running from the cow. For days she had been hemorrhaging. By the time she was hospitalized, infection had developed, and in those days there was nothing to fight infection. Sulfa and penicillin had not been discovered.

Such a loss to the family! We all adored her. Just writing these memories brings back the terrible empty ache I felt when she left us. So now, I'll go look at, and touch again, the things she gave me that I have managed to keep—a yellow sweater, a little doll dresser, a porcelain figurine of a young woman wearing "beach pajamas," and a collar from one of her dresses. These are the tangible things I have from her.

But the memories! Oh, the memories!

GRANNY MC

H. Ruth Coppinger

My father was tired at sixty-five. He had worked hard in the oil fields of Louisiana for many years. He welcomed being sixty-five. He bought a new suit for his retirement dinner and came home for good with his gold watch. But Daddy believed men did not live long after retirement.

As for Mama's family, they prepared for old age and death while they were still in their fifties. I clearly recall Mama saying to me when I was in my forties, "You'd better slow down. You're not as young as you used to be." For a moment it depressed me almost as much as the Avon lady who suggested I needed hormone cream.

And then there was my great-grandmother. Granny Mc was born before the Civil War, and by the time Great-granddaddy went away to fight for the Rebel cause, she had six children. Great-granddaddy returned home after the battle at Mission Ridge, wounded and in need of constant care. Granny Mc cared for her husband until he died, then left the farm and began traveling from one child to the next. She would arrive at each destination carrying one large and one small valise.

Granny Mc always received special treatment when she came to visit. A comfortable rocker was placed near the fireplace for her, along with a supply of good home-grown tobacco to fill her small pipe. After dinner she would sit and rock and leisurely smoke her pipe. She generally stayed a month or two, dispensing advice and weaving stories. Then she would climb into a buggy, her two bags in tow, and travel on to the next child. All the children knew what the small valise contained: Granny Mc's burial clothes. Before embarking on her sojourn, she had carefully hand-sewn a dress and undergarments so that if she died during any of her visits, her children could properly prepare her body and dress her for the viewing and burial.

The years passed, and one day Granny Mc inspected the contents of the small valise. The dress had aged and the threads had rotted. Granny Mc had outlived her burial clothes. In her eighties, still determined to prepare for the inevitable, she made herself another burial dress.

When my mother and her sisters aged, becoming frail and depressed, I could always elicit a chuckle by reminding them of Granny Mc and the remake of her burial clothes. They too had been preparing themselves for years. Despite their own dire predictions, they all lived past eighty.

On my birthday this summer I realized that I was now the oldest in that long line of well-prepared women. I decided not to dwell on the inevitable but to remember Granny Mc. I looked at her gold locket watch on its velvet ribbon, which will eventually be passed on to my daughter, and I smiled. I welcomed being sixty-five.

GGP

Janet D. Lake

As I sliced my banana into the cereal bowl this morning, I thought of Great-grandfather. Hardly a run-of-the-mill connection, but GGP was not a run-of-the-mill fellow. He was my grandfather, and great-grandfather to his ten great-grandchildren, and he said that bananas were to be sliced into the bottom of the bowl *before* you put the cereal in.

My earliest recollections of him are not altogether happy. He demanded instant obedience, absolute order, and he was *always* right. Pretty challenging for a child who was probably as strong willed as he was. In the genes, no doubt.

GGP was always the director of something or the executive secretary of something else. He had an office in the basement of his home. Oh, he worked in New York City, but the basement was headquarters for his thousand and one other activities. And I loved it. He had all kinds of paper, all sizes and colors. He had a typewriter, and he let me use it. He also had a spittoon shaped like a turtle, and if you stepped on the turtle's head, the shell opened and revealed horrible stuff, but it was fun to do.

When I was all grown up and had made him great (I gave him his first great-grandchild), he became one of my best friends. He retired in order to take care of my grandmother during her terminal illness, and the man who had never lifted a finger to help decided that a house could be run as efficiently as an office. He proceeded to do just that. After Gram died, my husband was serving in the navy in the western Pacific, and GGP came out to California "to put your household on a paying basis," he said. He organized everything—the kitchen, the daily schedule, and most memorably, the children.

My daughter was of an age to enjoy saddle shoes, and fashion said they had to be scuffed up. GGP said they had to be clean. *His* great-granddaughter was not going to be seen in such disreputable shoes. Every night he polished them; every morning I suggested to the tearful daughter that she just "dirty them up a bit" on the way to school. And every day we went through the same thing again.

GGP and I played canasta in the evening. Television was a new thing to him then, so we watched along with the children. While Gram was ill, he had taught himself to cook, and his specialty was sugar cookies. He made the best sugar cookies I ever ate. We would snitch the dough, and even worse, eat the cookies before they ever got cool. He'd pretend great annoyance, maintaining we didn't take time to appreciate them, just ate them, but I think he was secretly delighted.

GGP outlived all but one of his five children. He lived to dandle two of my grandchildren on his knee. There were many griefs in his life, but he never lost his sense of purpose and pride. He had moved in with his one surviving child, my aunt, who baby-sat for families that went away for prolonged vacations. At seventy-two, she was finding it a bit taxing. One morning, musing aloud, she wondered how she could break the news to a dear family that caring for their two-year-old was too much. GGP, then ninety-four, spoke up and said, "Just tell them your father won't let you."

In July of his ninety-eighth year he invited some friends from one of the senior centers he had founded years before to come have lunch with him. He and my aunt prepared a lovely luncheon, and then he took his friends on a walk through his beloved woods, enjoying the sounds and smells. The next day he was tired. Two days later, he simply did not wake up.

I'm sixty-seven now, but I expect I'll always slice my bananas into the bottom of the bowl.

THE STRAWBERRY FARM

Sid Levin

"Grandpa, we found these strawberries in the backyard. Can we eat them?" The little darlings were five and three, and I wouldn't have deprived them of anything. I went back to the yard with them to help them get their fill of berries.

That was in August. In September Carol called and said, "Jackie and David want to visit Grandpa, and they want some more of those terrific strawberries." My strawberry patch was through for the year. I quickly ran to the supermarket, picked out the biggest, ripest, reddest berries I could find, and salted them into the garden among the leftover weeds. When the kids arrived, we three went out to the yard and I helped them "pick" the berries. I was a sensation! Nobody could grow strawberries like their grandpa.

This scene repeated itself many times for over a year. Each trip of theirs was preceded by a warning phone call and a dash to the gourmet fruit market for the finest strawberries money could buy. My ranking as the best strawberry farmer in the world was unshaken until that fateful call in December.

"Grandpa, we're coming over this afternoon about two," Carol said. It was only twelve-thirty, plenty of time. When I got to the store, no berries! I rushed to another market, still no berries. At the third, same results. Now I was panic-stricken. My reputation was at stake.

Necessity is the mother, invention the product. I invented. I bought a box of cherry tomatoes, scattered them in the strawberry patch, and presto, the kids ate tomatoes that day. I kept my standing with them.

That was almost ten years ago. David is fourteen now, Jackie twelve. The other day, I mentioned the famous strawberry patch. They didn't even remember the tomatoes; all they recalled were the great strawberries Grandpa always grew. I had to confess and tell them the whole story.

My reputation as a farmer has now been destroyed. I wonder if I can get a government subsidy.

MATTERS OF THE HEART

Lynn Hamilton

FDR's sonorous tones poured out of the radio, filling the parlor. "That man in the White House," as Grandfather called him, was in fine fettle. Right in the middle of the fireside chat, Grandfather stood up and said, "I'm going to buy a piano."

"That's nice," said Grandmother, biting off the thread she used to darn his socks. She knew these daydreams: next week a boat, a special meerschaum pipe, or one of those newfangled Model-T Fords. She wasn't worried. She should have been.

Grandfather paid three hundred dollars cash for his Knabe piano.

"Three hundred dollars?" breathed Grandmother. "Why, you never had a lesson in your life."

"Nope," he said.

"Well, what in the world will you do with it?"

"You'll see." He smiled, flashing his gold teeth.

The Knabe arrived the following Monday morning. Grandfather stood on the porch and lit his pipe. Grandmother stared out the bay window at the men unloading the truck. The Knabe, wrapped in heavy blankets, was slid to street level as gently as a baby carriage. Grandmother took off her apron, tidied her hair, and went out to watch the piano inch up the sidewalk.

When the Knabe was in its place, Grandfather peeled off six fifty-dollar bills. The driver dashed off a receipt. "You got a good 'un," he said, nodding at the Knabe.

Grandfather sat down on the bench, rubbed his hands together over the keyboard, stroked the gleaming wood. He lifted the slanted front board with the music rack and pulled down the wooden prop. He sucked in his breath at the sight of the strings and hammers.

"So what are you going to play?" asked Grandmother with a tinge of snip.

"Gently, gently." His muffled voice wafted from the piano's innards. "In matters of the heart you must always get the best."

Grandmother went off to make soup.

During the weeks that followed, Grandfather kept the Knabe dusted and polished. Grandmother never heard him practice, not once. When visitors came, she made sure to show them the Knabe. "And you'd never believe how much money," she said.

At Christmas the whole clan gathered in the parlor for presents and cake.

"Play us a tune, Pop," said Uncle Don with a wink at Grandmother.

With a flourish, Grandfather sat down, paused, his hands held lightly above the keys, then began "Silent Night, Holy Night." We gaped as he changed chords, slick as a somersault in spring. We sang until the walls shook with sound. At the end of the second verse there was wild applause.

"Where did you learn to play the piano?" cried Uncle Don.

"Yeah, give us a little Charleston there," said Aunt Mary, snapping her fingers.

Grandfather beamed. He never learned to play anything else, but at Christmastime we always had "Silent Night."

Grandmother and the Knabe came to live with us when I was in the third grade. I learned that middle C was always where it was supposed to be. The Knabe was my solace during World War II and the long wait for my marine to come home. It was an accompaniment to the cries of my firstborn and the three that followed. I turned to it again when my brother went to Korea, our sons to Vietnam. And again when Dad died and Mama went along right after. Four generations have learned to make music on its yellowed ivories. It sings every time the family gathers at holidays.

Grandfather was very wise. If I listen closely I can hear an echo down the years. "In matters of the heart you must always get the best."

I look out the den window at the Marin Hills wrapped in clouds. Above, the sky is clear and cold. Below, Christmas lights are winking all over town. Our family will gather tonight, and the rooms will fill with music. I dust the old Knabe, buffing it to a rich mahogany glow. A Knabe is still just about the best piano you can buy.

Zaydie's Temper, Bubbie's Will

Sally Baler

I remember my grandfather, my zaydie, as a stern figure of authority, not very tall but quite good-looking. A white beard served as a frothy frame that set off his incredible blue eyes. His disarming smile gave him a roguish quality, but he possessed a temper that was known throughout the neighborhood and the surrounding towns.

My bubbie was a short woman with graying hair wound in a bun at the nape of her neck. A bit on the plump side, she always wore an apron around her ample waist. I can't recall a particular dress, only the apron. A hint of lip rouge was the only makeup she wore to brighten her heart-shaped face. It seemed to me she was never without a book clutched in her hands. It annoyed her when she had to put the book down to complete her household chores.

Zaydie was eighteen years old when he left his small village in Russia to avoid military service under the czar. He traveled to Minsk, where he worked at small jobs and felt secure in the anonymity the big city offered. One day he stopped at a public park and sat on a bench daydreaming. He became aware of two young women walking toward him, actually one in particular. They exchanged glances, and his heartbeat accelerated. He followed her home and waited outside her residence for two days.

On the second night, Basha Ginsberg came out of the modest house and invited him indoors for some food. Eight months later they were married. Two years later they left Russia for America. In Massachusetts, they lived with relatives in East Boston and then moved to their own flat in Dorchester because Bubbie was expecting her first child. Eventually she bore six, whom Zaydie described as three female children and three superb sons.

Bubbie loved America. She was delighted with her six-room flat, which was airy and warm in winter. She was enchanted with the indoor plumbing and the electric lights. She liked her neighbors, made new friends, and took pleasure in each new day.

My zaydie did not. He did learn to speak English, and after much family persuasion he shed some of his former habits of dress. But somehow he managed to keep his Russian image, especially in the winter, when he wore his Cossack-style fur hat, his knee-length boots, and his alpaca coat. With Zaydie, Russia was alive and well and living in Boston.

Each week and sometimes twice weekly, Zaydie entertained three or four of the local men in the front parlor. They discussed religion, money, their sons, and other important matters. Hour after hour Zaydie talked about his "wonderful Russia," which wore on Bubbie's patience. She did serve the men tea and home-baked sponge cake, but after the refreshments were consumed she hinted that it was time for them to go home. Soon Bubbie began to serve tea and cake earlier and earlier in the day.

Zaydie complained that she did not like his friends. "The next thing you know," he told her, "you'll be serving them when they walk in the door."

"I can't help it," she replied. "You are making me ill with these meetings. You keep bragging about Russia, and in the same breath you bitterly curse the czar. You tell them you are lonesome for the life you had there, yet you frighten them with horror stories of the pogroms. Make up your mind. If you love Russia so much, then go back."

Zaydie could be charming, but he was also an overbearing, strict master at home. He believed that the proper place for the woman of the house was in the house, where she should cook, clean, keep the Sabbath, and take care of the husband, sons, and other children.

Whenever Bubbie took issue with his behavior, he reminded her that he was "very Americanized." Didn't he eat hot dogs (kosher, of course)? Didn't he listen to Caruso on the Victrola? Didn't he smoke Helmar cigarettes instead of rolling his own? Didn't he deposit his money in the local bank instead of keeping it under the mattress? What could be more American?

Each Thursday after her shopping, Bubbie and I crossed Blue Hill Avenue to the Morton Theater, where we stood in the lobby while she stared for long moments at the colorful posters advertising coming attractions: Fanny Brice and Eddie Cantor heralding the latest *Ziegfeld Follies;* Clara Bow, Clark Gable, or Jean Harlow in their new films; and Pearl White living dangerously in the next thrilling installment of *The Perils of Pauline,* serialized weekly after the Pathé News.

Bubbie went to the Saturday matinee at the Morton Theater every week of the year unless a serious religious holiday fell on a Saturday. Every Saturday at noon my two sisters and my cousin and I walked to her house and were served a lunch of chicken soup with rice and leftovers from the Sabbath meal the night before. After lunch, Bubbie doled out eleven cents: ten for the movie and a penny to buy candy. Bubbie paid fifteen cents to sit downstairs so she could be closer to the screen.

Zaydie became somewhat of a madman every Saturday at noon. One time he slammed his fist through the door, causing the pictures to fall off the wall. Arms raised to the ceiling, head thrown back as if he were talking to God, he screamed, "Are you trying to destroy me? If you don't care about me, what about your grand- children? You are teaching them to act like Gentiles. Do you know any other woman who spends every Sabbath in a movie palace? You are making me the laughingstock of the neighborhood. God will punish you."

Bubbie told me later that he would have been wonderful in some of the movies she had seen that month.

One Saturday when Zaydie finally quieted down, Bubbie stood facing him defiantly. "I am leaving fifteen cents for the ice man," she told him. "We cannot miss the delivery or all the food will spoil."

"Aha!" he bellowed. "You will have to miss the delivery. I cer- tainly do not handle money on the Sabbath like some heathens I know."

Bubbie smiled and dropped a nickel and a dime on the table. She picked up her purse and walked to the door. Before leaving, she said, "When the ice man comes make sure he takes the money, and don't bite his head off. It's not his fault that I am at the movies. It's not my mother's fault, it's not your fault, and it's not God's fault. It's my fault. The need in me to go to the movies is too strong to fight. I will bear this sin and suffer the consequences." In a softer tone she added, "Louis, don't upset yourself. Make sure the man gets his money. At three o'clock, take a glass of milk and some crackers."

While Bubbie listened to Nelson Eddy sing "The Indian Love Call" to Jeanette MacDonald on the wide screen at the Morton

Theater, Zaydie tapped his fingers in nervous staccato at home as Tony, the ice man, slipped the latch into place after fitting the block of ice into the proper compartment. Zaydie spoke not a word when Tony picked up the money, but he turned his head away so as not to be contaminated by the sight of it.

Bubbie died when she was fifty-eight, long before her husband. In his last years he became a legend in the neighborhood as residents recounted for their children Louis Berman's dreadful behavior. He was a familiar sight on Woodrow Avenue as he daily walked with the aid of a cane along the familiar route to the synagogue. He was now nearly blind and in poor health.

Zaydie's Saturday morning prayers were for his wife, whom he missed. He felt closer to her on Saturday, he said. He felt she was watching him as he sang and prayed, the same way she watched her movies, and he was happy to perform for her.

Childhood

A STORY

Hannah Sampson

I know it was an early Saturday afternoon because I was minding two-year-old Francie in her go-cart, straining to see Papa's head among the crowd on the subway steps. There! I instantly recognized his rolling gait as he walked purposefully, like a sailor just home from the sea.

In a moment I was caught up in his arms and could smell the wonderful fragrance on his newly shaved face and his newly cut hair. His shoes were twin mirrors because he'd had a shoeshine while enjoying his Saturday luxuries at the barbershop. Papa was tall, very straight, and as good-looking as Rockliffe Fellows (a ruggedly handsome matinee idol). All my girlfriends were in love with him, so I had a lot of friends.

Now he emptied his pockets of the funny papers that were printed at the plant six weeks in advance of publication—another reason I was so popular. He took the handle of the go-cart, and I began to read as we walked home. When we arrived, he took Francie out of the cart and parked it under the stairwell, bouncing her in his arms. Francie giggled hysterically as we walked up the flight of stairs to our apartment.

Mama was waiting, as always. She had a quirky sense of humor. She was small and delicate, with fine, silky gold-brown hair, constantly in curls, to her disgust (we lived near the beach, and there was always moisture in the air). Her ideal was Colleen Moore, who had absolutely straight hair that she wore in a Dutch cut.

Mama took Francie and laid her on a small goosedown quilt on the floor. Papa touched Mama on her cheek.

"You smell good," she said. "Spent a fortune, I'll bet!"

"Only a small fortune." Papa grinned.

Mama fiddled around at the stove and soon served Papa. I'd already had my dinner. Then Mama put on her coat. "I'll be back," she said. She didn't usually leave the house after Papa came home, but he just nodded and ate.

I spread the funnies out on the floor near Francie and read the Katzenjammer Kids and Popeye. Papa finished eating and put *The Pearl Fishers* on our Landay record player, with Enrico Caruso singing his heart out. Papa said it helped him relax; then he lay down on the sofa.

I put Francie in her crib for her nap and went downstairs to play potsie with Louise. Then I got my double-dutch jump rope. Josie and Maria from down the block joined us. I went first because it was my rope.

> I sent my brother to the ice cream store,
> We ate it up and he went for more,
> We ate and ate and ate and ate,
> We got so fat, couldn't get through the gate.
> One, two, three, four, five, six, seven, eight.

Jumping, I suddenly saw Mama walking very fast up the street. She had a funny look on her face and a scarf over her head. She hurried by without greeting us, so I knew something was wrong. I grabbed the rope and ran up the stairs into the house.

Mama was in their bedroom, lying across the bed, crying her heart out. Papa went in and lay down beside Mama.

"What?" he asked, distressed. "What?"

"Nothing!" Mama yelled through her sobs.

"What *nothing*? Tell me. What?"

Mama ripped the scarf from her head and sat up, tears still streaming down her face.

Papa made a big mistake. He burst out laughing.

Mama looked at him incredulously, then picked up a pillow and banged him with it. He caught the pillow and hugged it, laughing harder.

Mama had had her hair bobbed!

"I told him, 'A Dutch cut, just like Colleen Moore,'" she wailed. "And just look at it!" And she began to cry all over again.

"So doesn't he know Colleen Moore?"

Mama blew her nose and wiped her neck where the tears had crept down. "He knows Colleen Moore. He cut it like Colleen Moore. Oh, it looked like Colleen Moore after he'd cut it. Then it *dried*. And it wouldn't stay flat."

Mama reached for the dresser and got her celluloid-backed hand mirror and looked herself over, and soon she and Papa were laughing so hard they woke up Francie. Mama's entire hair was a mass of tiny, wispy curls, with not a bang in sight. Like a little baby boy she looked.

"Let's face it," Papa said, "Colleen Moore you are not. Lillian Gish, maybe. Besides, I didn't marry some Irish colleen. I married Ada Berkelheimer with the curly hair."

I shushed Francie back to sleep. Papa and Mama were sitting side by side on the bed. Suddenly Papa reached into his pocket. "So, tootsie." He smiled at me. "You've been a good girl?" And he gave me money for the movies, reminding me to sit through only two shows and to come straight home.

I picked up Louise, and we saw an episode of Pearl White and something with Tom Mix, and we saw it all twice.

When I came home Papa had just been to the store and got our usual Saturday night supper: fresh kaiser rolls, sturgeon, lox, cream cheese, cream soda. It was the only marketing he did. He arranged the food on the good dishes and called Mama to come and eat. They usually sat at opposite ends of the kitchen table, but now they sat beside each other, exchanging soft smiles without words. How I secretly longed to penetrate this private enclave! Although I knew they loved me, I sensed that this was just the two of them and there was no place in it for me. I would always be just on the periphery of this mysterious silence.

Later on, I understood. As Robert Louis Stevenson said, "When parents are lovers, children are orphans."

THE DAY I RAN OVER RUBY AND FRANK

Inez Unruh

My father thought his children could do anything. He would show us how to do something once, then walk away and expect us to do it. It never occurred to him that it might be beyond our age range and strength. He expected us to rise to the occasion, and truth to tell, most of the time we did.

One summer day, however, his confidence came a memorable cropper.

It was the Dirty Thirties, during the drought and the Depression. We lived on a wheat farm, and a sparse harvest at best was right at the door. I was a skinny, undersized nine, the fourth of eight children. My youngest brother was six weeks old. My seven-year-old sister was wheeling him around the yard in the wicker baby buggy with the big hood. My fifteen-year-old sister was in the house cooking supper. My thirteen- and eleven-year-old brothers were in the barn with Mom doing the evening milking. My four- and two-year-old brothers were playing in a pile of dirt. Dad was working on the harvester and I was handing him tools when he decided to check the wheat for ripeness. His method was to walk through the field, break off a head, rub the beard between his hands, and chew a few grains to see if they were dry.

We lived on the crest of what passed for a hill in western Kansas, actually just a gentle rise. The farmhouse was next to the road, with a circular drive between it and a line of locust trees to the south. The barn and corral were beyond the trees. Our riding horse, Buck, was tied to the third tree from the end near the barn. Across the road to the north and east lay the quarter-section of ripening wheat. The roads were laid out on the section lines in mile-square grids.

We had a Model-T Ford. The spark and ignition were on the steering post. There was one pedal on the floor for locomotion. You pressed down and the car started moving, you let up and it slowed. Another pedal for the brake, and that was it.

Dad took me with him. We drove half a mile to the east, half a mile to the north. He set the spark, told me to take the car home, gave me a few brief instructions, and walked off across the field.

So there I was, barely able to see through the steering wheel, my leg stretched out full length to reach the pedal. At thirteen I weighed sixty-nine pounds, at nine I must have looked six. No matter, Dad told me to take the car home, so I took the car home. I don't remember being at all afraid.

When I came to the bottom of the hill, the car slowed. Down went my foot, and the car picked up speed. I careened around the corner into the yard and saw my sister dead ahead under the third locust tree with the baby buggy. I panicked, my foot froze, and I didn't make the curve. The car came to a screeching halt against the tree with the baby buggy and my sister underneath.

To my dying day I will recall in agonizing detail the buggy wheels floating slowly past the window. I see Buck rear back in the dust, breaking his reins and running away. I see my sister, dirty and torn, with tire marks on her back, crawl out from under the car. I see my mother and brothers come running, screaming and flinging milk buckets. I see them, the three of them, lift the car bodily from the buggy and tear the crumpled mass apart. I see my mother clean dirt from the baby's mouth, and I see him begin to cry as I sit crying and screaming on the ground.

A half-hour later my father strolled in, serenely unaware that anything was wrong. My mother was a verbal woman, and she made him extremely aware in a very short time and in no uncertain terms. For two days I burst into tears every little while, until my mother said, "Nothing happened! Now quit your bawling!" And I did. I quit so completely, in fact, that from then to now I have not cried enough to wet a handkerchief.

We tell stories at family reunions. "The day John rode the boar backwards up the loading chute." "The day Lillian fell off the horse." "The summer we raised the chickens." "The day Inez ran over Ruby and Frank." It's funny now, it gets funnier every year, but sometimes I remember the pain and the fear and the guilt. For a long time I thought it was my fault, that I should have been smarter and bigger and quicker. It left me with the subtle conviction that what begins as glorious adventure will probably turn into monumental disaster, but it has not kept me from adventure.

Sometimes I wonder if I could still drive a Model T.

LITTLE CHARLIE VELEBA

Herman G. Glick

Little Charlie Veleba was my six-year-old playmate, a Czech boy who wore his knickers above his knees. He had long black stockings, button shoes, and a flat black cap. He smelled like homemade bread. He was run over by a car.

My mother took me to the funeral parlor, and we sat in folding chairs. There were cardboard fans on each seat, with Jesus on one side and "Bartunek's Funeral Parlor" on the other. In 1924 air conditioning had not become a necessity, and the heavy, sweet fragrance of flowers was suffocating. That sickening aroma must be what death really smelled like, I decided.

All I could see of Charlie was a tiny yellowish face without his black cap. I don't remember if I felt remorse or sadness, but I was disappointed because I couldn't see where his skull was fractured. My mother urged me to speak to Charlie's mother and tell her how sorry I was.

"I'm sorry that Charlie died," I said. "Can I have his toys?"

Charlie's mother was Bohemian, but not from Greenwich Village. Her square face was expressionless. I thought it was because the hair was pulled too tight on top of her head. She believed in coal and oranges or nuts in Christmas stockings. Talking to her was like putting a letter in the mailbox. The words disappeared. There was no reaction to my first social venture in consoling a mourner, which seemed to be a puzzling failure.

A few days later, there was a sharp rap on our kitchen door. My mother was on her hands and knees, holding a candle to the frozen pipes under the sink. I had been busy freezing pennies in the ice on the windows. I opened the door, and there was that square face. She thrust a warm loaf of bread, wrapped in a tea towel, into my arms. "*Chléb*," she said—Czech for "bread"—and turned abruptly to go. Spinning around, she shoved a paper bag at me and vanished.

In the bag was a little European celluloid acrobat who did tricks when you turned him in the sunlight. The square face that showed no grief must have understood me, or else, in their silent farewell, Charlie explained it to her.

The Magic of Dreams

Edna C. Norrell

Edna envisioned herself bowing gracefully from the stage of the Grand Ole Opry to thunderous applause and a standing ovation. She was going to be a big star the summer she persuaded her daddy, against his better judgment, to order a $5.95 flat-top guitar for her from Sears. At twelve, dreams are important, and during the difficult, dark times of the Great Depression, dreams were about all she had.

The great day and the guitar arrived. Edna tore open the cardboard container and pulled out the most beautiful instrument she'd ever seen. Sears had generously included a pick, and she lost no time taking both out to the wash bench in the backyard. The strings seemed awfully loose; they flapped against the box, and she had no idea whether they were in tune or not. She tightened them up a bit and started right in playing. The old hound dog pointed his nose toward the sky, tucked his tail between his legs, and headed for parts unknown.

Edna decided to sing too; maybe a yodel would blend right in (she'd heard Jimmie Rodgers do that). The red rooster listened for a moment, shook his head, and lit out for the barn at a dead run, a flock of hens following closely.

Chickens couldn't be expected to know about the finer things in life. Hound dogs either. As Edna's playing got louder and her yodel higher, her mama rushed out the back door and told her to tone it down, she was probably scaring the wits out of Daddy out in the back forty.

Guitars, for some reason, were called "starvation boxes," and after listening to Edna for fifteen minutes, her daddy said he could understand why. A person trying to make a living playing one would in all probability starve to death. After a week he could stand no more.

"Honey, why don't you go see Grandma and Grandpa?"

"I was just over there last week," Edna protested.

"Well, they aren't getting any younger, you know."

So the guitar and Edna went to visit Grandma and Grandpa, who welcomed them with open arms, assured Edna they would love to hear her play, and lived to regret it. Ten minutes later Grandma remembered that Aunt Hettie was ailing. Edna's music was just what she needed to cheer her right up.

Aunt Hettie had a son named Isom, who was a year older than Edna and owned a banjo with two strings missing. According to him, he didn't need them; a real musician could play on what was left. He knew one chord on the guitar, G, and taught it to Edna. Boy, was she in business now, especially since Isom could play two tunes, "Redwing" and "Pop Goes the Weasel." Aunt Hettie developed a splitting headache and asked them to relocate.

Down in the pasture, Isom struck up "Redwing," Edna joining in with her one chord. Two cows and a mule made for the back side of the pasture. When Isom started in on "Weasel," Edna felt her yodel would help. She let loose with one that had a lot of highs and lows, voice breaking in between the highs. Isom said maybe she should leave off the yodels, they didn't exactly fit in with "Weasel," and that hurt her feelings. Edna thought her high notes were out of this world, and they just about were.

Three years later, Edna still hadn't made it to the Grand Ole Opry. In fact, she never did make it, but she sure had fun dreaming. Fifty years later, she taught her grandson the first chord he ever learned, G. He is a very good guitarist and has his own gospel band.

MY HIDEAWAY

Jackye Havenhill

Like sentinels guarding an outpost, they stood. Every house in our rural area had one, positioned a short distance from the back entrance. Whatever the status of the house—from the large, white, airy two-story clapboard with a vine-covered veranda to the two-room, run-down, weather-beaten shanty hovering in the corner of a plowed field—behind it stood the ever-present necessary outhouse.

Each was as distinctive as the residence it complemented. Some were erect, standing proudly with doors securely latched, while others leaned miserably, their doors hanging by a hinge. Some had no door at all. Many homes boasted large outhouses, smugly referred to as "two-holers," sometimes even "three-holers." Some people considered their outhouses improper topics of conversation and discreetly hid them behind a cluster of tall hollyhock bushes or a row of stately poplar trees. The camouflage helped but could not conceal the recognizable architecture.

Our outhouse was a special one. It was only a one-holer, but to me that made it even more private and more special. I lived on a dairy farm, and my father sold milk in town. Each morning he loaded ten-gallon cans of milk into the truck and hauled them to the processing plant. Since he sold Grade A milk, not only did the barn have to meet certain specifications of cleanliness, so did the outhouse. Ours was a concrete building placed over a deep pit. The floor was also of concrete. The well-hinged door had to be securely fastened at all times. As part of the government requirements the building had to be whitewashed, just like the barn, and lime was sprinkled into the pit at regular intervals.

This sturdy structure became my hideaway. Often during the summer, when the chores were endless, I sneaked to the outhouse to enjoy moments of quiet solitude. Stacked in the corner were outdated issues of the Sears, Roebuck and Montgomery Ward catalogues, battered and torn. Not only had my parents clipped from the pages items they wanted to purchase, my sisters and I had cut out paper dolls and dresses that we dreamed about.

It was in the outhouse that I became an addict of the short story. Mother had put year-old copies of the *Delineator*, a magazine for women, in the corner with the catalogues. I read a story on each trip, except when Mother's summons forced me to abandon it until the next escape.

My most memorable summer was in the late thirties. *Gone with the Wind* had just been published. It was the book of books. I literally devoured it. I would hold my copy coyly out of sight and make a dash for the outhouse, always careful to fasten the door, hoping and praying no one would miss me. It was in the outhouse that I fell madly in love with Rhett Butler. It was there that I admired Scarlett's courage and loathed her ruthlessness.

I would read and time would slip away. Soon, engrossed in my book, I would hear Mother calling me. I always answered obediently but ignored her for as long as I dared. When she pounded on the door and commanded me to get back to my work, her voice stern, I knew it was time for me leave Rhett.

Reluctantly, I would mark my place, close my book, and leave my secluded hideaway. When I returned to my drab world, I always carried my dreams with me.

Our Lake Is a Pond

Warren Platt

A crow perched in the latticework of Medicine Bow's water tower greets Billy and me raucously. A few clouds float overhead, drifting serenely in the warmth of the Wyoming sky. It is August 1922, and we are both about ten years old.

We pause for a moment at an inviting pile of junk. The rusting hulk of a deserted car sits jauntily at one side. It's all that's left of our old Maxwell touring car. I climb onto the sagging seat and press an imaginary horn.

"Ooga-ooga," I yell.

The battered torso of an abandoned Model T nearby, weeds and grass competing with the rust, invites the attention of Billy, and he runs to it.

"I'll race ya to the lake," he challenges.

Imagination changes the dusty purple of sagebrush and the spindly stalks of greasewood into gigantic trees. Scent of pine replaces the aroma of sage, and two mighty cars spring into life and roar to the lake.

An overflow pipe from the water tower feeds a fairly steady trickle of water into a crooked depression fifty yards or so away. A muddy, weedy, curved pond results, maybe a hundred feet long by thirty or forty feet wide and nowhere more than knee-deep.

We jerk off our shoes and socks and step gingerly into the water, making sure there are no wriggly live things under our feet. Warm, gooey mud oozes up between our toes, giving us a thrill of pleasure. We work our feet forward, and a brownish cloud spreads. A few feet away, the beady eyes of a water dog warily follow our progress. The redolence of muck and decaying weeds, fetid, familiar, and welcome, surrounds us. A large green frog on the edge of our makeshift raft garrumps and dives into the water as we approach. There are buzzing sounds of insects, and a couple of devil's darning needles drift by.

We hop onto our raft, Billy at one end and I at the other, head out of the lake into the mighty Mississippi, off into the world of Tom Sawyer and Huckleberry Finn. The small shrubs become cottonwood and live oak trees on the far riverbank. An eddy marks a shallows, beyond maybe a big fish. Billy stops poling.

"Shh," he whispers. "Warren, I think there's a gator hiding in there." He points to a clump of cattails at the edge of the river.

"Sure is," I whisper back. "Get your spear ready so we can fight him off."

It's a bitter fight, but we're winning when we spot Heck coming down the slope to the pond with something half hidden in his hands, his eyes a little shifty as he glances around.

Now, Heck's not one of our regular group, and my mother has advised me not to have much to do with him. He's older, tends to get into trouble, to do things and propose things that aren't strictly in line. However, my mother isn't here.

"What ya got, Heck?" I inquire.

He sits down on the bank and importantly holds up a handful of long, wicked-looking black cigars.

"Gosh," Billy gasps, "where'dja get those?"

Heck holds one to his nose and sniffs, like he's seen 'em do at the saloon. "Remember old Charlie's house, that had the fire? Well, he had a lot of boxes of cigars, and they got soaked when they put out the fire. He had 'em spread out in the sun to dry. I snitched these."

"Whatcha gonna do with 'em?" Billy asks.

"Smoke 'em, of course." He grins. "Dare ya to try one."

Heck strikes a big wooden match and starts to puff, pretending like it's old stuff for him. He blows some smoke out and passes the cigar to Billy, who looks at it sort of funny, draws a little smoke, gasps, and gives it to me. Well, I know better, but my honor's involved, so I take a puff. The putrid smoke catches in my throat, and I try not to gag as I hand the cigar back to Heck.

"Boy, that's somethin'," I manage. "Dare ya to finish it."

"Aw, you're both sissies," comments Heck, and with much bravado proceeds to smoke.

Billy and I draw away from the drifting, stinky smell and watch with a mixture of fascination and admiration.

Then a strange thing happens. Heck's face turns kind of green, and his head's weaving around a little, and he begins to retch. He's sick, and boy oh boy, I mean sick. We stand around a while until Heck yells at us to get the heck out of there and leave him alone.

When we get back up to the water tower, the crow in the girders has been joined by several others, with their strident, mocking cries. I look at Billy and Billy looks at me, and we laugh and laugh and laugh.

CHILDHOOD MEMORIES

Robert Christin

I was lying on the bed in my mother's room while she and my aunt got ready to go out. I knew this was a special occasion because they had so many things on the dresser and the vanity table: jars and jars of stuff, creamy stuff they rubbed on their skin, on their faces, on their cheeks, makeup for their eyelids and eyelashes, red lipstick for their lips, and combs and brushes of all different sizes for their hair.

First they took their baths and came out in robes, their hair wrapped in large towels so they looked more Arabian than American. Then they put on panties and bras and garter belts and stockings, and then they fixed their faces and their skin and their hands, and after all that they began to dress: first a corset, and on top of it a slip, and finally, amidst all the powders and creams and paints and crayons and lotions and balms, they slipped into their bright dresses. When at long last they emerged, they looked spectacular and the room looked awful, with powder on the dresser and the floor in front of it and all over the vanity table and the chair.

They were always late. My father would call up the stairs,

"Edith, are you coming?" and Uncle Bill would yell, "Peg, please, for God's sake, let's go!" My mother and my aunt would yell back very sweetly, "It won't be long," except that as they said this they were starting their baths, and they said it again and again while they were dressing. Now and then, because they were hurrying, something fell or spilled, powder on the bedspread or fingernail polish all over the dresser, and Peg would say, "Damn, damn, damn," and then go right on applying her rouge or combing her hair. I always liked watching this ritual of theirs because it was like being backstage before a magic show and finding out how the magician got ready and maybe even how to do some of the tricks.

When the women were ready they started down the stairs together, high heels clicking on the oak steps almost in unison, like soldiers marching, and when they got to the bottom in all their splendor my father and my uncle didn't seem to notice how much they'd changed but only said, "It's about time." Mom and Peg didn't seem to care.

As they walked out the front door and onto the concrete porch, they carried themselves differently, my mother very sweet when she was all dressed up, never cross or angry at me or anyone else, smiling and looking ever so pretty. Sometimes Old Man McGee next door would be on his porch, and he would look over and say, "Where did those two beauties come from? Come here, Maggie, there are two dashing women visiting next door. Have a look." And Maggie McGee, who seldom dressed up and was always sweet, would say, "Why, Win, that's Edith and Peg, and they sure are dashing beauties. Where are you going, lucky ladies?" And my mother would yell back that they were going to a dinner dance at the Neil House sponsored by some charity my father's boss's wife belonged to.

And the two actresses, the two movie stars, my mother and my favorite aunt, walked back and forth on the front-porch stage as if they were appearing at the Hartman Theatre, glancing around to see whether any other neighbors were watching their performance. Then the men came out, they all descended the steps toward the car and waved goodbye, and I went in to join the baby-sitter and my brothers and sister for a quiet evening in the littered household where the kitchen was a mess and the dishes were still on the dining room table and if we all pitched in and cleaned up, Ruth, our sitter, would let us stay up late.

If You Have a Skeleton...

Laura Arbeit

I snatched the little doll with the porcelain face from my sister's lap and hurled it against the metal brace she wore on her paralyzed leg. "I hate you worse than poison," I screeched.

The shattered prettiness stared up at both of us from the stone steps. Ella gasped and screamed, "You killed her....You killed her!"

My mother appeared in the doorway and quickly perceived that I was the villain. "How could you do that to your sister? She's worked so hard on the doll's clothes. How *could* you?"

"She's not my sister. I'm a princess, that's what I am!"

It was not the first time I had said that in my nine-year-old life. Perhaps it was one time too many for my mother. She wiped her hand on her apron and slowly, deliberately slapped my face. Stunned at this unexpected development, I didn't shed a tear. The stinging sensation on my cheek felt good. It was palpable evidence that this woman who faced me was really the wicked witch who had stolen me from my kingdom. In the teeth-clenched tone she used only when pushed to the end of her patience, she said, "Pick up the doll. Now it is yours. And Ella may take whatever she wants of yours in exchange."

The sound of my sister's sobs goaded me into yet another act of defiance. I scooped up the broken doll I had coveted minutes before. I ran to the garbage can, threw it in, and replaced the lid with a loud bang. "There! She's dead and buried."

My mother's face told me she was furious. I walked past her and up the stairs. I went to the bathroom, locked myself in, and vomited. I waited until I had stopped trembling, then washed my face and went to my room, where I threw myself on my bed. I whispered into the bedspread, "I am a princess. I am, I am."

Papa's voice startled me out of my incantation. "Leah'la?"

I jumped up and ran to his open arms. And suddenly jerked myself away. "Oh, Papa, if I was the wrong baby, then you're not my papa either!" I was terrified by this exercise in logic.

Apparently Papa was too. "What are you talking about? ... The wrong baby?"

I refused to answer and turned away.

Sternly, in his professional actor's voice, he roared, "Out with it! I want the whole story."

Mama's exasperation with me was an everyday thing. I had learned to live with it. But Papa's anger took my breath away. "But you know," I pleaded. "You were at the hospital when they brought the other baby that looked just like Mama. The pretty one."

"Where did you hear this gibberish?"

I hesitated. His eyes locked into mine. There was no escape. "It was a long time ago, when I was really little. I was supposed to be taking my nap. Mama was talking to Aunt Esther."

"And what was it Mama said?"

"She said sometimes she thought about the baby they brought her first, the one that looked like her. She wondered how she was growing. Oh, Papa, Mama's voice was so sad. Then Aunt Esther said, 'Those hospitals! I told you to give birth at home like I did. They're always making mistakes.' Something like that."

"Go on. What else do you remember?"

"Papa, is it true? Did they mix up the name tags?"

It seemed like forever before Papa responded. Finally he took me by the hand to the bureau with the mirror. He pulled over my desk chair and hoisted me up on it. Our faces were reflected in the mirror, side by side.

He said, "What color are my eyes?"

"Blue."

"And yours?"

"Blue."

He asked, "Have I got a nice nose?"

I giggled. "No. It's too big. Just like mine."

"And my smile?"

"It's a teeny bit crooked."

"And yours is straight?"

"Papa, Papa, I look like you, don't I?" I didn't wait for an answer. I hugged him and did a happy little jig on the chair.

My mother's voice put a stop to that. "Is this the way you punish her? Fine. Fine."

"I think our princess has been punished for too long."

"But Max! What about the doll?"

"Minna darling, a wise man once wrote,

> "'If you have a skeleton hidden away,
> In a closet and guarded and kept from the day
> In the dark; and whose showing, whose sudden display
> Would cause grief and sorrow and lifelong dismay,
> It's a pretty good plan to forget it.'"

"Typical. We have a behavior problem and you spout poetry. Max, she's not ever going to know the difference between reality and her dreams if you let her get away with—"

"No more talk! Our little one has inherited my temper and imagination as well as my crooked smile. Someday she will be a fine actress and will play as many princesses as she chooses."

I swallowed the lump in my throat. And said what I'd never said before. "Mama, I'm sorry. I'll 'pologize to Ella too."

My mother sniffed. "Words are cheap. You'll forget you ever said it."

"I'll save my whole allowance. I promise. Then I'll buy Ella a new doll. Honest. Just let me be an actress!"

"See, Minna, it's in the blood. She takes after me, doesn't she?"

"She certainly does! I don't understand either of you. Come to the table. I made noodle pudding."

A PIECE OF CAKE

Walter J. Pierce

It had been a tough day. Jim had failed to turn in his homework in the morning, and things had worsened progressively.

It was hot when he got home from school. His sweater hung from his shoulders over his book pack. He opened the door and went inside.

"Mom!" he shouted. No answer.

Where was she?

"Mom?" he yelled up the stairs.

He checked the door leading to the cellar. It was locked. He was disconcerted. Moms were always home. He had to pitch in the game tonight. He had to eat early so he could be there. It was a big game.

He took a deep breath. "Ma-ahm?"

Still no answer.

He tried the kitchen, a favored room for any growing sixth-grader, where he always found security. This time he found temptation that went beyond his ability to resist: a chocolate layer cake with plump English walnuts sprinkled liberally on its fudge like icing. It was beautiful, and its chocolaty smell was overwhelming. He wolfed down a generous slice cut from the part where the most walnuts were massed. Pouring a glass of milk and making it disappear almost instantly, he hurried to his room, put his homework assignment on the table, and changed into his baseball uniform. He was just about to leave when Mom returned from grocery shopping.

"Help me with these bags," she said. "I'm having a party for Aunt Fran."

Jim grabbed a bag full of ice cream and headed for the kitchen, where the fridge waited for his burden.

Mom had no sooner entered the kitchen when she shrieked, "You cut my cake! I baked it especially for your aunt, and you ruined it! You march right up to your room and stay there! No dinner for you!"

Panic overtook him. "Mom, I have to pitch tonight! The guys are counting on me!"

"I was counting on that cake," she shot back.

"Please, Mom, let me play. They need me," he begged.

Her eyes seemed to bulge in anger. "Who said you could cut my cake?" she demanded. Then her voice grew controlled, full of determination. "You will do as I say right now. You'll go straight to your room and stay there. And don't let me hear another word out of you."

Defeated, and fearing that further protestation would lead to additional punishment, Jim ran upstairs to his room, slammed the door, and started to cry. He had to pitch. He saw his homework on the table. He looked out the window. Game time was approaching at high speed. Tears paralyzed him.

Then an idea hit. He could crawl out the window, shinny down the rainspout to the garage roof, climb down the fence to the driveway, and—pitch. Mom would never know. He opened the window and put a pencil in the sill track so it wouldn't close too tightly; he needed room to get his fingers under the sash when he returned.

His plan worked perfectly. He arrived in time to warm up.

His fastball was working, and his slider was enough of a change-up to keep the batters guessing. He wanted to try his curveball, but he knew the coach would bench him if he threw one. The coach claimed his charges were too young to put that kind of strain on their arms. Of course, Jim knew better. He was stronger than most sixth-graders.

Jim allowed two runs to score. One was a homer. If the right fielder had only prepared for this game, he would have been in the right place to catch that ball, Jim mused. And the other run was unearned because his second baseman made what Jim considered a stupid error.

At bat, Jim was two for three, with two RBIs and one run scored. He gloated over his victory as he hurried to retrace his steps to his room. He'd struck out their best hitter twice, and if only the right fielder had played that hitter properly, he might have had a shutout. If only people did what they knew they should do!

He climbed the fence to the garage roof, shinnied up the rain-spout, opened the window, and entered his room, which was now dark. Satisfaction that he had not been caught blended with elation from his pitching success. He had fooled his mom and dad; Dad was surely home by now.

I can make things easy when I want to, he crowed to himself.

Jim heard sounds of a party as he moved cautiously to the light switch by the door. When the light came on, the first thing he saw, sitting beside his undone homework, was a generous slice of chocolate layer cake with plump English walnuts sprinkled liberally on its fudge like icing.

THE BUREAU OF BALLS

Arn Shein

It's one of those dates when everyone can tell you exactly where they were and what they were doing when all hell broke loose. On December 7, 1941, I was glued to my radio, listening to a football game. I couldn't get enough of sports.

Three months before the attack on Pearl Harbor, and less than a month after my thirteenth birthday, the Brooklyn Dodgers, my beloved "Bums," became National League champions. It was their first pennant in my lifetime and their first in twenty-one years. I was a good student, but I had a great inducement: I knew that if I got straight A's on my report card, I would be allowed to go to Ebbets Field on weekends to see my favorite team in action.

I really didn't want to clutter my mind with too many other things, and certainly not with that little disturbance called World War II. I discovered that if I read only the last ten or eleven pages of the *New York Daily News* and knew exactly when to turn on my radio, I could avoid the war almost completely and concentrate on the truly important things in the life of a thirteen-year-old boy: Would the Brooklyn Dodgers win or lose?

A good chunk of my teen years was spent at Ebbets Field, where I would arrive early, sit in the left-field stands near the foul pole, and collect baseballs during batting practice. I didn't catch very many balls myself, but when batting practice ended, I would walk over to those who had and tell them I was from the Bureau of Balls. It was my job, I said, to return the baseballs to the Dodger players.

"You know how it is, the war and all."

To this day, I have no idea what the war had to do with horsehide, but I was a big kid for my age, and the people who caught the baseballs always seemed to believe me. I guess they thought they were being patriotic. Whatever the reason, I used to go home with a lot of balls.

Eventually I became sports editor and columnist for a daily newspaper, but even in those early days I must have been a pretty good storyteller, because Mom and Pop never doubted me when I told them that I brought home so many baseballs because I outran the other kids. My unsuspecting parents left this world without ever knowing that their son was a self-appointed employee of the fictitious but highly efficient Bureau of Balls

THE COAL CHUTE

Arlene Lewis

The entire world remembers October 29, 1929, as the day the stock market crashed, the beginning of the Great Depression. My family remembers that day for a different event.

My mother, one of eight children, was part of the immigrant wave that came to the United States in the early years of the twentieth century. After their marriage, she and my father moved from the Lower East Side of New York to the "suburbs" of the Bronx, in the Grand Concourse area. Her parents and her brothers and sisters soon followed. Aunts, uncles, and cousins lived within a radius of three blocks, forming a close, protective family unit, a fortress of love, warmth, and care.

On the day of the crash, my mother dressed me all in white: white blouse with ruffles on the scoop neck and puffed sleeves, white cardigan sweater, tight white leggings, white anklet socks, and high-laced white shoes. Then, because she had innumerable errands to run, she left me with my favorite, good-humored, cheek-pinching Aunt Rose. I loved staying with her, because it gave me the opportunity to play with her son, Allan.

I was an eighteen-month-old chubby baby who with great determination had just begun to master the art of walking. Every step was an arduous ordeal. My fat thighs rubbed one against the other. My body weight was too much for my wobbly legs to support. I required frequent rest stops. In contrast, my cousin Allan, just five weeks older than I, was a thin, wiry, athletic boy who had been walking for months. Desperately I attempted to keep up with him. I worked hard! I walked. I waddled. I staggered. My breathing was labored. Fatigue set in. My plump, pudgy legs just wouldn't move anymore.

I was right in front of a basement window in the apartment house where Aunt Rose lived. The window was not a pull-up kind but a push-in kind. It should have been locked from the inside but had been left open for a coal delivery. The chute to slide the coal through the window was still in place, ready for a second shipment. I sat down on the brick ledge, leaned back, somersaulted through the window, and landed face down on a freshly delivered pile of coal.

When Aunt Rose became aware of my disappearance, she started screaming hysterically, "Arlene, Arlene, where are you?" She frantically attempted to question Allan, despite the fact that he couldn't talk!

My terrified grandparents walked all around the block, crying over and over, "Arlene, Arlene, where are you?"

Aunt Pauline and Uncle Joe scoured the front lobby of the building, calling, "Arlene, Arlene, where are you?"

Aunt Leah and Uncle Morris went to Jerome Avenue to look under the elevated trains. Aunt Bertha and Uncle Dave poked into alleys. Uncle Irving stopped people on the streets, and Uncle Moe stopped traffic to make inquiries. Panic was beginning to set in as the unsuccessful search dragged on. They were about to contact the police when Uncle Joe stuck his head in the open cellar window. He thought he saw a hint of something white on the pile of black coal. Could it be?

Snakelike, he slithered through the window and down the chute, to find me sound asleep. I was carried upstairs tenderly, carefully examined to make sure there were no broken bones, and quickly changed out of my coal-blackened white outfit. When my mother returned, the only hint that something was amiss was the fact that I was wearing Allan's clothes.

I was lucky I wasn't hurt, lucky the second delivery hadn't come to suffocate me, lucky I wore white to give Uncle Joe a chance in all that blackness, and just plain lucky to be alive. My relieved parents were very grateful for all those miracles, and for the way the whole family rallied in the crisis.

I have no real memory of the coal chute incident; my only recollection is of my family telling the story ad infinitum. But I have had fun with it! To this day, I tease my cousin Allan, insisting that he pushed me down the coal chute. When I was in third grade, I won first prize in a contest, writing about the episode. And here I am, writing about it again.

ALL WOOL AND A YARD WIDE

Gertrude M. Taylor

Twice a year my father hopped off the 5:15 from New York with a neatly tied box tucked under his arm, label showing: "Brokaw Bros.–Men's and Boys' Fine Clothing." Both my father and my grandfather worked for Brokaw Brothers, and their employee discount was too good to pass up. It took me a while to catch on to the fact that I was wearing the latest models for little boys, sailor reefers in spring, and in winter a classy gray chinchilla-like set complete with matching hat and leggings.

One day, en route to first grade with Charley, Emily, and other chums, the truth came out. Charley announced in clarion tones, "Yaw, that's a boy's coat ya got on. It buttons like mine! An' yer hat has earflaps like a boy's." Curly-haired, snub-nosed, with one sock perpetually at half-mast, Charley was an ever-present pest, one of my love-hate friends, and his taunt wilted my small ego considerably. Silence held for a moment; then, with the ready cruelty of childhood, the rest of the crowd took up the cry and chased me all the way to school. Even Emily, with her golden curls, starched pinafore, and velvet-collared blue coat, deserted me.

After a surreptitious survey of my girlfriends' coats, the light dawned. I *was* wearing a coat that buttoned the opposite way, and a roller-brimmed hat with earflaps. There were tears that night, but my mother and father failed to see the importance of my complaint. The coat was beautiful, warm, and sturdy, so why was I upset by a bunch of silly kids? Daddy was an expert on material and assured me I wore the best. "Why, young lady, that's botany cloth, all wool and a yard wide." The next morning I was firmly buttoned into the offending coat and sent off to school, but I did manage to tuck the earflaps up under my hat.

For some reason, Charley held his fire, but I panicked every time he opened his mouth or looked at me across the reading circle. At the end of the day, those of us who wore leggings had the doubtful privilege of starting early to climb into them. They had to be fastened up the side with a buttonhook, which took considerable time. I was doing fine, only missing a couple of buttons here and there, when Charley cruised by with a devilish leer and muttered sweetly, "Well, *they* button on the right side, anyway!" At least he noticed me.

Winter eased into spring, and it was time for that natty navy-blue cheviot reefer, with a dashing insignia on the left arm, de rigueur for both sexes. I was allowed to go to the corner to meet Daddy's train, but the day I saw him carrying that ominous box, I almost ran home and hid.

"Well, hello there, kitten. Guess what I've got!"

I could already smell the rich wool and feel the slightly scratchy rub of the collar across my neck. "Daddy, I'm not going to school anymore if I have to wear a boy's coat. I won't, I won't!"

Somehow we got home, but it was a wet trip, and tears and temper flooded the house. Then came the moment of truth. The box was opened, the swathing of tissue removed, and my mother held up the beautiful all-wool sailor reefer. It had an elegant lining, a fancy Brokaw label, and brass buttons. But there was a difference: two sets of buttons marched down the front. Two sets of buttonholes matched them. I was saved! So were my parents. A double-breasted coat solved the problem, and I was in fashion—girl's fashion.

I shall never forget the brothers Brokaw and those wonderful woolen samples my father brought home, some small enough to make cozy covers for my dolls' beds, plaids, stripes, and plains, and some large enough to protect my legs from marauding mosquitoes when we sat on the porch in the dusk and watched the fireflies blink their secret Morse code. I can almost reach out and feel the rich nap, trace the muted red-and-white plaid running through the soft navy blue. The poignant smell of honeysuckle, the persistent staccato of katydids, all mingle with the memory of tears and triumph. Yes, life was all wool and a yard wide that particular summer.

THE VELVET COAT

Elizabeth Szoke

My mother was an extremely generous person. She would have given the shirt off her back to anyone in need. She not only gave money to beggars on the street, she had regular days when they would come to the kitchen for alms. Mondays, Tuesdays, whenever, they would crowd into the kitchen to get their due. But there was another streak in my mother that caused my sister and me to rebel, a Puritan spirit that established rules we knew were incontestable and disregarded whenever we could.

My mother had ideas as to what young girls should or should not be doing. They should have tasks in the morning. They should never read before lunch. They should practice the piano for two hours every day. They should put away their clothes so the maid could clean. They should water the plants, run errands, set the table, and help mix the cake batter, the electric mixer not having been invented yet.

To escape our prescribed chores, we hid under the bed reading Boccaccio and Dostoyevsky and fighting about the heroes of the novels. My sister's favorite was Prince Myshkin from *The Idiot*, but I thought he was a sissy. We also read English stories and called Lady Windermere "Luddy," the Hungarian way.

We couldn't leave our room without my mother admonishing, "Turn off the light, don't waste electricity." By the same principle we had to eat every bit of food dished out on our plates with the accompanying reminder of the starving Chinese children. Once I asked in my most insolent voice, "How about the Eskimo children, Mother?" The way she looked at me, I never asked again.

But the worst of all the unpleasantnesses of my young life was the clothes I had to wear. They were always hand-me-downs from my sister's outgrown wardrobe. The seamstress let out a few inches on the side and lengthened the skirt, the cleaners removed the spots, and my mother brought them into my room with a satisfied smile. "Just as good as new," she said as I burst into tears. It didn't matter that I damaged these dresses, dropped food on the skirts when no one was looking, felt like Little Orphan Annie. No use, I had to wear them.

The garment I most hated was my sister's coat, which I knew would soon be mine. It was black velvet with a white fur collar and had a velvet bonnet to go with it. I also hated it because she wore it with such an air of elegance and superiority, and I knew that by the time she left it to me, it would be faded and out of style. I screamed in disgust, "I don't want the stupid coat and the funny bonnet!" But my protestations as usual went unheeded.

When I finally became owner of the horrible coat, I wanted to drown it in the river below our house, but I was afraid someone would fish it out and I'd have to wear it as was. I thought about burning it but was afraid of the conflagration it might cause. Then a wonderful opportunity presented itself. My aunt and uncle lived about a two-hour train ride away from us, and they invited me to stay with them for a few weeks.

My parents took me to the train. I wore the fatal coat. The bonnet sat crookedly on my head, and my mother straightened it as the train pulled in. I kissed her goodbye, my father brought my small valise into the compartment, and the train slowly moved away from the station. I deliberately chose a compartment empty of passengers, drew the curtains, and lay down, pretending to be asleep. No one entered, and I really did fall asleep, awakening to sounds and voices that told me we were nearing our destination. I gathered my belongings and put them in my valise. Except my coat. No one anywhere. Carefully I wrapped the coat in some big brown paper I'd brought with me, knelt down, flattened the package, and pressed it under the seat.

I hurriedly went to another compartment, where from the window I could see the silhouette of my roly-poly aunt, my balding uncle, and my two cousins. They greeted me joyfully, and two spirited horses took us home in my uncle's carriage.

When we got to the house, my uncle took my suitcase upstairs. My aunt looked at me and asked, "Where is your coat? You brought a coat, didn't you?" Miserable hypocrite that I was, I said, "Of course I did. Gosh! Where is it?" I ran to the bedroom, looked into my suitcase, retraced my steps to the entrance. The coat, not so mysteriously, had disappeared. This spoiled the evening—that is, for my relatives. I was jubilant. I couldn't believe my luck.

I slept like the proverbial log. In the morning my aunt knocked at my door to call me for breakfast. I dressed quickly and went into the dining room, where breakfast was about to be served. All of a sudden my eye caught something big and black spread over one of the chairs. It was my velvet coat with the white fur. My aunt was radiant. "Isn't it wonderful? There are still some honest people left in this world. They traced the coat to our house and sent it! They deserve a big tip!"

I joined in the celebration of the coat's happy return and resigned myself to the inevitable. I finally stopped wearing the coat. I simply outgrew it just a few months before I was to be married.

THE WHITE DRESS

Esther Schuman

We children never thought of ourselves as poor, though we knew we did not have many things we longed for: no bike, no roller skates, no piano.

Cast-off clothing was what we wore. Our mother did not have the skill to remodel the dresses and skirts given to us by our wealthier (and fatter) cousins. We accepted these garments without a murmur and unearthed many a side street so as to avoid the cruel laughter of our fellow students. I was ten years old, and I was always being called up to the school assembly stage for a prize or certificate. I became adept at holding behind me folds of a too-big skirt as I walked to the platform.

But the sun shone for us. We were never hungry. Life was wonderful, and we happily spent hours figuring out the most candy we could get for our penny-a-week spending money.

One day my adored music teacher, Miss Vossler, announced, "We will have a gala assembly performance next week of Handel's 'Hallelujah Chorus.' Esther, you will be up center, front row, with the sopranos. All girls will wear white dresses." Great, wonderful! I knew the music already. But…white dress?

"I don't have a white dress," I told Miss Vossler.

"Oh, that's all right," said a classmate, Evelyn Vanderveer (I will never forget her name). "I'll bring you one. I have several."

Yes, Evelyn brought me a white dress, and it fit. And I stood in the front row singing my heart out, with my mother in the audience.

The next day that white dress was washed and ironed to a fare-thee-well and wrapped carefully in the best brown paper we had. When I presented the package to Evelyn Vanderveer, she recoiled. "Oh, I don't want that back. I *gave* it to you."

Glory be, I had my own dress! I raced home and burst in on my mother.

"Mama, Mama, the dress is mine. Evelyn doesn't want it back!"

Silence. What is this look on my mother's face? Why are the tears flowing from those beloved eyes as she holds me in her arms?

There was a while of growing up before I understood why my little mother cried.

THANK YOU, EMMA LOUISE

Juanita H. Songer

Emma Louise was a pretty little girl. She had nice clothes, and her mother kept her neat and clean, but she was such a nuisance! It was always too hot or too cold, or she had a scrape or blister to complain about. And complain she did, all the time. She was younger than most of us and would not have been included at all if she hadn't been a neighbor of Carol Blakely. Carol's mother had told her to sort of look after Emma Louise.

It was nearly the end of the school year, and we had a free day so the teachers could tally our grades and get our report cards ready. To celebrate, a group of us decided to hike up a nearby hill and have a picnic. It was lovely up there at the top, trees for shade, flat places for running and eating, flowers for picking. It was a beautiful day, sunny and breezy.

The first cloud appeared when Carol arrived with Emma Louise in tow. Hardly halfway up the hill, Emma Louise began to lament the fact that she was sweating. Weren't we all? All afternoon it was always something. She couldn't find a good stick to roast a wiener. It made her hot to stand close enough to the fire to cook it. The stick broke and the wiener fell into the fire. She scorned the blackened marshmallows so delicious to our taste. We called her a pantywaist and a crybaby right to her face. I'm sure she had a perfectly miserable day.

On the way home, we stopped in the school yard to get a drink from the fountain. I had brought a small thermos my father used when he was fortunate enough to get a day's work with a road crew, and it was empty. Emma Louise, in a sudden effort to be ingratiating, filled it to the brim and forcefully jammed in the cork. The fragile liner shattered. All of us heard it. There arose a chorus of "Now you've done it! Shame on you!" and one dire threat: "Her daddy will give her a whippin'!"

I was heartsick. It was the time of the Great Depression, and I knew there was no money for a new thermos. This meant that Daddy, a bookkeeper by profession, would have to do hard labor without even the small luxury of a hot or cold drink with his lunch. But I also knew that he doted on me and would not punish me for an accident.

I looked at Emma Louise and she looked at me, her eyes brimming with tears and her lips trembling. To my own surprise, I heard myself saying, "No, he won't whip me. You didn't mean to do it."

Everyone scattered except Emma Louise. As I bent to get a drink, I heard her ask timidly, "Does everyone love you?"

Instantly I faced my own bossy, contrary self, and I didn't care much for me. I knew I wouldn't win any popularity contests either. "Of course not," I answered. "I don't guess very many do."

"Well, I'd think they would. You're so nice." That is what she said, but I knew what she meant was "Thank you."

I was so embarrassed, but for the first time in my life, I felt the surge of joy that comes from being a true giver. Though the gift is only a smile or a forgiving word, two people are instantly richer. Suddenly I liked Emma Louise. And myself, too.

A Gift from the Heart

Ruth C. Wintle

Life was harsh during the Depression of the thirties. That summer in the Ozarks, day followed endless day of relentless, blazing sun. Month after month not a drop of rain fell to cool the parched land. Crops withered and died. Worry lines deepened on Dad's face, and new frost appeared in his dark hair. Mother didn't smile as much, or sing as she worked. There were tears in her eyes as she explained to me and Lyle, my seven-year-old brother, that there would be no gifts that Christmas.

"No gifts?" we chorused. "Not even a doll? Or a Barlow knife?"

"We'll just have to be grateful for a roof over our heads and hope that the food holds out till spring planting time," Mother said.

As Christmas drew near, I kept hoping that somehow a miracle would occur and there would be presents under the tree. It would have to be a miracle. I was nine—too old to believe in Santa Claus.

Lyle's behavior became very strange. He started sneaking off to the attic and locking me out. Once he almost slammed my fingers in the door. I retaliated by yelling, "I hope you *don't* get any presents for Christmas."

Christmas Eve we hung our stockings in the traditional way, even though we didn't hold out much hope, but maybe, just maybe...

Next morning when Dad shook the grates in the kitchen stove—the signal that Christmas had officially arrived—there were no shouts of merriment or sounds of children's feet rushing to see what Santa had left. We stayed in bed, delaying the moment of bitter truth. When no one was looking, I slipped in to examine my stocking, wishing with all my heart there would be the teeniest bulge of a present, even a pencil. But that stocking was as flat as Dad's wallet.

After our simple Christmas dinner at noon, Lyle suggested we go walk our trap lines. The pelts from the animals we caught in those traps provided our only spending money during those lean years. We bundled up in our warmest wraps and set out in the knee-deep snow.

Ignoring Lyle's cheerful chatter, I vented all my bitterness and disappointment on him. "If I was an only child, there might be enough money for a doll," I told him. I knew how much he wanted a bike for Christmas, but he figured he'd survive. "By golly, when I get my old-age pension, I'll get me a bike," he joked.

Down the hill, across the frozen stream, through the woods, and over two rail fences we went, stopping to look at each trap. They were all as empty as our stockings.

We trudged homeward, half frozen, just as darkness was approaching. While we were thawing by the open fire, a few secret signals passed between Mother and Lyle, and then he disappeared, returning almost immediately with a hastily wrapped package. With a shy grin and a "This is for you, Ruth," he thrust it into my hand.

I tore off the wrapping. There amid scraps of paper and string it lay—a beautiful doll blanket. My happiness was clouded by guilt as I remembered the hateful things I'd said to him that afternoon. Tears welled up as I thought of the long hours he'd spent in that cold, unheated attic, away from my burning curiosity, as well as that of his friends, who would have made his life unbearable if they'd discovered he'd taken up needlework. There, he had painstakingly stitched in pink, blue, and yellow flowers. The crocheted edge was a bit more than his childish hands could manage, so he had arranged with Mother to get me out of the house that afternoon while she finished it for him.

I soon forgot about everything but the joy of that gift. It was just an ordinary flannel doll blanket, but the simple, uneven stitches embroidered a tapestry of love. It didn't matter that I didn't even own a doll.

A BIRTHDAY BONANZA

Irene K. Murdock

It was the year I turned five. I was enrolled in afternoon sessions at kindergarten, and my mother had secretly arranged with my teacher to have a surprise birthday party for me.

On the big day I was sent off to school after lunch, all scrubbed and shiny.

Shortly afterward my mother arrived, carrying individual ice cream cups (we called them Hoodsies in those days) and a huge beautiful birthday cake, complete with pink candles. Then my father appeared, eager to share in the celebration, smiling cheerfully as he gazed proudly and adoringly at his little daughter, the star of the occasion.

"The doctor! The doctor!" cried one little boy, bursting into tears. One by one each of my classmates joined him until the entire group was dissolved into a weeping and wailing throng.

My father was a family doctor. He made house calls and was an intimate part of life for most of the people in the neighborhood. Not too many months earlier, as the first day of school approached, he had vaccinated most of the children in the room, and they were obviously fearful that he had come to repeat that painful and inglorious act, subjecting them to the cruel needle once again.

I watched, stunned and dismayed at this unexpected turn of events, which threatened to spoil my beautiful day. What was a little girl to do to stem that awful tide and avert a complete disaster?

In one quick motion I hopped up on a chair, commanding attention. My mind was wrestling with a first awareness that we all play many roles in life—husband, father, doctor, friend—depending on the circumstances. Five was a fairly early age to grasp this abstract concept, but somehow the occasion lent itself to special insights, and drastic action was required.

I stood tall and straight on that little chair, summoned all my resources and newfound understandings, and made the first public speech of my life. "That's *not* the doctor," I said emphatically. "It's *my father*, and he's come to my party. And if you don't stop crying you can't have any ice cream and cake!"

The response was instantaneous. A sudden silence cloaked the room. Not a tear fell, not a sob was heard, not even a whimper. The sun shone again, and peace and quiet reigned. The festivities resumed joyfully, and my fifth birthday was one of the happiest of my whole life.

The Burglary

Joanne Randolph

Burlington Avenue ran east and west, dividing La Grange in two. It ran parallel to the tracks of the Burlington Railroad, which moved passengers and freight out of and into Chicago from the west. When we were small children, we would look westward down the tracks, squinting our eyes, and pretend we could see California, and even the Pacific.

La Grange in the 1930s was a wonderful place to dream of the places we'd someday be. With the Great Depression grinding on, keeping many of the fathers out of work and keeping everybody home, dreaming was a favorite occupation.

Along Burlington Avenue was a long finger of shops, a gas station, Thorsen's Realty, Van's Drug, where all the high school kids hung out, and a car dealership that did little business. We lived across from the Stone Avenue Station, where our father boarded the train to go to work in Chicago. There was always something going on around there, partly because of the passing trains, partly because we were so near the shops, and partly because we had nine children in our family.

One day in 1931, when I was about four, my older sisters and brothers were out visiting their friends, and I was left home alone —except for my mom, who was always home. It was a hot day in July, and I had been lying on my back in the grass, looking up at the clouds to find snowy animals and fairy angels. A freight train rumbled by, and I counted the cars as they passed, getting up to 106 before being interrupted. The interruption was Jean and Todd, whose father ran the Cherry Dairy, an ice cream shop about three doors away. They were older than I by several years and had very adventurous spirits. They usually thought of fun things to do, and I usually was not included because I was the youngest kid on the block. So when they came looking for *me*, I was really excited and pleased.

On the west edge of our yard was a tiny building, perhaps ten feet by fifteen, called Walter's Popcorn Stand. We never met Mr. Walter, but we all knew Alice, the lady who worked there. She opened up after the heat of the day passed, and sold popcorn, peanuts, and candy till 9:00 or 10:00 P.M. Alice often gave us "left-overs," as we couldn't afford to buy anything. She always acted like she didn't like kids, but she kept giving us the popcorn, so we figured it was okay to be coming around.

But on this hot day, Alice had not yet opened the stand. Jean and Todd had walked past, found the window standing open, and decided they would climb through to get some candy. But neither was small enough to fit through the window, and neither was strong enough to lift the other, so they came looking for me.

It was easy to get in, but when I got there it felt spooky. It was very quiet in the deserted little shop, and it seemed like the whole world had stopped doing whatever it had been doing. I began to have second thoughts, and though it never occurred to me that we were hurting Alice, whom I loved, and who was so kind to us, it did occur to me that we were sneaking, so we must be doing something wrong. Nevertheless, I headed for the candy counter and grabbed candy bars with both hands, delivering them through the window to Jean and Todd, who eagerly stuffed them into their pockets and sent me back for more. I was on my third trip to the candy counter when Jean and Todd looked up Burlington Avenue and saw a police car. They screeched in fear, clutched their pockets tightly, and ran down the alley beyond the popcorn stand, leaving me alone inside with nobody to pull me out and a police car slowly coming to a stop outside.

In 1931 policemen didn't have car radios; they had to check in with headquarters from a call box, which was a telephone in a locked box mounted on a pole. There was just such a call box a few feet from the popcorn stand, and I had often seen policemen using it, but today my guilt and my fear made me think the car was coming just for me. I was so frightened that I started to cry, then bawl, louder and louder, so that when the car stopped and the officer got out, all he could hear was my wailing, coming from what looked to him like an empty popcorn stand.

He came to the window and reached in for me. Half of me was scared because he had caught me, and half of me was happy to have a grown-up to take care of things, though I was crying so hard I could scarcely explain what I was doing there. He marched me home and told my mom where he had found me, and then the two of them went into another room to talk. When they returned, the officer told me to sit down and wait until "the other policeman" came to take me to jail. I climbed up on a chair and sat, so exhausted from my wailing that I couldn't make a sound.

All day long my mother went about her housekeeping, neither looking at me nor speaking to me. I had become invisible to her, I no longer existed. When my father and brothers and sisters came home, one at a time, I could hear whispered accounts of my shame, and when they passed by me, I was invisible to them too.

Finally the house began to darken and I knew the day was ending, and still "the other policeman" didn't come for me. I never knew why, but I was awfully glad he hadn't.

BILL'S SWAMP

Leonard Weyant

You can't hike into the Hudson Highlands from my father's old farm in Fort Montgomery, New York, without passing Bill's Swamp. Time has allowed beech, birch, and aspen trees to grow and suck out most of the water, so it's more a wet woodland now. At its edge stands a majestic tulip tree, straight and tall, as if put there by God as a memorial to the events that took place.

My father's farm was really not much of a farm: we had a few chickens, a couple of cows, a pig, and two horses, Bill and Jim. The horses were our mainstay. For generations my father's family had been in the wood business; they would buy standing timber, hire woodchoppers to cut it in cord lengths, and then haul it to the Hudson River docks to be taken by barge to the brick companies, which needed firewood to bake their bricks. The horses were required to pull the heavy wagons up into the highlands to retrieve the cordwood. This was no easy task, and my father was not a lenient teamster. He drove the horses hard, and by the end of the day all they wanted to do was lie in the pasture and eat a little grass.

But we children, being high-spirited and adventurous, would not let them rest. We wanted to go horseback riding. Jim wouldn't have any part of us, but Bill would cooperate, so naturally he became our favorite. We would all take turns getting on his back while the other children threw small stones or sticks at him to make him move. Bill would walk us reluctantly around the field, and sometimes, if we threw enough things at him and made enough noise, he would run a little, to the rider's delight.

Afterward we always tried to find some delicacies for Bill to show our appreciation. We'd climb the old apple tree and get him choice apples to munch on, or steal some sweet corn from the fields, or sneak some sugar from the kitchen.

One summer there were New York City children vacationing in the country. Naturally they were attracted to our farm and the horses, and we were eager to show off. We wanted to show them how to ride, so it was up to Bill to accommodate. We walked him around with one of us on his back, but that wasn't enough. In our attempt to display our superior horsemanship, we intensified our efforts to make him move faster. As we threw stones and sticks at poor Bill, the city children joined in, throwing larger rocks and making louder noises.

Bill was not used to all this extra prodding. Maybe he was scared or just annoyed, or maybe some unknown force within rejuvenated him into believing he was a colt again; but whatever it was, Bill stood straight up on his hind legs. The passenger slid to the ground, and then Bill bolted across the field as if he were a thoroughbred leaving the starting gate.

We all ran after him, yelling and shouting in disbelief, but rejoicing in the thought that Bill had abilities unknown to us. We followed him into the woods, and there we lost him. We searched in all directions, to no avail. We were about to go home when someone heard a whinny in the direction of the old swamp. When we arrived, there was Bill, up to his belly in the middle of that murky quicksand, kicking and squirming and neighing, with a look of hopeless fear on his face.

What could we do? There was no way we could begin to help Bill out of his predicament. The only recourse was to retreat home and tell my father, and that I dreaded, for I knew he would surely kill me, or possibly throw me in the swamp with Bill. But everyone else ran away, so I had to be the messenger bringing the bad news.

When I told my father, he jumped right up without a word and ran to the swamp. He looked at the hopeless situation and then turned to me with fire in his eyes, demanding to know how this had happened. Too frightened to speak, I stammered inaudibly, waiting for the inevitable. I knew he was going to do something awful to me, but he just grabbed me by the shoulders, stared directly into my eyes for a moment or two, and said, "The only thing we can do now is shoot him." I'd never seen my father cry, but that day there were tears in his eyes. He dropped me to the ground and went home. Bill was still kicking and neighing.

I sat there at the edge of the swamp with tears streaming down my face as I yelled to old Bill how sorry I was and then cursed God for letting Bill get in this trap. In a few minutes my father returned with his rifle, and I ran sobbing toward home. Halfway there, I heard a rifle shot, then another. I stopped, and suddenly the realization hit me that I would never see Bill again, never ride him or bring him sweets. My whole world was ending, and I vowed never to go near that terrible place again.

Well, time heals all wounds. Gradually my broken heart mended, and I did return to the swamp and the highlands, but the memory of Bill will never leave me. And when I stand next to that monumental tulip tree, I know that God too felt sorry for old Bill.

CALICO

Adair Wiess

Violette first taught me to count and name colors in French. She pronounced me "a vary smard pupeel" and let me play with her "chatte," Calico. Most of the kids in my neighborhood were not allowed to associate with Violette or her husband, the Judge. On weekends their noisy revels and frequent quarrels rang out on our quiet street. But my parents took no notice, perhaps because my father practiced law before the Judge. They drew the shades at night so that only their silhouettes were visible, and the livid mark on Violette's cheek was the lone reminder of what I witnessed.

One day I went next door only to find that Violette was too

cross to teach me any new words. "Eet eez eempozeebahl," she fumed. "Calico eez a houz chatte!" She motioned for me to follow her to the screened-in back porch. There, in a pasteboard box filled with scraps of quilting fabric, lay Calico, contentedly nursing four darling kittens. I knelt beside the box and rubbed a finger along their downy backs.

Violette shared none of my delight in the maternal scene. "Zeez keedens I do nod need. I musd ged reed of zem." She pushed me toward the front door. Instead of her usual "adieu" she said, "Eef you or your frenz vand a keeden, lad me know," and shut the door in my face.

When Mother came home, I broached the matter of the kittens. "Don't bother me about Violette and her pets," she said angrily. "In Depression days like these, we do well to feed ourselves."

Since my father was an expert at solving other people's problems, I sought his help with what I considered an urgent matter. Father was very dear to me, terribly witty, with a cheerful, easygoing disposition and a lovely, musical laugh. Running the four blocks to his office, I hurried up the narrow hallway to his suite of rooms, burst through the door, and threw myself into the comfort of his arms. He held me close and listened patiently to the story of Calico and her kittens.

"You will let me have one, won't you?" I pleaded. "And help me find homes for the others?"

After a disconcerting pause, he hugged me and announced, "We'll come up with a plan. I promise."

The end came sooner than even I had imagined. I was alone at my desk on a rainy afternoon, practicing my penmanship. The phrase I was working on is as clear in my mind today as it was over fifty years ago: *The dear old cow gives us sweet milk to drink.* I was trying to make my letters match the copybook when, mingled with the drumming of the rain, I heard the anguished yowling of Calico and the mewling cacophony of the kittens. At that moment Violette came from the porch and deposited something in a washtub under the backyard faucet. By the time I reached the door, she was coming out with the second kitten.

I raced back and forth along our common fence, begging her to stop, but she took no notice as she stoically carried the last two kittens out. In a final attempt to halt the grisly proceedings, I screamed, "I'll take them, Violette! I'll take them all right this very minute!

128

Daddy said I could," I lied. She went inside without a word.

I ran to the street, where my parents were just pulling up in our Ford, and threw my arms around Mother, sobbing. "Violette's drowning the kittens, Mama! Stop her! I want you to stop her this minute!" She gave me a little shake, then pushed me out of her way. I rushed around to my father, pulling on his coat as he tried to get out of the car. "Please do something, Daddy! You promised! You did!"

He put his arms around me. "There are some things in life you simply have to accept," he said, "and this is one of them."

I broke away from him, gasping for breath, as if I too were drowning. At the front door I turned back and yelled, "You're a liar! A liar! A *liar!*"

When the Judge came out at dusk and transferred the tiny corpses from the tub to the trash bin in the alley, I was at my desk, writing.

> Her name is Calico. She has lovely patches on her fur.
> For a little while she was the mother of four kittens.
> She licked them and loved them like a good mother should.
> When they nursed, she was happy. Now she is alone once more.
> But she will always love them. She will never forget them.
> And I won't either.

THE BICYCLE

Blanche Caffiere

At age thirteen my life was not worth living because I didn't have a bicycle. My mother had good reasons: (a) they were expensive, and (b) I didn't know how to ride.

Reason (a) vanished when my piano teacher said she would sell me her old Columbia for five dollars since it was just sitting in her basement. When I joyfully told Mother, she thought up one more barrier. "Well, you can get it if you earn the money." She felt safe because she thought I had no marketable skills.

Esther, my big sister, had overheard the conversation about the bike with more than a neutral ear. She'd always wished she could ride a bike. She was engaged to be married and had a cedar hope chest in which she was storing linens, cut glass, and other household niceties. She knew that I could crochet. "If you'll make me some lace for a set of pillow slips, I'll buy the bike and we can share it," she said. Esther was a legal secretary earning ten dollars a week, so this was quite a bite out of her paycheck. I loved to crochet and I snapped up the offer.

The bicycle was too big for me but was the perfect size for her. We got it on a Sunday and spent most of the day just trying to balance. Esther's progress was much more impressive than mine, but she got overconfident, lost control, and rode headlong into a cement wall. The next day she was black-and-blue, so swollen and stiff that she had to stay home from work. "I've had it with that bike," she said. "It's all yours as soon as you finish the lace."

I mastered the art of riding even before the crocheting was finished. I went everywhere on that bike: to piano lessons, to the store for last-minute items, to school. There was one thing missing —I had no girlfriend to ride with.

At last Louise Bourgault came into my life. We were sophomores at Lincoln High School and were in the same gym class. I found out that she had an older sister and a bossy older brother, as I did. Best of all she owned a bike and loved to ride. We went everywhere together, but most of our rides were dull to Louise; she wanted more daring stuff. Once she hoisted her bike onto a narrow wall surrounding a pond, waving at me and yelling, "C'mon up, Blanche. This is fun. Don't be a sissy." That did it. I laboriously lifted my heavy Columbia up to join her. Two times around were enough for me, because just then Louise lost her balance and jumped to the ground, her bike crashing after her. Like Douglas Fairbanks, she landed on two feet without a scratch. How I admired this girl who was teaching me to live dangerously.

The next time I saw Louise, she had a yellow flyer advertising a bike trip to Snoqualmie Falls. The Fisk Bicycle Company was sponsoring it—obviously a gimmick to sell more bikes. When I presented the idea at the supper table, the response was a cold silence. Finally my worldly-wise brother, nine years older, spoke up.

"Ma, if you let that kid go up there on that old bike, you should have your head examined," Ralph declared. "That bike is a clunker, and she could break down any minute."

"A bicycle mechanic is going along, and there's a truck you can ride if you can't make it," I said.

Taking a gulp of coffee, Ralph set his cup down forcefully. "All I can say is that you and the mechanic will be seeing a lot of each other. And who is chaperoning this fiasco?"

I tossed my head. "Eleanor Cruttenden is going, and her mother and father are the chaperons. They go to our church." That was my trump card. Mother thought anyone who went to our church was above reproach.

In those days there were no sleeping bags. Mother dug out some old army blankets and a cotton sheet, and we made a bedroll. She also dyed a white wool middy blouse black to match my voluminous gym bloomers. Next morning at seven o'clock she and Ralph came to the front porch to see me off. The weather was threatening, and Ralph was shaking his head. Mother said, to convince herself, "Now, Ralph, Blanche will be fine. The angel of the wild things takes care of her." Ralph was unconvinced.

It was difficult to make an impressive getaway with the blanket roll over one shoulder. I couldn't take my hands off the handlebars to wave goodbye, for a fall then might have ended the whole adventure. When I came to curvy Interlaken Boulevard, a postman didn't see me and I swerved to miss him, losing my balance and landing at his feet. The blankets cushioned the fall, and I was all right. As he helped me up, he asked, "Where are you off to?"

"Snoqualmie Falls," I said confidently.

"Snoqualmie Falls! You'll never make it, sister."

Two men from the Fisk Bicycle Shop were at the ferry landing at Leschi. Eleanor was beaming as she walked her shiny red bike onto the ferry, and Mr. and Mrs. Cruttenden were proudly pushing a tandem. Louise was raring to go, dressed in corduroy pants and a black turtleneck, a boy's cap sitting jauntily on her short-cropped blond hair. Few girls wore pants then, but Louise did, and she carried a jackknife too. She didn't move like a girl, she swaggered. How I envied her.

After a short ferry ride to Kirkland, we shoved off in earnest for the falls. Louise and I rode together for a short way, but she kept complaining about how slow I was. I would pump harder, but

I couldn't keep up with Louise or Eleanor, or even the two girls from Queen Anne High, whom we regarded as total foreigners because they were not from our school. I fell farther and farther to the rear. Louise would come wheeling back, circling me and saying, "C'mon, speed up a little."

The gloomy weather finally brought rain, and I began to think Ralph was right. I looked at my hands on the handlebars. They were black. The dyed middy was running. Louise showed up again to tell me that the girls from Queen Anne were a bunch of sissies —they were riding in the truck! I didn't dare tell her that I'd been thinking of doing the same thing. Suddenly she said, "That mudguard of yours is scraping on your back tire. No wonder you're so slow." She whipped out her jackknife and cut the cords, which had shrunk and were pulling the mudguard closer to the tire. I pushed on the pedal and shot forward like a rock from a slingshot. "That's it," said Louise. "Now you can keep up."

By noon the sun had come out, and we stopped by a pretty little stream to eat our soggy sandwiches. Then onward and upward. The rest of the way was all up a steep grade. It was raining again, and the leaders announced through a megaphone that we would soon be turning off the main road. We would go down a path for about a mile to a barn where we would park our bikes, then hike on to the cabins.

A pleasant plumpish woman welcomed us into the pungent barn. She took one look at me and said, "You're wetter than a diving duck. Here, let me loan you this pea coat." She brushed away cobwebs as she helped me into it. As we left the barn, Louise said, "Whew, that is the stinkiest old coat I've ever smelled. Obviously it's from World War One." Soon others were holding their noses, but I was beyond caring.

I trudged through the last lap before the cabins, picturing a blazing fire, white ruffled curtains, and hot soup, like the flyer had promised. But the cabins were dark and had to be unlocked with stubborn keys. Mrs. Cruttenden struggled to get a fire going in the ancient stove, and one of the girls lit the little oil lamp that stood on a shelf in the corner as we began to prepare the evening meal. My pancake mix was so wet it needed just a tiny bit of water to make it ready. The pancakes were pale gray and raw in the middle, but with a little honey they tasted as good as Aunt Jemima's finest. Bedtime followed immediately.

The next day dawned beautiful, blue sky, full sun. Breakfast was cocoa and a piece of damp bread. I was requested please not to wear the pea coat. Everyone was peppy and eager to hit the road for home. As we had predicted, the Queen Anne girls rode in the truck.

The trip home was mostly downhill and called for a lot of braking. My spirits were up, and I went faster and faster, passing Louise and Eleanor for the first time. Something was wrong! My brake was not responding. Panic swept over me. Angel of the wild things, where are you? The thought came—stretch your foot out and drag it on the front wheel. It worked. I heard Louise yelling, "Blanche, wait for me!"

EGGS, CHICKENS, ESPECIALLY SETTING HENS

Earlene Stone

The chickens were Mama's domain and her only source of pin money. Therefore chickens and eggs were stressed. What we did was trade the eggs at the country store for luxuries, little things we didn't ask Daddy for, like a pretty vase or ribbons and a penny's worth of candy for me. I remember two or three pieces of china and glassware that stayed in the store a long time before we could get them out—like an egg layaway.

There were no such things as incubators then. A chicken yard had a fair-sized flock of hens and a couple of cock-of-walk roosters of a good breed for meat and eggs. If too many young roosters were hatched, we ate them. Hens that quit laying were fattened to roast or make a gumbo with.

The hens let it be known about twice a year that they wanted to set on eggs. They started to lay in hard-to-get-to places and guarded those eggs like mad. They wanted to set! Well, sometimes

Mama didn't want them to set. She wanted her eggs every day. Or maybe she had enough chickens to feed just then and didn't want any more.

It was my job to gather the eggs and feed the chickens. It was easy to collect the eggs in the barn where Daddy had built about six laying boxes. What frightened me to death was going under the house to look for eggs in the holes the hens had scraped out to set in. I went armed with the broomstick Mama used to stir her boiling laundry, testing the ferociousness of the hens by poking them. If they refused to budge and pecked at the stick, I knew I was in for it. As I crept nearer, I'd swing the stick over their nests, hoping to dislodge them, but all they did was flutter their wings and take a stab at my face, stretching their necks and pecking away with their beaks. I was terrified they'd pluck my eyes out! I'd crawl away crying and screaming that I wasn't going back under there.

Then Mama would say, "Maybe I'll let you spend a whole nickel on candy." And my mouth would start watering for chocolate cream mounds, jelly beans, gumdrops, licorice. I could get ten candies for a nickel. I loved peppermint sticks too. Back I'd go under the house to fight those old hens. If I could get the meanest one to flee the nest, the others would usually follow suit. When I got a good whack at her head with the stick, she'd uncover her eggs, dizzy and goofy. Then I'd swing at her body. She'd finally get out of there, and the others would be afraid of the same, so one whack usually did it. Once they were gone I'd gather the eggs quickly. Sometimes I'd get a dozen from three hens because for days I'd been telling Mama there were no eggs under the house, just to keep from going there.

We took the eggs to the store about twice a week because we didn't want them spoiling on us. I'd go with Mama, and we'd spend an hour shopping around for something we could afford. If there was nothing we wanted, Mama was given a credit slip. The last thing we always did was stop at the candy counter. The grocer let me pick and choose and mix my candies. I took a full ten or fifteen minutes sometimes. He and Mama would look in his catalogue to see what she could order.

Let me tell you, I earned my candy money on the farm!

The other job I hated was dusting the hens with lice poison. If lice were found in the laying nests, all the straw had to be burned and the nests sprayed with poison. Then the hens had to be caught and held by the wings and dusted all over and slipped into a cotton sack with only their beaks and their eyes out. That way the chicken lice died and fell in the sack, which could be burned or washed. It was really Mama's job, but I had to be there to hold the can of poison and give her moral support.

I didn't mind feeding the chickens. They'd come from all over late in the afternoon. I'd rattle the corn in the bucket and call out, "Keedy, keedy, keedy!" And they'd be so colorful and happy. I felt empathy for those poor critters then.

The only other time I loved them was when they were pot-roasted or fricasseed.

Till the Cows Come Home

Anthony Marinaccio

During the Depression, just before the end of Prohibition, I lived on my grandparents' farm in upper New York State. In order to survive the lean years, my grandparents had been forced to turn their 205-acre farm into a summer resort and winter hunting lodge. They made their own whiskey to serve to their guests, and they also supplemented their income by selling milk to the local creamery.

Early one summer morning, when I took the cows to pasture, I noticed that most of the grass on our land was burned from a drought we were experiencing. I decided to follow the stream that ran past our land to county-owned property where the grass was still green. I left the cows to graze for the rest of the day, congratulating myself on my wonderful idea.

At dusk, when I returned for the cows, I was horrified to find them lying on the ground, motionless. I raced to the main house as fast as my legs could carry me, screaming at the top of my lungs. My father ran back to the cows with me, discovering to his chagrin that they were alive but in a drunken stupor. Apparently the runoff from my grandparents' still had found its way into the stream where I'd taken the cows to graze.

Everyone at the farm had a good laugh, except for me. I was punished by having to stay in the meadow with the cows until they sobered up.

Now, when I hear of people drinking whiskey with milk, I smile.

A Corncob Bigger Than a Henhouse

Polly Tooker

I know now that the date was August 31, 1932, but at the time I was just an eight-year-old helping her daddy husk corn on a sultry day. We were at my grandfather's farm in Vermont, where my mother always brought us in the summer. My schoolteacher father had a summer job as athletic director at a YMCA camp, but he joined us when camp was over and always helped with whatever needed doing. And what needed doing this day was canning the bushels of corn that had been picked earlier that morning.

My daily chore at the farm was to keep the woodbox filled, a matter of carrying three or four sticks at a time from the roof-high stacks in the woodshed to the deep bin just outside the kitchen door. Daddy had helped me with the wood, tossing two sticks into the bin and then giving me time to line them up and step back quickly before the next two came flying in. Now we were husking the corn, and Daddy had worked out a way to chop off just the very end where the husk was attached so that the pale green covering could be slipped off easily even by my small hands. Every now and then my mother would come out and collect what we had ready, taking it back to the steamy kitchen for blanching, cutting, packing in pint jars, and processing. Hot, sticky work on a hot, sticky day.

On one such trip she rested the pan on her hip, looked up at the sky, and said, "I hope we can get all this done before the eclipse."

I picked up the new word. "Daddy, what's a clipse?"

"E-clipse," he corrected me carefully, and sat there a moment looking at the ear of corn in his hands.

"You see the henhouse across the road?"

Of course I saw it, the low, red wooden building with rows of perches inside, where my grandmother and I collected eggs.

"Which is bigger, the henhouse or this ear of corn?"

That was an easy one. "The henhouse," I answered promptly, and waited for the next part of the game.

He held the ear of corn a few inches in front of my nose, and my field of vision was filled with the even yellow rows. "Can you see the henhouse now?"

"No."

"Then does that mean the corn is bigger than the henhouse?"

I knew the corn was the same size it had been a few minutes before, but so was the henhouse. This was heavy thinking for a little girl, and I needed the next question.

"Which one is closer to your eyes?"

Now I had it!

"That's what's happening this afternoon," he continued. "The moon, which is much, much smaller than the sun, is coming between our eyes and the sun in such a way that it will just exactly cover the sun and blot it out for a few minutes, even though the sun, like the henhouse, is much bigger."

We went on with the corn, but I held up every ear I husked and made it blot out the henhouse.

Later that day we all stood on the side lawn, away from the trees, and looked up at the sky through overexposed negatives and pieces of smoked glass. The men had come in early from the hayfield, and it was a relief to feel the day getting cooler. I didn't know exactly what I was supposed to be looking for, and I felt a little disappointed when I finally saw the big gray circle with a dent in one side, like an apple with a bite taken out. Eventually the bite consumed the apple and the unseasonal night was on us.

My mother leaned down to me in the stillness and said, "You must remember today, because what is happening right now won't happen here again for a long, long time, certainly not in my lifetime and perhaps not even in yours. So you remember what today was like and don't ever forget it."

I looked around me, impressed by her seriousness if not quite sure what I should think about remembering. But I didn't forget the weird, grayish yellow light, the slope of the side lawn at the end of the farmhouse, and the little group of us standing in the cool semi-darkness, talking in low voices and looking up at the sky through bits of smoked glass.

SUMMER SOLSTICE

Lydia Hartsock

Early in the morning, on June 23, Mrs. Grunt-manis, the cook, entered my small room and awakened me. We were spending that summer in Lielupe, on the banks of the Lielupe River, on the Baltic bay in Latvia.

"You have to get dressed quickly," said the cook, "if you want to go to the swamps. And don't let anyone hear you!"

I opened one eye and looked at her, trying to remember what it was all about. Mrs. Gruntmanis set one of her willow baskets on the floor and handed me my clothes. Her wide chest, held taut by a starched apron, reminded me of the geese on the neighboring farm. Her hands, pink and freckled, smelled of yeast as she helped me into my clothes.

As we trudged through the dew-covered grasses that reached up to my knees, Mrs. Gruntmanis handed me a piece of Saint John's cheese and a slice of dark bread. The cheese was speckled with caraway seeds that lodged between my teeth as I stuffed the sweet-sour breakfast into my mouth.

Tall grasses gave way to a bog covered with forget-me-nots. The swamp sparkled like a blue lake, so thick were the flowers growing there. We took off our shoes, since our feet were sinking into the moist earth.

When I saw the mud oozing between my toes, I grabbed the

cook's willow basket and cried out, "I'm sinking! I want to go home!"

The cook's strong arm swept down and hoisted me onto her back. "Hold tight," she said, and leaving her baskets in the bog, she deposited me on a small hillock covered with buttercups. Then she went to fetch the baskets and said, "You pick these, and I'll go back for the forget-me-nots. They don't grow well on dry land. When your basket is full, call me."

Rocking from side to side, water reaching halfway up her legs, the cook waddled through the swamp, picking armfuls of flowers for her basket while I picked buttercups whose thick stems oozed a milky liquid. I was so intent on filling my basket that I almost forgot about the cook, until I looked up and saw her, the size of a small handkerchief, near the river's edge. Her stiff apron stood out like a sail in the blue distance.

"A-uu," I cried. "My basket is full."

When we got back, the laundress was busy getting the house in order. A young sapling birch had been chopped down and was standing in a corner, its bright yellow leaves sparkling and exuding an aroma that only birches have. The tree seemed to absorb the mustiness of rooms that had been shuttered and dank throughout the winter. The magic of this day had started.

That afternoon we went to the meadow, stopping at a large oak tree. Where the branches were low enough to grasp, we picked armfuls of dark green leaves with young acorns still attached. No house was allowed to be without the birch or the oak on Saint John's Day, the sacred trees of the ancient Letts.

Back at home, a large bowl of dark dough was rising on the kitchen stove. The bread would be baked before sunset on wooden paddles, covered with pungent river reeds. While the dough swelled and puffed, we braided ropes of oak leaves for the front door, garlands of buttercups and birch leaves for the table, and smaller wreaths of forget-me-nots and buttercups for our hair. Rag rugs that had been beaten to a brilliant blue against river stones and dried in the sun were scattered about the clean pine floors. Mrs. Gruntmanis placed medicinal herbs in jars on the kitchen and porch windowsills, for only if they were picked before Saint John's Day would they retain their curative powers. No ritual was omitted as a middle-class summer house was turned for one day into a peasant hut.

As the bread was cooling on oak paddles and the sun commenced to set, a group of young people dressed in native costumes of white linen, girls with flowers in their hair and young men with oak leaves, stopped at our door to sing: "Ligo…" Ligo was a pagan goddess who brought blessings to the farms and farm animals as well as to the harvest and the rest of nature.

We joined the singers and proceeded to the nearest farm, where the cows, foreheads and horns adorned with flowers and leaves, bellowed near fences and barns. Here another group, young and old, joined the first group of singers and proceeded to yet another farm, the teasing ditties always ending with "Ligo…" And then, across the hills and from the shores of the river, we heard more voices, echoing each other, rising and falling, losing and finding the refrain.

Approaching a small rise in the meadow, we saw a wooden barrel filled with tar hoisted atop a large pole. It was burning brightly as other groups of old and young gathered around to continue their song and dance until sunrise.

I hugged my knees close to my chin and looked at the flames shooting skyward out of the barrel of tar. The warmth felt good when the mists began to rise from the valley below. My head started to droop, and I felt a strong arm gently around my shoulders as I leaned against the ample chest of our cook, which smelled of starch and freshly baked bread.

It was midnight that I missed, because I had fallen asleep on Mrs. Gruntmanis. And it was midnight that I had looked forward to so much, when we would visit the stables and hear the miracle of the speech of horses, on the only night of the year they were given human voice. And I also missed the sight of the blooming ferns in the deep forest, for these too only bloomed on June 23, when nothing was the same as during the rest of the year. All I heard through my deep sleep was the refrain "Ligo, Ligo"—melodies and words that had reverberated throughout the centuries for over four thousand years on the amber shores of the Baltic Sea.

In Search of Shadows

Myrtle E. Jeska

When I close my eyes, I see again those glorious nights of full moons reflecting on jewel-encrusted snows. White rabbits darting over hard snow defied the laws of gravity until they froze to listen with cocked ear to the barking of a dog in the distance. I feel still the pangs of frigid air, so piercing one could not draw deep breath. Cold was measured not by thermometers but by the crunch of footsteps in this pristine white world, by the snapping of branches as they fought to survive.

It was country, and we were country folk. We did not see our world as unique, because we knew no other. We took for granted the magnificent landscapes that appeared as changing panoramas in whichever direction we looked. Fresh air, unpolluted and clear, filled our lungs with energy.

As children, marching single file on well-packed paths, we shoved each other into snowdrifts, mounds that might be brittle as glass or soft and fluffy as fresh marshmallows. One by one we threw ourselves into irresistible drifts of white pillows, leaving snow angels behind to sleep.

We built snow forts that magically turned into enemy strongholds imprisoning innocent victims. Sometimes we were victorious as we attempted to demolish the wicked fortress with an endless barrage of snowballs and rescue the captives. If not, we suffered the terrible tortures inflicted upon us as we refused to divulge the innermost secrets of our king. It was a world of enchantment and make-believe, a world that belonged only to us.

When night fell on our winter wonderland, kerosene lamps flickering yellow in distant farm windows warmed our light hearts. Evenings often brought boys and girls from neighboring farmhouses together to go skating on Minnehaha Creek. We were prankish as kittens but pure as the snow as we laughed, pushed, huddled, and hugged to keep warm, and sometimes to establish territory next to the person we "liked."

Minnehaha Creek lay silently frozen beneath giant trees with barren, grotesque limbs, trees so old they held the secrets of a land where Indians had lived, hunted, fought, and died. Hollowing out a snowdrift, we piled up branches and logs and fed the fire until it blazed. We laced our skates with icy fingers and rose to feel the freedom of flying over the creek like birds carried on mountain currents. The cold was forgotten as we skated alone, or in long lines or pairs, sometimes hiding behind the huge trees in the ghostly shadows to whisper in the innocence of young love. Arm in arm, we skated back to the fire to add more logs and toast our feet before we glided once more.

Minutes changed into hours, live coals turned to yellow embers. All too soon it was time to bank the fire. As we walked home, a song hummed softly by one was soon picked up by another until a chorus of jubilant voices rose high into the vast emptiness of the winter night. Stardust from myriad glittering constellations fashioned a gossamer cobweb around us and encased our hearts in a silver cocoon.

A time of poverty and depression, yes. But a time in space that money could not buy nor grander memories replace.

ROOFTOPS

Dorothy Friedman

I've been to Hollywood rooftops of pink blossoms and jade leaves, of mountain views and piano bands, but never did they have for me the winged radiant quality of those summer nights on the tenement roofs of Sackman Street in Brooklyn. "For everything," Papa said, "God provides an answer."

When the tiny rooms of our small railroad flat were boxes of solid heat, the twelve families in our house made an exodus to the roof like angels ascending. Dressed for sleep in pajamas and nightgowns, the men loaded mattresses on sweaty backs, the women carried the linens and pillows, the children the chess and checkers sets, ropes, musical instruments, even an occasional telescope. Tanta Pessimira, who lived alone, said, "Now I can show the beautiful nightgown my Sybil sent me from Washington, D.C." It was lacy enough to be somewhat risqué, and Mama said to Papa, with a wet eye, "Only a stone should live alone."

Wonderful nights, tar and brick and cool-breathing stars and a moon that polished the roof with a white gloss. Every fifteen minutes the Livonia Avenue elevated train sped by, an explosion of life in the air, almost level with the roof, and now and then I caught a glimpse of a boy and girl huddled together. My eleven-year-old heart patiently sighed for romance. I'd stand looking down on the earth, lit by yellow globes of light, and watch the spray of blue sparks in the wake of the clanging trolley. Then I'd turn, mesmerized by the life on the roof.

"A knife, a fork, a bottle and a cork, and that's the way you spell New York!" the younger girls sang as they skipped rope. Rosie's grandfather sat off in a corner davening from his Bible, his moonlit face like corrugated metal, head bobbing up and down. Occasionally he stopped his prayers to blow his nose in a huge red-checked handkerchief. Mothers nursed babies, fathers played gin rummy, and Bessie's little brother squirted anyone who looked at him with his water pistol. Warm, freshly baked cookies in a straw basket on a white tablecloth for all the children, and Mama admonishing, "Take only one, leave some for the others." The older boys sang and teased the girls. Joey flipped a coin: "Tillie, if it turns up heads, will you go to the movies with me tomorrow? Look, Tillie, it's heads." And Tillie laughed, and said without looking, "If you promise to be nice." It was a first date, and someday they would marry. Abie, who could build radios, put his arm around Bessie and said, "If you let me kiss you, I'll help you with your homework." Lucky Bessie! That year I had a crush on Abie.

Herschel played his accordion, and the kids danced around the skylight. "Dinah, is there anyone finer ..." The boys broke in and danced with the girls—"In the State of Carolina ..."—and some nervous mother called, "Stay away from the ledge." The breeze had the gentle feel of water, and I'd think, If only I could live up here forever.

Turning Points

WHAT'S A BANANA?

Esther Trigger

"Next year in America" was the concluding prayer of every Passover seder that I remember in Pinsk, Poland, until the age of nine.

I can still see that first welcoming speck of light in the black distance of a moonless night in February 1932. For endless hours my eyes wait for the golden land to burst forth. Very slowly, as in a dream, the light creeps toward me. It grows bigger and brighter until there is a panorama of light that looks like a glimmering magic kingdom suspended in the darkness of sea and sky. People are overflowing the deck, shouting, laughing, crying, hugging, and wondering what tomorrow will bring.

The next thing I know, I am riding in a shiny taxi with my New York cousin, Myrel. My eyes can't believe these fast-moving mechanized miracles driving in endless procession, because my mind's eye is still seeing the horses and buggies of Pinsk. My ears are adjusting from the soft voices of crickets singing in the marshes around our house to the clatter of engines and the startling sounds of horns, sirens, and whistles. Cars and people move in every direction as far as I can see. They flow like ocean waves, stopping, starting, and waiting together.

"How do they know when to go?" I ask Myrel. Gesturing into the air, she describes red and green lights, but I am ashamed to admit that I really can't see them. I am craning my neck to look at the huge, uncommonly shaped buildings huddled together and reaching to the heavens. There are so many signs and billboards I don't know which side of the cab to look out of.

My brain is in a box where yesterday, today, and tomorrow bounce off each other. I am really in America. I am crossing a bridge, and I can't see the end. Tomorrow I go to Chicago, where I will fly into Pa's arms and he will hug and kiss me like he did before he left—two years ago.

The cab stops at Myrel's house. She must be very, very rich. She has an inside toilet and it flushes water. Again my mind's eye involuntarily flashes to Pinsk, to our outhouse almost covered with snow. Myrel has electric lights in every room, and she has her own radio. I heard a radio once, in downtown Pinsk.

Myrel brings forth a glorious bowl of fruit. In Pinsk I was allotted one slice of orange only when I was sick; the rest was carefully wrapped and hidden. Here I see five of the biggest, freshest, most beautiful oranges I can imagine. Dispersed among this colorful display are strange, elongated, golden-yellow specimens. Pointing, I flaunt the one English word I know: "America."

"This is a banana," laughs Myrel. She unfolds the thick skin, letting each section fall gracefully like the petals of a flower. As the creamy white center comes to view, she offers it to me.

The banana fits comfortably in my hand and feels smooth in my palm. I sample its fresh, sweet inner essence, and as it melts in my mouth it permeates my soul. I taste the flavor of an answered prayer.

ELLIS ISLAND PURGATORY

Manuel Zapata

No one on Cherry Street, a bit of Spain in the shadow of the Brooklyn Bridge, a neighborhood subsequently wiped out to give way to the Alfred E. Smith housing project, was willing to accompany him to that purgatory in the bay. "And don't you go anywhere near that place either," he was cautioned, "for they could ship you right back to Spain too, along with your brother. The best thing to do is forget him. Forget about that letter they sent you. It could be a trap."

But Manuel couldn't forget about Jose. He had sent him enough money for a second-class steamship ticket, along with some very simple instructions, but something must have gone wrong. He had gone to meet Jose at the pier and had waited in vain for hours. Now he knew from the letter that Jose had been taken to *la isla*, where they took all the immigrants whose entry status was in question, usually the ones who arrived in steerage. It was assumed that those who could afford the more expensive accommodations were less likely to become burdens in this land of promise.

Jose's left hand was partially impaired from a childhood illness. Manuel had told him to conceal it with his overcoat, but maybe they had discovered it. How was he to prove that despite the handicap Jose could still work as hard as any man? What Manuel needed was an interpreter, for he could hardly speak a word of English, being a recent immigrant himself.

Manuel was unable to find a single volunteer. Among those who spoke some English, none was daring enough to go with him. Someone suggested getting a lawyer, but no one knew where to find a lawyer who could speak Spanish, or who could be trusted, for it was thought that lawyers were part of a system that was now threatening to keep newcomers out. Everyone feared that great judgment hall in the middle of the harbor, and even after they had passed through, it continued to be perceived as having the power to bring an abrupt end to an immigrant's pursuit of a piece of the great American pie. At least, that was part of Ellis Island's reputation in 1920, not altogether undeserved. And now Congress was considering legislation to exclude almost all immigrants who did not come from an Anglo-Saxon background. Manuel had been lucky to get in. He wanted his brother to make it too, before the "golden doors" slammed shut.

As for Jose, he was confident that his older brother would somehow get him released. Meanwhile, they were feeding him three full meals a day (although there were some things he would not touch, like corn, which was only fit for chickens and pigs), and he had a clean bed to lie in (even though he didn't sleep well because his bones weren't accustomed to the soft mattress). He spent hours looking through the large windows at the huge buildings and wondered if his brother lived in one of them and if he had to climb all those stairs. He was impressed by the size of the towers and wondered if they were safe. Yet he was disappointed by the overall gloomy view before him, as seen through a curtain of black smoke billowing out of hundreds of chimneys. He had expected New York to be bright and cheerful and beautiful. Instead, it reminded him of a small city he had once seen that had known a great fire.

He watched the many ships that came and went in the harbor, and kept thinking back to the morning he entered it without really seeing it. He had gotten on a long line and spent hours waiting to be processed. The heavy folded overcoat weighed on his crippled hand. He badly wanted a cigarette, and turning away from the processors, he chanced it and rolled one between his fingers. That's when he must have betrayed himself, for when he arrived at the processing table the officials signaled him to switch the overcoat to his other hand.

Manuel walked along South Street past piers, the fish market, warehouses, and tall buildings, down to the ferry that would take him to the island he had hoped never to set foot on again. He had tried his best to spare his brother the same frightening experience. The threatened curtailment of immigration had created a panic, and thousands of human beings from all over the world were attempting to get in under the deadline, as yet unknown.

On the island, once inside the big building, he walked among the crowds hoping to hear an American-looking individual speaking Spanish, but without success. Pacing back and forth in that babel of humanity, he must have aroused suspicion, for he was approached by a person he estimated had to be important, a man in a dark suit with a white shirt and tie and a fountain pen in the pocket of his jacket. This man addressed him in a stern yet soft manner, but he couldn't understand a single word. Fear overcame him when he felt a light grip on his forearm and he was led into a room where an interpreter began to query him in broken Spanish. He produced the letter and was asked why he had come to claim his brother alone, without someone who could speak English. He explained how his attempt to find such a person had been futile. When the interrogation was over, he found himself walking between the two men down a corridor and up a stairway into the Great Hall. There a guard was given instructions Manuel didn't understand. Manuel was told to keep his eyes on a specific door.

He watched the door. People went in, people came out. After ten minutes that seemed like ten hours, Jose came through the door. Manuel embraced him, very happy and very scared. Maybe now we both go back to Spain together, he thought.

Through the interpreter the official with the fountain pen said something along these lines: "There's no doubt in my mind that he is your brother. The release papers will be signed. Then you can take him with you, but I want you to parade him around Cherry Street and tell everyone how you got him released all by yourself. And tell them that we don't bite people here."

In the late 1920s Manuel—my father—helped build roads for

the millions of automobiles rolling off the Detroit assembly lines. He went on to feed the insatiable appetite of the coal furnaces of a copper refinery, six days on and one off, and in twenty-seven years he failed to report to work only once. Occasionally he made reference to an America that catered to the Anglo-Saxon, but with tamed resignation. Later on he saw how the doors of opportunity opened up to me and to his grandchildren, one of whom graduated from the United States Air Force Academy.

When Jose retired he returned to the land of his childhood, where his Social Security pension went a long way. That's when his love for America blossomed to a degree he would never have believed possible. He joined an organization of retired immigrants for whom the Fourth of July and Thanksgiving became the most sacred of holidays. There is no patriotism greater than that which is measured by the yardstick of firsthand experience.

WORDS IN A
BLUE NOTEBOOK

Eula Lee Maddox

I was six years old, a dirty, barefoot child patting out make-believe tea cakes from mud in the yard of the sharecropper shack where I lived with my father, my two sisters, and my grandmother. I was eating my biggest tea cake when the landowner and his hunting friends came across the field, stopped about twenty feet away, and started talking about me as if I were a dead dove or a shot quail.

"What is it?"

"Jesus, it's eating dirt. It lives in that?"

"Hey now, I know," the landowner said. "A curse. Trash. The South's disgrace."

I quit chewing and grabbed up my mud tea cakes with both hands and slammed them at the men's faces.

150

"I am not so a curse and trash and the South's disgrace," I said, "and I ain't no it. I am me."

The landowner swore at me and said if I didn't cut it out he'd give me a whipping. The others laughed. One ran over and dropped a dollar bill in front of me. I snatched up the dollar, wrapped it in soupy mud, and hit him between the eyes with it.

They walked away laughing.

The next year I started first grade and learned to read and write. "I am me" was the first sentence I wrote on my own. At the end of second grade my teacher gave me a little blue notebook "for making A-plus on all your work."

I wrote my name on the blue cover, found the words "curse," "trash," and "disgrace" in the teacher's *Dictionary for Children,* and copied the definitions on the first page of my blue notebook. On the inside cover I printed in big capital letters, "I AM NOT A CURSE. I AM NOT TRASH. I AM NOT THE SOUTH'S DIS-GRACE. I AM ME."

Every day through grade school and high school I kept the blue notebook near me, usually in the bottom of the book bag my grandmother made me from leftover quilt scraps. Anytime I was tempted to slack an assignment, I'd see my words on its inside cover and I'd see the landowner and his friends laughing at me.

By the time I was a sophomore in high school I was on fire with the dream of going to college even though I knew it was impossible. I filled all the blue notebook's pages with outlines of college courses, clothes I'd wear there, even friends I'd make.

A week after graduation I found work as a salesclerk thirty miles away. I packed my few clothes in my book bag, wrapped the blue notebook in a square of sacking cloth, tied it with heavy cord, and asked my grandmother and my sisters to "keep this bundle for me till I get settled."

The next year my grandmother died, and shortly thereafter I found a job on a college campus five states away that allowed me to take two free classes each semester. I'd send for the bundle, I wrote my father and sisters, soon as I got settled.

Eventually, I knew I was as settled as I'd ever be. I asked my sisters about my bundle. Neither could remember it. I took a week off and went back and searched the rubble of all the sharecropper shacks we'd lived in, but I found nothing remotely akin to my blue notebook.

Never mind. I'll always see my words on the inside cover of the blue notebook as clearly as the day I wrote them. Then as now, I am me.

CHOICES

Bernice Mosbey Peebles

When I was very young, in the 1920s, I heard someone use the word "nigger."

"Mama, what's a nigger?" I asked.

"It's a dirty, nasty person," she said.

Although I had been taught not to call names, I couldn't resist the temptation when a new boy, Willie, entered our second-grade class. He was "colored," the term used then, dirty, unkempt, with uncombed hair and a runny nose. No one in our class looked like that. One morning before school started, a group of children formed a circle around Willie, crossing their forefingers and chanting, "Willie is a nigger! Willie is a nigger!" I joined in. Jennie, a white classmate who was not in the circle, pulled me out.

"Bernice, *you* mustn't call that boy a nigger," she said, "because you're one too, only we don't call you that."

After school I told Mama what Jennie had said. (I don't recall telling her what I had done.) Her terse comment was, "Yes, sometimes they refer to colored people as niggers." From the tone of her voice, I knew better than to ask why she hadn't told me that before.

By the time I was eight, I was acutely aware of stereotypes about blacks and spent a great deal of time attempting to refute them. There were colors I wouldn't wear, foods I wouldn't eat, and I refused to sing or dance. My brother Julian, four years older, had no such problems.

One day in music class the teacher reprimanded me. "All colored children can sing," she said.

"Well, I can't."

My downfall had to do with watermelon. I had seen cartoons

of black people with big red lips, eating huge slices of watermelon and grinning. I resolved never to admit that I liked watermelon, although I had tasted it secretly and loved it.

We owned a house in a rural town in upstate New York, and we were the only people of color on our street. Grandma and Grandpa lived down the hill, a nice, safe country walk in those days. Once, soon after we moved in, I was on my way to visit them when the man across the street called me. He looked gruff and had a huge reddish mustache. "Come here, little girl," he said.

In the 1920s, no child in my hometown had reason to be afraid to "come here." Child molesters had apparently not been born or lived elsewhere. I went over to see what he wanted.

"Do you like watermelon, little girl?"

"No, sir!" I replied, and ran off, sad that my new neighborhood housed people who were going to make fun of me.

When I got home, Julian was bent over our kitchen sink, eating a huge slug of watermelon. Although I begged, he wouldn't give me any, so I screamed and yelled. Mama came running to see if Julian was killing me, and of course I tattled on him.

"Julian, your father and I have always taught you to share with your little sister," said Mama.

"Yes ma'am, but I'm not sharing this. Mr. Brown told me he offered her some and she got insulted. If she's so dumb that she doesn't know what she likes, she's not getting any of mine!"

Mr. Brown grew the biggest, juiciest watermelons you ever saw, right across the street. He lived until I was grown up, but I never did taste one.

BACK OF THE BUS

Mildred Pensak

I boarded an interstate bus in Washington, D.C., to return to New York after a visit, and settled myself in the center. All the other passengers were scattered in seats in front of me. All but one, a young Negro woman with her three children.

I looked back and saw her in the absolute rear of the bus with her little ones around her. The infant was in her lap, and the two youngsters were standing, hugged to her knees. With all those empty seats in the front, middle, and rear, she didn't feel free to let the children sit down on this very long ride. Maybe she couldn't pay for their tickets and was afraid to set them down.

I signaled her to come forward, but she shook her head fiercely. I tried again, but she was adamant and remained remote and lonely back there. Finally I went to her and asked her to come sit near me, offering to hold the children's hands to help them walk. Her eyes opened wide as she tilted her head toward the driver, and the fear in her face told me everything.

Washington, D.C., wasn't south enough for me to have thought about segregation, but obviously it was happening there too. As I spoke to her the bus driver yelled back at us, "She can't sit anywhere else. She belongs there. That's the law!"

I am a quiet person, not known as a fighter, but his words stunned me so much that I shouted back, "She's coming forward with me, like it or not." He yelled. I yelled. And on it went until the young woman gathered courage and nodded that she would join me. She had not said a word in all that time.

Nor had anyone else. That was another tremendous shock to me. The driver was threatening to put me off the bus, along with the young woman, and no one defended us. She came forward with the children and arranged everyone comfortably in the seat across from me. The many hours' ride was eased for them.

When we arrived in New York City, I got off the bus with the others. Not until I was in the street did they tell me, "You did the right thing. You were right."

"It's a little late to tell me that now," I said.

Soon after, Rosa Parks took her stand.

FIGHTING FOR DEMOCRACY

William Rapacka

In the winter of 1943 I lived in the city of Newark, New Jersey, and like any boy of seventeen, my big ambition was to join the army and fight the Nazis and Japs in direct conflict, hand to hand with the evil forces. Besides, my favorite stepbrother was in the army, and I admired and tried to imitate him in every way. But the army wouldn't take you until you were eighteen years old, so another year or better at least I had to wait. No, not me, I said, I'll trick my way in. I went and changed the date on my birth certificate and registered for the draft.

Drafted I was and entered the army sometime in June of 1943. Shortly before I left, my stepbrother came to bid us all goodbye, and I felt bad when I heard him tell our father that he did not believe he would come out of the war alive.

Still, I went into the army gung-ho to beat the hell out of our enemies, who stood in the way of democracy, justice, liberty, equality, etc. I was shipped to Mississippi and loved all the adventure of this move I had made. By the standards of the poverty I had lived in, I thought army food was the greatest. The clothes fit, and I was even getting paid for the privilege of going to kill Germans and Japs. Basic training to me was a cupcake filled with cream. I loved being a soldier and saw myself as a great part of a great army that was fighting tyranny and injustice.

One day basic training ended. Lo and behold, the great fence of our camp opened up, and this young, ignorant, uneducated buck went off to see the world with his three buddies. I will never forget how we went into a restaurant in Jackson and I gorged myself on two T-bone steaks. I had never had T-bone steak. For that matter, I had never had a broiled steak; I don't think I even knew what "broil" meant. After the big feast the four of us started to look the town over. We went from street to street, looked in window after window. Stomach full, money in pocket, and a proud U.S. Army uniform on my back—the world was mine!

As we walked down a street in the center of town, we saw a crowd of people in a circle making comments and grunting and cheering. My youth and curiosity drove me toward the crowd, with my buddies following. I expected a street dance or someone hustling something, fortune-telling, selling monkeys, whatever. To my complete surprise what I saw was a black woman, thirty or thirty-five years old, lying on the concrete sidewalk with this huge man in blue farmer coveralls holding her in a deadly grip and shaking her violently. Three or four feet away stood a little girl child about two years old, crying hysterically, with her dress pulled up to her mouth and tears streaming like a water faucet.

The man yelled, "Nigger, tell me you're sorry. Tell me you're sorry!" She looked up at him and shook her head from left to right. He punched her in the face as hard as he could, repeating, "Tell me!" I yelled at him to stop, but my buddies grabbed me and said, "Don't get involved. You're down south, Bill."

Before I could shake myself loose, a policeman broke into the circle. He shoved me into the crowd and said, "Keep out of this, soldier." Thank God a cop is here to stop this beating, I said to myself. Then the policeman asked the supposed farmer, "Jesse, what the hell is going on here?" Still holding the woman, Jesse said, "This nigger bumped into me and won't say she's sorry," and then he shoved her like a dog to the concrete, her head hitting with violent force. The policeman gave her a healthy kick. "Nigger, get up and get out of here or you'll be in trouble." Turning to Jesse, he said, "Come on, get going. She's had enough." As Jesse was leaving, the cop inquired about his family and how they were doing. I went to help the black woman, but again my buddies grabbed me and told me not to get involved.

Well, I didn't get involved and went about my business of trying to be a good soldier, but I could not get that picture out of my mind. Finally I went to the C.O.'s office and said I wanted to see the captain. The master sergeant at the desk asked why. I said it was personal, and he said, "Listen, private, if the captain had to see every soldier that comes in here over the most trivial matter, he wouldn't have enough hours in a day, so tell me what it is or get the hell out of here."

"Sarge, I'm underage, and I want a discharge out of this army as soon as possible."

"Rapacka, if you're joking it's your ass. You better not be kidding around," he said, and he knocked on the C.O.'s door and sent me in.

"Private, what's this all about?" I proceeded to tell the captain about being underage and said I wanted a discharge because I didn't like the army anymore. He saw through my story. "Private, your record shows that you are a good soldier and may even go up for Pfc. shortly. Now tell me, what is it, trouble at home or what?"

I looked at him and told him my whole experience in town. I said that I could never take pride in wearing any kind of uniform after seeing that policeman's act of injustice. After fifteen or twenty seconds the captain got up and gave me a look that only a sympathetic father could give a son. "I'll have your discharge processed as quickly as possible. Dismissed." I left the room, walked past the grumbling sergeant, and was discharged in about two weeks. I could never get my patriotism worked up again to anything close to what it was before.

My brother Casimir never did make it back. He died on Europe's battlefield, and the place was supposed to be Malmédy. My parents couldn't write, and I never found out the details. I got back in the war later as a merchant mariner and even had the good fortune to run into my old company in New Guinea in 1944, by a freak chance. But that incident in Jackson will follow me to my grave in my mind.

CROSSING THE LINE

Edward Miller

When you're a teenager, music is food for the soul. You never forget the music of your teenage years, no matter how lousy it was. I remember "The Hut-Sut Song": "Hut-Sut rawlson on the Rilla Raw and a brawla brawla suet." And I remember "Mairzy Doats": "…and dozy doats and liddlams e divy." But mostly I remember Fats Waller, Meade Lux Lewis, Albert Ammons, Pete Johnson, Pinetop Smith, Leadbelly, Jelly Roll Morton, and that great music of my youth, boogie-woogie and the blues.

Once in a while you could hear good boogie on the radio, but not as often as I liked. At seventeen, I had a job as an orderly at Wesley Memorial Hospital, so I had money enough to buy almost any recording I wanted. I also bought the classics, like Bach's Toccata and Fugue in D-minor and Beethoven's Fourth Symphony. My dad and I both liked classical music.

One day I went to the local record store over on Lincoln Avenue near Belmont. I was interested in buying a small two-record album of boogie music by Albert Ammons and Pete Johnson. When I asked for it, the guy at the sales counter gave me a funny look.

"You're outta yer mind, kid. Ya gotta go down inta the Black Belt if ya want any a' that stuff."

I'd heard of the Black Belt, the area on Chicago's South Side below Thirty-fifth and above Sixty-third. My mother had told me it was a disgrace that all the blacks were forced to live in that small zone of the city. I asked her why and got the standard answer: "Nobody knows."

Whites weren't welcome in the Belt, but I wanted some Josh White as well as that boogie from Ammons and Johnson. I took a chance and rode the elevated down to Thirty-fifth. It was a black neighborhood all right. I stood out like a sore thumb. I guess a black kid would have felt the same way in an all-white neighborhood. I really felt alone. I also felt extra small and scrawny. I was only about five feet five in those days, and skinny too. I looked like a wimp compared to the people I saw down here in the Belt. Wishing that I was big, really big, I shrugged my shoulders and walked into a record store about half a block away.

It was the eyes. I never got such dirty looks in my life. I could feel resentment almost like a hammer. I think I was holding my breath.

"Whut you want, *boy?*"

That last word came through gritted teeth holding an unlit half-smoked cigar that stank. The guy was actually wearing a derby, like I'd seen in advertisements for *Amos 'n' Andy*. His shoes were yellow-tan, with the best shoeshine I'd ever seen. His hands were on his hips, and his tieless white-shirted belly hung over his belt. Everyone else in the long, narrow shop turned to look at me. The eyes!

"Can I buy any Pete Johnson or Albert Ammons here?"

"Whut?"

"How about Turner? Meade Lux Lewis? I wanna buy some Fats Waller, but not today."

"You like Turner, Ammons, Johnson, Lewis?"

"You bet. I really like boogie, and I can't find any of the good records where I live. Can I get them here?"

"Sure can, kid. Whut you looking for?"

"'Boogie Woogie Maxixe,' by Meade Lux Lewis."

"I got that. Whut else?" He dug out the record.

"You got any Huddie Ledbetter—any Leadbelly?"

He smiled, really friendly now. "You bet, kid. Which piece you after?"

I laughed. "Any. Just grab one. I haven't got any of his music. I've never been able to find it. How about Josh White?"

By the time we were through, I'd bought seven or eight records and my boogie album too.

"Anytime you want music by black artists, come down and see me, boy. If I ain't got it, I'll get it for you." He looked at me. "And don't feel uncomfortable, kid. You'll be okay here anytime you wanna buy some real music."

"Thanks a lot!"

Now I had some of the best music I've ever owned, American music at that. As I left the store and headed for the el station, I heard someone saying from the shop, "How about that! A white boy with music in his soul."

DIFFERENCE

Betty Swords

The pediatrician told me that my four-year-old Stevie was "just a vegetable." He would not develop any more. I mourned Stevie's blighted life, the damage caused by lack of oxygen during delivery. He could never be normal—whatever that is.

In the fifties, the mentally handicapped had only recently begun to "come out of the closet." Parents had much to learn; we had so many unanswered questions. That's why I was excited the night a local TV station sponsored a roundtable for parents of the mentally handicapped, with a telephone call-in. I drew a hassock right up to the TV so I felt like part of the discussion.

Oh, yes, I knew the problems they spoke of: the difficulty of finding the appropriate school (some had even had to change jobs and move to a city that offered special education), the tremendous cost of private schooling if the child wasn't eligible for a public program or the waiting list was too long. And how do you give handicapped children the extra time and attention they need to learn the simple things—dressing, feeding, and bathing themselves—without feeling that you're depriving your other children? How much responsibility can you place on siblings before they start to resent and hate the "different" child? How do other people relate to the child? As one distraught woman said, "I can get my family and friends to understand why Georgie acts different from most eight-year-olds, but not that darned clerk down at Safeway!"

And then there was a fear I'd not even thought about. An eighty-year-old woman called in to ask, "When can I die? I can't let myself go until there's someplace for my fifty-five-year-old son to live aside from an institution." In fact—terrible question—would everyone be better off if these children—my child—*were* put in an institution? And what kind of guilt did those parents suffer?

The next panelist to speak was Rabbi Samuel Adelman, of Beth Madrash Hagodal synagogue of Denver. I'll never forget his words.

"You've all talked about the problems connected with the retarded child, but no one has spoken of the *pleasures* these children bring us."

There was a shocked silence from the others on the panel. I wondered how he could say such a thing when I thought of all the heartbreak.

The rabbi continued. "When we accepted our daughter for what she was instead of lamenting what she was not, we learned to appreciate her special qualities—a sweetness and innocence, a tremendous capacity for giving and receiving love. Tragedy can be a pit of despair into which you sink or a mountain on which you climb to the heights."

Rabbi Adelman's words haunted me for a long time before I was fully able to accept the truth of them. I too recognized the sweetness and innocence of my child. (If it takes a higher IQ to produce lies, deceptions, and cruelties, do these special children have something we can learn from?) And I recognized Stevie's uniqueness: an unusual rapport with animals. In the morning a gaggle of neighborhood dogs met to see Stevie off on his special-education bus, reassembling in the afternoon for his return. The first time they gathered I feared for Stevie, because I could barely see his head over the back of a big dog. But not to worry! "All dogs are my friends," he told me.

When Stevie heard his older brother studying Spanish from a TV program, he was puzzled until we explained: if Ricky went to Spain or Mexico, he would be able to speak their language.

"Me too!" Stevie was glowing.

He had enough trouble with English, his brain damage being in the area of speech and language. "Spanish is hard to learn," I said, but he interrupted.

"Not Spanish," he said, his eyes sparkling with excitement. "I learn *Tarzan* so I can talk to all the animals in the jungle!"

Stevie has always had a similar rapport with young children, who adore him. As an adult, he uses that empathy to write imaginative fairy tales about unicorns and wolves and their friendships with children. I've typed up some of his stories and made copies for his friends.

What I learned from the rabbi extends beyond Stevie; the truth he spoke applies to all parents, especially those who haven't accepted their children for what they are: the father who wants his awkward son to live out his athletic dreams; the mother who wants her daughter to be the belle that she wasn't; the parents who try to make a musician out of an unmusical child. These parents haven't bothered to discover what their children are really like.

Yes, Stevie has limitations—but so is each of us limited to some degree. Poor eyesight may prevent us from being pilots; we may be too tall to be jockeys and not tall enough to be models.

On the other hand, we all have strengths; *that's* where we should place the emphasis, for ourselves and others. Surely you've never read a review of a production of *Hamlet* that said, "John Doe is an absolute klutz at any and every athletic sport, and a dunce at chess as well, but he did a magnificent job acting the role of Hamlet."

SAY GOODBYE, BOBO

Doris B. Gill

It was like many other quiet summer afternoons. The children and I were having a "literary hour" beneath our favorite maple tree. Five-year-old Steven looked up from his coloring book. Scrutinizing his work with satisfaction, he said, "Bobo escaped from the zoo today." He didn't sound frightened or even surprised; he might have said, "It's raining." But he said it, I later recalled, as if it were a fact and nothing could change it. Before I could respond, four-year-old Jeff exclaimed excitedly, "I hear the popsicle man!" The bell rang out across the quiet suburban lane, and Bobo was forgotten as the children scampered down the sidewalk, clutching coins for the iced treat.

A few days later I was cleaning the back screen door, which looked like a child had targeted it with rotten apples. Steven galloped by on his stick horse, chasing imaginary cowboys and Indians. "Whoa," he said, reining in his steed as he noticed the screen splattered with decaying remnants of fruit. "See, Bobo was here and messed on the door."

I tried to explain that Bobo was secure in his cage at the Seattle Woodland Park Zoo, but Steven wouldn't believe me. I decided it was time to visit Bobo in person. The next day, a shirt-sleeve-weather afternoon, was perfect for a picnic in the park. After lunch we went directly to the Ape House, and there was Bobo. The boys leaned on the railing for a front-row glimpse. I watched Steven to see his reaction. He smiled weakly, trying to enjoy Bobo's antics, and seemed satisfied that the huge ape was safely ensconced in his glass-and-metal enclosure.

A crowd had gathered for the zoo's most popular attraction. Ignoring his audience, Bobo turned his back, pounding his leathery chest in feigned ferocity. The giant of the jungle glanced sideways and slyly checked his spectators' response, looking pleased as everyone recoiled uncomfortably. Steven inched toward me for safety, but before I could take my frightened son's hand Bobo resumed his theatrics. Turning his bullet-shaped head, he looked directly at Steven with his piercing, deep-set eyes. He rolled his almost human hand into a powerful fist and bashed the unbreakable glass. The crowd stepped back in unison. The woman standing next to me said, "I sure wouldn't want that overgrown monkey looking at one of my kids that way," and grasped her baby stroller a little tighter. Steven bolted from the Ape House, and we finally caught up with him at Monkey Island. He looked a little pale but soon seemed to forget his ordeal as he watched the playful monkeys.

That night, after the children were tucked in, Steven began crying. When I went to him, he howled, "Bobo was in my room!" "But Steven, you saw Bobo in his cage. He's locked up tight, he gets a shock when he touches the glass." His azure eyes were filled with tears as he sobbed emphatically, "He did get out. I did see him."

I wrapped him in his favorite down quilt and rocked him in the chair that had comforted him through teething and colds. The streetlight beamed through windblown leaves, distorting images in the dark room. I tried to imagine what Steven believed he saw, picturing that great hairy beast dominating the small bedroom, his hot breath on the face of the terrified child.

The next day I switched bedrooms with Steven, moving him to a lighter side of the house, and told myself optimistically that he would outgrow his unwanted guest. It was no wonder he was having problems. The year had not been good for our family, and Steven seemed to be feeling it more than Jeffrey. First losing his father, through divorce—what do you tell a five-year-old when his daddy doesn't visit? As if that were not enough for a little boy to manage, he was facing surgery to correct obstructions in both kidneys.

As the months passed, Bobo became firmly entrenched in our household. Steven was in the hospital much of the time that year. The nurses reported that Bobo had checked in there too. Ironically, there was a monkey tree outside Steven's hospital window. "That's Bobo's nest," he told me matter-of-factly as the nurse took his blood pressure.

A year passed, the surgeries successfully completed. Steven was flourishing, looking forward to being old enough for Little League. But Bobo was still our star boarder, and I was beginning to think we would never get rid of him.

One autumn evening, after the boys were settled in bed, Steven yelled. I was tired and had been planning a quiet night. As Steven's cry turned into a loud wail, I walked into the kitchen and began opening cabinets in desperation, not really knowing what I was looking for. I had to find an answer. Bobo had overstayed his welcome. Then I spied it. Would it work? It might. Steven couldn't read much yet.

As I entered the room, Steven uncovered his head from his hiding place beneath the blankets. He hugged Bananas, his dog-eared stuffed monkey, as if for protection. Tears streamed down his flushed face. I turned on the small lamp and held out a brightly colored can. "Do you know what this is, Steven?" He rubbed his eyes, adjusting to the low light, perplexed by my smiling expression. "I have a special surprise for you," I whispered. He stifled a sob as he examined the can. "This is just our secret. It's called Gorilla Be Gone. All we do is spray your room each night and Bobo will never come back."

Steven watched skeptically as I sprayed the dark corners of his bedroom. After I applied the final touches to the ominous closet, he said, "How do I know Bobo will stay away?" Taking his forefinger, I placed it on the sprayer nozzle. "This will be your secret weapon. Now you are as strong as Bobo." I put the can on his nightstand, within his reach. As he snuggled into his feather bed, I handed him Bananas and kissed him good night.

At last Bobo said goodbye—thanks to a can of air freshener!

LA DOLCE VITA

Phyllis Major

Even now, thirty years later, I remember the details of that remarkable Saturday morning. The day began in a quite ordinary way, as had dozens of Saturdays before. As I dressed, I began clicking off in my mind the usual list of chores. In the background I heard Sam shaving as he prepared to leave for his office. I could only wonder how many bowls of cereal nine-year-old Lennie and fourteen-year-old Mitchell would go through before I got to the kitchen. I half listened for the doorbell to announce the arrival of Dorie, my Saturday morning blessing, a neighbor's teenage daughter who came regularly to help with the cleaning and polishing.

I remembered our date that evening. Weeks ago Sam and I had arranged to meet Al and Liz in Hollywood for *La Dolce Vita*, the new Fellini film all our friends had been urging us to see. Marcello Mastroianni at his best in gloriously decadent Rome. *La Dolce Vita*—"The Sweet Life"—would be a sweet antidote to the Saturdayness of it all.

Soon Dorie arrived and we began our work. We moved through the morning in silent harmony, nodding or chatting a moment in passing. Every half-hour or so Mitch or Lennie dashed in, attacked the refrigerator, and ran out clutching Cokes, cheese, and bologna to share with friends waiting outside. By noon Dorie and I were ready to relax over bowls of soup.

About 12:30 the phone rang. Sam was calling from his law office. His voice sounded strained.

"Hi, honey. I've got a problem here. Are you free this afternoon? It's an emergency!" His words came fast. "There isn't much time. I just had a call from a desperate woman, one of my old clients. She's been struggling to take care of herself and her five little children, including twin boys just three months old. No husband. Finally, after a lot of agonizing, she realized she simply had to do what was best for everyone, so she arranged with a good local family to adopt her twins. They were supposed to pick up the babies this morning, but they just phoned her to say that they couldn't go through with the adoption. Period. Meanwhile, she has the twins all dressed and bundled up. She can't take it anymore! She's physically and emotionally exhausted, at the end of her rope. So she just called me, desperate for help, wanting to know if I could find the twins a good temporary home right now—today! Then Monday I could start looking for a good adoptive family. She trusts me...." He paused to catch his breath. "What d'you think, honey? Could we take those babies in? Just for the weekend?"

"How old did you say they are?"

"Three months. I promised to call her right back."

Three-month-old twins? In this house? A dozen questions skipped around in my head as I strained to remember the size of three-month-old babies. I no longer had any of the boys' baby

clothes, no crib—maybe an old blanket. I had given away everything years ago. Maybe I could…

"Are you there?"

I laughed. "Sure, honey, it's okay! Pick us up in half an hour.
Dorie and I'll be ready."

I gulped. Only thirty minutes to get everything together! Slam-
ming down the receiver, I turned to Dorie, who had been eaves-
dropping all the while. The housework was forgotten.

Back at the phone, I madly dialed friends. "Do you have an
extra crib in your garage? Can you spare a baby blanket, shirts,
sheets, diapers? I'll take anything!"

The boys came in for another go at the fridge. I told them
what was going on. They were amazed by the whirl about them.
"Babies? Twins? How long will they stay? Whose room?"

"Don't bother me now."

I dashed through the house, instructing Dorie to clear some
furniture out of the den to make room for two cribs, one from a
friend and one from a rental agency. I could scarcely remember
anything about babies, let alone twins. One of my friends suggested that I phone Mrs. Cassett, a member of the local Mothers of
Twins Club. I never knew such a group existed, but that afternoon
I was very grateful when a calm, relaxed Mary Cassett answered
my frantic questions.

"Don't worry," she said. "It's challenging, a lot of work, but it's
much easier than you think."

Well, maybe *she* thought so. After all, her twins were already
two years old. "But how do I feed them both at the same time?"

"Nothing to it. You prop them up in their infant seats and feed
them with one spoon."

"One spoon?" I was aghast.

"Sure, just load it up, shove it one mouth, load it up again,
shove it in the other mouth. That's all there is to it."

"But," I pressed her, "what about their bottles?"

Mary was patient. If they wanted their bottles at different
times, obviously there was no problem. But if they both got hungry at the same time—"and twins usually do"—all I had to do was
cradle one baby in one arm, nipple in his mouth and bottle
propped on his belly, while with my free hand I offered the second
bottle to the other baby lying flat next to me. On the next feeding,

I simply switched babies so I could cuddle each one alternately.

"If you have any more questions, just call me. You'll do fine," Mary said cheerfully.

Outside, Sam was honking the horn. I thanked Mary, and Dorie and I ran to the car.

After an interminably long ride, we arrived at the house. Sam introduced me to the mother, who was obviously strained and upset. I felt awkward as I tried to reassure her. Then we went over to see the twins. It was eerily quiet for a long minute or so. I bent over them, and to my astonishment I saw one chubby towheaded blond, thumb stuck in his mouth, and next to him, his thinner, very active, very brunet little brother, who turned out to be the elder by two minutes. I had had visions of two cherubic look-alikes. I could never have anticipated such distinctly individual infants. Soon we were all going over the necessary information about feeding, sleeping, bathing, dressing—the all-important routines to which they were already accustomed.

When we parted, Dorie carried the blond twin, and I the little brunet. As we started out the door, I looked back at the mother. I could see the three older children hovering in the background. At that moment, I felt her loss as keenly as if these were my own babies whom I had to release to strangers. I noted how beautifully she had dressed them—how pretty were their little outfits, how bright their wrapping blankets. I knew she wanted the best for her sons, and I also knew she trusted Sam to find them exactly the right adoptive parents.

I gulped and looked at Sam. It had been a long time—more than nine years—since I had held a baby in my arms. In those first awkward moments I felt self-conscious, but I needn't have worried. My arms remembered well. Soon the little brunet was nestled quietly and comfortably up against my body.

We stopped at the home of my girlfriend, where we picked up some extra blankets and crib sheets. She took one look at the twins, then at us, and broke into peals of laughter. Only days later did we learn why. Obvious to her, a mystery to us.

At last the five of us came home. At once we were surrounded by Mitch and Lennie, who had set up the two cribs in the den. They were curious and delighted with the babies—but brunet and blond "twins"? And so tiny? Was I sure they were three months old? After checking to be sure the twins were in fact boys, they left to resume their play.

Sam put sheets and blankets on the cribs and brought two Boston rockers into the den. Dorie and I took the babies to the kitchen to give them their first feeding. I wasn't about to try that "only one spoon" bit yet. Then Sam and I took the babies into the den/nursery, settled into the rockers, and began the first bottle feeding. Intently I studied the little blond I was now holding. His wide-awake eyes peered up at me equally intently, still that hazy gray-blue color of all newborns. I was curious—would they remain blue or change to brown? The twins emptied their bottles rapidly. We carefully placed them in their cribs, tummy down, and waited for the milk-bubble burp. Then we covered each warm little body with a blanket and softly left the room.

Outside the den, we looked at each other. Sam asked if I really wanted to go to Hollywood to see *La Dolce Vita*.

I grinned at him. "No, honestly, I don't. But Al and Liz are expecting us, so let's go. Dorie will baby-sit. We'll see them when we come home."

The freeway trip into Hollywood seemed faster than usual, and soon we were watching Marcello and his sophisticated friends enact their anguish in a heavy tattoo of sensuous, erotic images. Over coffee later, I could hardly join in the excited chatter about the film. It all seemed unreal. We told Al and Liz about our week-end babies. Amused, they watched us leave earlier than usual.

Back on the freeway, I urged Sam to drive faster. Maybe they would need another bottle? After all, Dorie was alone with them. Sam looked over at me and stepped on the gas. In the silence of the speeding car, scenes from *La Dolce Vita* flickered and sputtered in my mind's replay of the film. As I looked out the car window at the dark Palos Verdes hills ahead of me, those film images blurred into the reality of the dark nursery.

When we got home, I ran inside and warmed up two bottles of milk, just in case. Sam joined me in the den. At first all we could see were the two little bodies huddled under blankets. So still, just the sound of their breathing. That unique, wonderful smell of infants filled the room. We looked down at them. First the blond, then the brunet head popped up and looked back at us, sleepy eyed, from behind the bars of the cribs. Our footsteps must have awakened them. In an instant we gathered them up, blankets and all. We went over to the rockers, each holding a baby in our arms. We didn't speak. Nothing to say. We listened. The only sound in the room was the sound of our greedy little sons, busily sucking away on their bottles—the sound of *la dolce vita*.

OUR NIGHT OF MAGIC

Charlotte Carpenter

A slow but steady rain came down all that wintry morning and froze where it fell—on the ground, the trees, the buildings. By midafternoon the rain had stopped and we looked on a crystal world.

We were accustomed to the white hoarfrost of winter, but this was something else—a hard, clear coating of solid ice. Our five children, ages five to sixteen, returned from school exclaiming about how good the sledding would be on the steep hill in our pasture.

They took out at once, but they never reached their destination, for between home and hill lay a gently rolling, treeless meadow. Here they found that their sleds would speed over the ice from fence to fence with only the weight of their bodies to keep them going. What fun they had. When they came home to chores and supper, they were so excited. "Mom and Dad, you've got to come with us down to the pasture tonight," they said. They had never seen ice so slippery that they didn't need a hill for coasting on their sleds.

Why should fortyish parents risk life and limb going out on a dangerously slick night? They begged until we simply could not refuse them.

Gingerly we made our way to the meadow. Even with rubber footgear, we found it hard to walk. The sleds we pulled kept sliding into the backs of our legs. It was very cold, and Father, the practical one, carried an armload of wood to build a fire.

We will never forget the unbelievably beautiful sight that met our eyes when we reached the meadow. The moon and stars, shining brilliantly as they do only on clear, cold nights, turned the meadow into a lake of glass. We built our fire at the top of a slight incline. The ice reflected us, and the leaping flames danced in the ice.

Again and again the children and sleds flew over the ground. If two rode together the sled went faster, so fast the riders could barely turn in time to avoid crashing into the fence. The littlest ones rode back to the starting point, easily pulled by older brothers. We parents envied them—the hardest part for us was walking back after the ride. We left most of the sledding to our children and stayed near the fire, absorbed in the dreamlike magic of this night.

We all felt so good as we started back that we hardly noticed our cold feet and tired bodies. "Will the ice still be here tomorrow?" one of the children asked. "Probably not, if the sun shines," I answered. And sure enough, by midmorning the ice was gone, leaving only an expanse of brown grass.

To this day, when we're in the meadow, whether it's covered with the luxuriant green of summer or the white snow of winter, we remember that night's wonder. I harbor a brief doubt, in spite of six other witnesses, for the experience seems like something we must have imagined.

My husband and I learned something that night—to enjoy an interlude of joy when it comes, not to put our children off when they find something wonderful, so unusual that it may never happen again, not to say, "We're too busy now, it will have to wait." We go with them to glimpse the moment—a new calf, a robin on the lawn, a butterfly or bug. We share their excitement over a ballgame, a school play, or graduation. For now we know this:

Refuse to take the time and you miss something precious to hold in memory, perhaps just the meaning of the mind. A magical sledding on glass in the starlight may happen only once in an entire lifetime.

MY FIRST JOB

Carole Hall

While the town slept, a layer of thick black ice covered the streets. A gray dawn brought no respite from the chill of that memorable winter day—the first day of my first job. I was fifteen, and for the princely sum of seven shillings a week, I had been hired as a very junior assistant at the drapery store in town, where I would sell yard goods and men's shirts, cotton reels and overalls, ladies' goods and scents, lingerie and corsets.

Back then you walked to work. Cars were few and far between, and expensive too, so "shank's pony" was the order of the day, and you the better for the walking. That morning the ice was so treacherous that I had to hug the walls of houses and struggle to secure each foothold. Only the most nimble traveled the streets and accomplished their destination; everyone else crowded doctors' offices and hospital emergency rooms with strains, sprains, and broken bones. Town buses slid wickedly like ponderous beasts to lurch against the nearest solid object and there to stay. It was a formidable day for a wee slip of a lass.

As I walked through the front door of the store, my glasses fogged up and not a thing was visible to me. I was late. Two hours late.

"Well, I see you've finally made it! Next time use the back door," said Mr. Fred Sharp, the store manager. "Get a move on, then. Floor needs a good sweep. Just because we're a bit late on account of weather doesn't mean we can shirk our duties, does it?"

Shaking my head in agreement, I looked about wildly for a broom.

"If we let weather rule us, we'd get naught done, would we, eh?" Mr. Sharp, a bit on the deaf side, tended to shout a little to get his points across. "And you'd better polish the brass door handle. Can't have smudges all over everything, can we, now?"

Not knowing what to do first, I just stood there.

"Go on, then, away with you! And put some elbow grease into it. I want to see me face in that handle!"

When I asked how to go about the polishing, Mr. Sharp stared at me with immeasurable sad patience.

"Brasso, lass! You use Brasso! And don't be taking all day at it either." Then he leaned down and peered at me through steel-rimmed spectacles. "You're not a numbskull, are you? What would you do if I told you to go borrow a rubber hammer and a bag of glass nails from the cobbler up street and fetch the lot back to me, eh?"

The saints preserve me, but I swear a mischievous elf jumped into my mouth and without a by-your-leave began dropping cheeky words from my very own lips.

"I'd say you'd be wasting your time, Mr. Sharp. What would a fine gentleman like you want with a rubber hammer and a bag of glass nails? But if you wish to be sending me on a fool's errand I'll not be telling you no, just asking you please to wait till the weather is more clement!"

And then I winced at my impudence. My own mouth is for putting my shoe in, I thought sadly. I need this job, and for sure now I'm to be sacked. My mother won't be at all proud, and she such a saint when it comes to patience with me!

Suddenly there came a loud guffaw from Mr. Sharp. Made me fair jump, it did. His laughter rang true in the cold morning air, rippling with merriment, free and unbridled. Head thrown back, he laughed the sweetest sounds while I stood in astonishment and stared at him.

When he finally stopped, the laughter bubbling down to a few chuckles and him having to blow his nose like the honking of geese, he placed a warm hand on my shoulder and said, "By gum, you're the real McCoy, and no mistake!"

I took myself off into the empty store and swept the brown floors and hummed as I polished the brass handle. No other employees came in, nor did any customers. The brutal freeze lasted all that mad March Monday and kept folks close to hearth and home.

Mr. Fred Sharp taught me the intricacies of the dry-goods trade. He also taught me that all life is a learning experience and knowledge is for sharing. Sooner or later we're all teachers, and everything has a first. I kept my first job for six years. Didn't pay much as jobs go, but as a learning experience it was unparalleled.

DELIVERANCE

John Coleman

"Oh, John! Does this mean they're going to put us out on the street?"

I took the letter from my mother and read it carefully. That was exactly what it meant.

I was the oldest of six children, all born in a little mining village in Scotland, of Irish parents. My father, George Coleman, had died three months before in the Glasgow Royal Infirmary. He had been injured in the coal mine, but there was no report of it, and he tried to keep on working to feed his family. Our house and the grocery store where we shopped were owned by the coal company. They deducted the rent from your wages. Now, since we had no bread-winner, they were getting no rent.

My mother and I decided to go to the collier's office and say that my father had died of pneumonia and we had no claim on them. Our visit was not in vain: we were granted free rent for six months, and I was offered a job in the coal mine. I was only thir-teen, and my mother got quite upset. I calmed her down and said to this very grim man who was interviewing us that I would get an exemption from school. He gave me a typewritten letter to present, guaranteeing me a job.

My mother worked on a farm, gathering potatoes. A horse pulled a machine that unearthed them. She collected them in her apron and deposited them in large baskets to be taken back to the farm and sold to wholesale merchants. When nobody was watch-ing, she would put potatoes under the hedges at the end of the field. Under cover of darkness my younger brother and I would take a burlap bag, creep along the hedges, and steal quietly into the night. We had potato pancakes for breakfast, potato scones for lunch, and boiled potatoes for supper. My aunt would supplement our diet with tea, bread, and sugar.

When I presented the collier's letter to my teacher, Miss Donelly, of Saint Augustine Roman Catholic School, she grabbed me by the arm and towed me to the office of the headmaster, a Mr. Paterson, exclaiming loudly, "Can't you do something about this outrage? This is my best pupil, and he is being taken out of school to work in a coal mine." Mr. Paterson replied, "Yes, I have the same feeling, and I am trying to change the child labor laws." Some years later he was elected to Parliament and did just that.

The next Monday morning I appeared at the pithead at 6:30 A.M. I shall never forget going down in that cage for the first time. My stomach came up to my mouth as the cage seemed to drop into the bowels of the earth, darkness and roaring water on each side of us. A lifetime later, when I was visiting Niagara Falls, it all came back to me.

I stood on the pit bottom, my legs shaking. I was approached by the underground boss, who told me to work with a miner whose drawer had taken the day off.

The miners worked at the coal face, digging and shoveling coal out to the drawers, who loaded it into a hutch, or small freight car, and pushed it out to the main road, where it was attached to a haulage rope and taken to the pit bottom, to be put on the cage and lifted up to the surface. If somebody's drawer didn't show up, you worked with him.

All work was piecework, your wages governed by the amount of hutches you filled. We all had numbered metal discs with string attached, to insert in the hutch so the surface manager could keep a record of our output. In my case it was a little different. The coal miner would pin all the hutches and get credit for everything. He had to guarantee ten shillings for my day's work, which was fine with me, though if I'd worked with three different men I had to scuttle around to collect from all of them on payday.

I was getting used to this life, and things were beginning to improve at home. With my pay we could buy more nourishing food. But from October to late March I found it very difficult. It would be dark when we went down the mine and dark when we came up. When we stepped off the cage in April, I would shout, "Presto, it's daylight." We would stop and listen to the birds singing in the trees and shout up to them, "Hi, hi!" But the old miners would be stumbling and falling over the railroad tracks as they exclaimed, "I can't see a thing." Six months in darkness was just too much.

I will never forget the day an iron girder fell and closed the mine shaft. We were entombed! Word spread rapidly, and a bell system loudly notified everybody to make for the pit bottom. Mr. Jack, the boss, told us to keep quiet and explained how we would make our way to another mine, where we would be hauled to the surface and to safety. Mr. Jack said the escape route was clear of gas; they had released a canary into the tunnel, and it had returned.

Pat McLaughlin, who was my father's good friend and had always watched out for me, came up and asked, "How are you doing, John?" He told me to stay close to him and keep in front. We set off with Mr. Jack leading on Wednesday at 1:00 P.M. We arrived at the other pit bottom and were hauled to the surface at 3:00 A.M. on Friday morning. It was a horror going through that tunnel. Sometimes we had to crawl on our bellies with water pouring from the roof. Sweating, with mud on our clothes, we were all a sorry sight. As we entered the tunnel, we were all singing, but before we reached our destination we were arguing and fighting.

When I alighted from that cage that Friday morning, my sister Mary and her husband, Frank Mann, were there to take me home. Pat McLaughlin had collapsed from exhaustion and was sick for some time afterward.

When I would sit in the pit bottom looking at those old miners, I would think they looked old beyond their years. I would tell myself there must be a better way to live. I tried everything— the police department, the post office, the railroads—but all to no avail. Pat would say to me, "John, stop knocking yourself out. You will be a coal miner all your life. That's all there is for you and me in this country." He was right. There was no way out. I lost all hope.

Then a miracle struck. Pat and I were walking home from the coal mine one day when a well-dressed man stopped in front of Pat and grabbed his hand and shook it. They talked and laughed for quite some time. When Pat and I resumed our journey home I said, "What was that all about?" He told me that the man had worked in the mine with him. He had emigrated to a town called McKeesport in the U.S.A. I said to myself, "This is it!" I had hope that if that man did it, so could I. When I got home I asked my mother if she knew anybody in the United States. She said her mother's brother went out there when she was a little girl. I asked if she had his address. She laughed and said he must be dead by now. "I think it was Vienna, Missouri, the last we heard from him. His name was Frank Duffin." I sat down and wrote a letter to Vienna.

I continued to work in the coal mines, always hoping I would hear from somebody. A year passed, and one day as I came home from work my sister Agnes said to me, "Whom do you know in America?"

"Nobody, I wish I did."

"Well, somebody knows you, as there is a letter to you from America on the mantle."

The letter was from a son of the man I had written to. He was living in St. Louis and had returned to Vienna with his wife to visit relatives. He was told by an acquaintance who worked in the post office that there had been a letter for him for over a year with a foreign stamp on it. He instructed this man to send it to his address in South Saint Louis. We corresponded for a long time. He sent me a ticket, invited me to come to Saint Louis, and said he would get me a job at Laclede Gas Company. I arrived and have spent my life here happily, all the poverty and hardship behind me.

To quote Tennyson, "To strive, to seek, to find and not to yield."

TRIUMPH AT BLUE RIVER

Don McKee

I was standing at the mill gate with a batch of leaflets as the second-shift workers came on. "The United States government protects your right to join a labor union," the heading on my handout proclaimed.

Passing out leaflets was nothing new to me, for I was a national representative of the Textile Workers Union of America (CIO), working out of Rock Hill, South Carolina. But this was my first appearance at the Blue River Mill, and initial literature distributions were always scary for me. You never knew what was going to happen. As I greeted the Blue River workers, I tried to look calm and relaxed. Inside, I was anything but.

Just before the shift change, a man who was not wearing overalls came out of the factory and put out his hand to accept a leaflet. He did not move on but stood right in front of me reading it.

"I'm deputy sheriff," he suddenly snarled, "and I want you to get the hell out of here. This is private property."

"But I'm outside the gates and have a right to…"

"Not while I'm the deputy. Now get the hell off."

With a quick jerk, the man grabbed my leaflets and flung them in the air. As they fell to the ground, he swung and struck me on the jaw, then shoved me down a couple of steps in front of the mill gate. As I struggled to get up, he reached into a back pocket and pulled out a hammer. Clenching it tightly, he grabbed my front collar with the other hand and started pushing me away from the mill entrance.

"Now *move* or I'll give it to you!" he shouted.

Expecting a blow at any moment, I slowly stepped backward, intent on his hand, now quivering as it clutched the weapon and readied it for a swing upward. The deputy, keeping his grip on my collar, followed each retreating motion. His face flushed with fury, he never relaxed his hold on the hammer. It was about seventy yards from the gate to where my car was parked. Step by step, my assailant propelled me in that direction.

Back at the mill gate, a crowd had gathered to watch the strange drama. And it certainly was a strange one. People opposed to union organization had seized my papers before during mill distributions. Fists, an arrest or two, even a brick had been directed against my person. Once a shotgun had been aimed at my head. But a hammer? In the year 1947, that was something new.

Still, there it was, held low in a shaking hand, ready to land on my cranium. The retreat continued.

Finally, when we got to my Chevy, the deputy let go of my collar and tried to open the car door, but it was locked. Perhaps uncertain what to do next, he just stood there. That brief moment of relaxation brought a surprise. Whether because of his success in removing me from the mill gate or because we were now so far from the crowd in front of the factory, the deputy tucked the hammer under an armpit, reached inside his jacket, and pulled out a small notebook.

"Now, what's your name?" he asked, fingering a pencil.

"It's Don McKee."

"That's M-k-k…?"

"No. M-c-K-e-e. McKee."

"Where you come from?"

"You mean before I came to South Carolina?" Anything to keep the conversation going.

"Yeah."

"My home's North Carolina."

"North Carolina!"

"Yeah. Chapel Hill."

For a moment there was silence while he scribbled in his notebook. To preserve the newly arrived calmness, I asked, "And what's your name, officer?"

"Reese. It's James Reese. I'm the deputy sheriff in Blue River."

"Well, Mr. Reese, I know Courtney Smith, the county sheriff. Guess you work for him."

"Sure do. You know Courtney?"

"Yup. Last month when a deputy ran me off during a literature distribution at the Aragon Mill, I went to see Mr. Smith—and he ordered the deputy to let me alone 'cause he was violating the United States Constitution."

"The Constitution?"

"Yeah, the First Amendment."

"The First..."

"Yeah. It protects the right to distribute leaflets."

"At a mill gate?"

"Course. Ever heard of *Lovell* versus *Griffin?* In that case the Supreme Court..."

"Tell you what I'll do, son," Reese interrupted. "You can distribute your papers at the gate but not on the top of the steps." And with that, he put his hammer back in his pocket, turned, and strode toward the mill.

Stunned by the turn of events, I watched him go. What had brought the unexpected change? Where did all that hostility go? What made it evaporate so rapidly?

But there was no time for explanations. Somehow, retreat had turned to victory. Walking back to the front gate of the mill, I picked up a handful of the union circulars, stood at the bottom of the steps, and began to pass them out again. From inside the gate, Deputy Reese watched. So did the crowd of workers, most of them from the first shift. Reese didn't move. He just stood there.

As I gave out the sixth or seventh leaflet from my small bundle, a sudden shout came from the crowd. People began clapping their hands and applauding. Unsure of the reason for the ovation, I waved, then continued passing out the handbills.

Were the workers applauding the end of the entertaining show the deputy sheriff had put on? Was there sympathy for a victim who had survived a devastating attack and somehow turned the tables on the attacker? My silent hope was that the cheering was for the First Amendment, even though I knew it could not be. For momentarily at least, the First Amendment had triumphed in Blue River.

GOING TO NEW YORK

Charles Polacheck

In the spring of 1939 I was twenty-five. I was working as an actor on the WPA Federal Theatre Project in Chicago. When the WPA shut down I was offered a summer job as an actor-director on the social staff of Camp Unity in Dutchess County, only fifty miles from New York. I grabbed it.

To be in New York, the center of the American theater world, possibly to work with the famous Group Theatre, that was the height of my ambition. I arrived in New York in May, just in time to see the Group's production of *Golden Boy.* I ate my heart out watching my classmate from the Goodman Theatre, Mladen Sekulovich (now known as Karl Malden), in a small part that I coveted. But at least I was in New York!

After a summer of directing a play every week for eight weeks, I found myself back in New York with no job and no money. I finally got a poorly paying job with a marionette theater that performed in the public schools. One day in November I noticed in the theatrical column of the *Times* that Elmer Rice was casting his new play. Since Rice's daughter Peggy was a classmate of my sister at the University of Chicago, I asked for and got an audition. I read for the part of a young Jewish taxi driver in Scene 2. Rice said he liked my audition but since I had no experience on the New York stage, he would let me know in two weeks.

I thought I was being fobbed off, but my out-of-work actor friends who met daily in the coffee shop beneath Walgreen's drugstore on Forty-fourth and Broadway assured me that Rice was the only producer in New York who told auditioners the truth. If he said he might use me, then he really might.

Two fateful weeks passed without a word. I was worried on two counts. First, would I land the job? Second, if I did, would I have to leave the marionette theater stranded? What to do? If I called Rice and pressed him for an answer I might antagonize him. Then I remembered that I knew a young playwright named Phillip Robinson who worked as an assistant publicity man in Rice's office. I called him, but he was in a rush. "I have to go to Boston, and my train leaves soon from Grand Central," he said. "Come to the office now, and we can talk on the way to the station."

I rushed right over to Rockefeller Plaza. When I walked into the waiting room, Rice's secretary was standing in the inner doorway. She looked at me and said, "Oh, you're Charles Polacheck. Wait here." And she disappeared.

After a few minutes Phil Robinson came into the waiting room. "Oh, there you are," he said. "Let's go."

As we walked over to Grand Central Station, I told him my problem. He said, "The best thing to do is sit tight and wait for Rice to call you." I thanked him, and he got on his train to Boston.

Then it hit me. Rice's secretary did not know that I was there to see Robinson. What if she had told me to wait because Rice wanted to see me? Should I run back to the office and ask her? Should I call her? I raced to the nearest phone and called my landlord to see if there had been any mail or messages for me. "No, nothing."

At nine o'clock the next morning I received a postcard asking me to appear in Rice's office at ten! I was prompt in my arrival.

"Well," said Rice, "you're a kind of difficult fellow to reach." After I explained the misunderstanding, Rice asked me if I would like to work as an assistant stage manager and do bits and walkons. I would also understudy Martin Ritt, who became a well-known movie director. The play was called *Two on an Island*.

So there I was with a bona fide job in a Broadway play my first year in New York. We went into rehearsal the following week and opened early in 1940. The cast was led by Betty Field (who later became Mrs. Elmer Rice), John Craven, and Luther Adler of the Group Theatre, who had played the lead in *Golden Boy* the previous spring.

I later discovered that the real reason the play was rushed into production was that the Group Theatre was preparing a new play by Odets called *Night Music* that had exactly the same theme and plot: a boy and girl finding each other and love and happiness against great odds in New York City. We opened *Two on an Island* six weeks before *Night Music.* In spite of the fact that Odets's play was considerably better than Rice's, *Two on an Island* was a hit and *Night Music* was a flop and closed in two weeks. This failure drove the final nail into the coffin of the Group Theatre. It was permanently disbanded.

So—I had come to New York not to join the Group Theatre but to play a small part in its demise.

A REAL PRO

Robert O. Shannon

My life in a small southern town in 1945 was high school, girls, work, and baseball. All the towns in the area supported a baseball team, and mine was no exception. Our team was good, since it was composed of veteran players too old for military service and a few youngsters like me.

Graduation was only a few weeks away, and I was not sure what career to pursue. My favorite activities were baseball and working with animals. Animals had always been an important part of my life, their companionship and unconditional love as priceless to me then as today. My family wanted me to attend college and study veterinary medicine. For most of my young life, the thought of becoming a veterinarian had been foremost in my mind. But that would mean more school, and frankly, I was about saturated with classes and studying.

Then there was baseball. My knowledge of professional baseball was limited to radio broadcasts of games in faraway places like Saint Louis, Detroit, and New York, but I had a personal fantasy that someday I would play in these places. My father had played baseball as a young man and had shared his love of the game with me. Dad died in 1941, but I will never forget how we huddled close to the radio, eating fresh boiled peanuts and listening to those big-league games.

Graduation day came and went. My dilemma about what to do continued. Surely there must be someone who could point me in the right direction. One afternoon, after I performed well in a game, several fans came up and treated me like a celebrity. Suddenly I was Bobby Feller or Dizzy Dean, and all I could think about was the glamour, fame, and fortune I would find in professional baseball. Baseball it is, I decided. That night, when I told my mother, she calmly remarked, "Do what you think is best, but be certain you fully understand what lies ahead of you."

Several days later, my great-uncle Sherrod Malone Smith stopped by for a visit. Uncle Sherry had been a professional baseball player for twenty-two years, fourteen of them in the major leagues. He was an outstanding pitcher for the Brooklyn Dodgers, the Pittsburgh Pirates, and the Cleveland Indians. Baseball fans will remember him not for the many games he won but for a game he lost, game two of the 1916 World Series. Two left-handers took the mound that day, Smith for the Dodgers and a young pitcher by the name of George "Babe" Ruth for the Boston Red Sox. They battled for fourteen innings before the BoSox won, 2–1. Now in his fifties, Uncle Sherry was a favorite visitor, particularly when he reminisced about Ty Cobb, Tris Speaker, Babe Ruth, Walter Johnson, and other greats of that era.

On this hot Georgia afternoon, Uncle Sherry inquired about my baseball ventures, and I modestly outlined my abilities as a pitcher of future major-league stardom. He listened attentively and then suggested we go to the backyard and "toss a few." Quickly I rounded up an old catcher's mitt, a glove, and a ball. Uncle Sherry put the right-hander's mitt on his right hand, which looked terribly awkward, but it was all I had to offer. He didn't complain as he assumed the catcher's position about sixty feet away.

I decided to begin with a "Rapid Robert" fastball, hoping the old ballplayer wouldn't get hurt handling it, especially considering the raggedy mitt on the wrong hand. Rearing back, kicking my leg high in big-league fashion, I released a fastball with all the force I could muster. He caught the pitch easily and returned it, shouting, "Now throw your fastball." Golly, I thought, that *was* my fastball! Once again I pumped and fired with full force. "Put more zip on it," he yelled. After several more pitches, Uncle Sherry signaled for a curveball and caught my slow-moving roundhouse with a big chuckle. "Babe Ruth liked those kind. He would hit them out of Cleveland Stadium into Lake Erie and laugh all around the bases."

"Let me toss you a few," he said. As I squatted down, Uncle Sherry leaned back, cocked his right leg like a pistol, and delivered a fastball that nearly pounded me into the house. Although I managed to hang on to the ball, my hand was steaming. "The old fastball has slowed down," he remarked with a smile. By the time I caught several more of his "slowed-down" fastballs, my hand was beginning to resemble chopped steak. Then he threw me a knuckleball. I knew it was moving toward me, but it appeared to be immobile, indecisive as to where it would go. The ball zigzagged up, down, side to side, and in several more weird gyrations. Fearing for my life, I swung the mitt at the pitch and knocked it to the ground. Never had I seen anything quite like it. Uncle Sherry continued to smile.

Later, as we sat on the back steps, he spoke with fatherly sincerity. "Remember, Robert, there are thousands of youngsters trying to make the big time, and only a few will succeed. It's a long, hard road unless you're a super-talent like Bob Feller, Joe DiMaggio, Stan Musial. Also, making the big time doesn't mean you'll last, and then what? Get an education first, but keep playing baseball. It will all fall into place in due time. No one can take an education away from you."

Uncle Sherry left shortly after our conversation. I never saw him again. He died in 1949. That night I slept fitfully, thinking of the day's events. Sherry Smith had made his point without ever saying, "No, you don't have it." I entered college in the fall and in 1950 received a degree in veterinary medicine. I knew that night as I know now that I made the right decision. Life as a veterinarian has been enjoyable, rewarding, challenging, and productive. I'll always be grateful to the big southpaw who reached back on that hot summer day and demonstrated to a seventeen-year-old what professional baseball is all about.

Did Uncle Sherry just happen to be in the area that day, or was the visit orchestrated by my dear mother? I've often wondered.

A LUCKY TRAFFIC LIGHT

Irving Stern

For twenty-eight years, three months, and twelve days I drove a New York City taxi. Before you ask the usual question, I'll give you the answer. Yes, I did have famous people in my cab: celebrities, politicians, ladies of the evening in the daytime, blue-collar workers, white-collar tycoons. They were all in the back seat.

Now, if you were to ask me what I had for breakfast yesterday, I probably couldn't tell you. One fare is so vivid, though, that I'll remember him all my days in this world, maybe even in the next world. His name was—but I'm getting ahead of myself.

About ten o'clock on a sunny Monday in the spring of 1966, I was cruising down York Avenue. The morning rush was over, and with the beautiful weather it was kind of slow. Talk about fate! At Sixty-eighth Street, just opposite New York Hospital, the traffic light turned and I stopped. From the corner of my eye I spied a well-dressed man dashing down the hospital steps, hailing me. The light turned green and the car in back gave me a little honk, but slow as it was, I wasn't about to lose this ride. Now a more impatient, longer honk and a cop's whistle from someplace. Finally the man reached the door of the cab, jumped in, and said, "LaGuardia Airport, please, and thanks for waiting. I'm in a bit of a hurry." Wasn't everyone.

"I'll take the FDR Drive and the Triborough Bridge and have you there in fifteen minutes."

"Great, great," he said.

Was this guy a talker, a mummy, a newspaper reader? I wondered. It didn't really matter. On Monday mornings LaGuardia is jumping, and with a little luck I might get a back-to-back. That would make my day. As I expected, there was hardly any traffic going uptown on the drive, and we were moving nicely.

After a few minutes, my passenger started a conversation with the other usual question, "How do you like driving a cab?" Having been asked this question at least a thousand and one times before, I gave him the stock reply. "It's okay. I make a living, meet interesting people sometimes, but if I could get a job for a hundred dollars a week more, I'd take it, just like you would."

His reply intrigued me. "I wouldn't change jobs if I had to take a cut of a hundred a week."

This I couldn't believe. "What kind of work do you do?"

"I'm in the neurology department at New York Hospital."

Many times on a long ride, a kind of rapport develops between passenger and driver. Quite often I had received advice from accountants, lawyers, plumbers, all kinds of people. Maybe this fellow—I'd try. We weren't too far from the airport now.

"Could I ask a big favor of you?"

He didn't say anything.

"I have a fifteen-year-old son who's really a good kid. He's doing very well in school. The problem is that we'd like him to go to camp this summer but he wants to get a job."

He still didn't say anything.

"But who's going to hire a fifteen-year-old, unless you know someone who owns a business, and I don't. For sure, I don't want him bumming around the streets this summer." Now for the $64,000 question. "Is there any possibility that you might get him some kind of a job? Even if he didn't get paid," I added lamely.

We had reached the airport, and he still wasn't talking. I was starting to feel foolish. Finally, at the ramp to the terminals, he said, "Well, the medical students are doing research on abnormal sleep this summer. Maybe he could fit in. Have him send me a résumé." He fished around in his pocket. "Hmm, I don't seem to have a card. Give me a piece of paper, and I'll write my name on it."

We were at his terminal now, with all the confusion that goes with a busy airport. I tore off a piece of my brown lunch bag, and he scribbled something on it and paid me. That was the last time I ever saw him. Before the cab door even closed another fare jumped in. I shoved the brown paper into my shirt, and away we went.

It was a hectic day in the city, as always. Around the dining room table that evening with my wife, son, and seventeen-year-old daughter, I suddenly remembered the piece of paper, pulled it from my shirt pocket, and proudly said, "Robbie, this could be a good summer job for you." He looked at it and read out loud, "Fred Plum, N.Y. Hosp."

My wife: "Is he a doctor?"

"I don't know. He didn't say."

My daughter: "Is he an apple, maybe?"

My son: "Is this a joke?"

That night, after I yelled, screamed, and threatened to cut his allowance, Robbie wrote the letter with his qualifications. The fruit jokes continued for a few days, and the whole episode was gradually forgotten.

Exactly two weeks later, I arrived home from work to find my son beaming. Excitedly he handed me a letter addressed to him on richly embossed paper. The letterhead read, "Fred Plum, M.D., Head of the Department of Neurology, New York Hospital." It requested him to call Dr. Plum's personal secretary for an appointment for a possible summer job. Now I was a hero.

Robbie got the job, worked for two weeks as a volunteer, and then was paid forty dollars a week. His white lab coat made him feel a lot more important than he really was as he accompanied Dr. Plum around the hospital doing minor tasks for him. The summer passed, and the following year he worked at the hospital again, this time with more responsibilities.

As high school graduation neared, Dr. Plum was kind enough to write a letter of recommendation, and much to our delight, Robbie was accepted by one of the finest Ivy League colleges, Brown University. Again that summer he worked at the hospital and gradually developed a love of the medical profession. During his last year at Brown he decided to apply to medical school, and Dr. Plum wrote beautiful letters attesting to his ability and character. He was accepted by the New York Medical College, got his M.D. degree, and did a four-year residency at Columbia-Presbyterian, specializing in obstetrics and gynecology.

While he was in medical school, Robbie had married a lovely teacher. As chief resident at Columbia-Presbyterian, he delivered his own healthy baby boy—but that's another story. And to think it all started with a taxi ride.

A Dollar That Made a Difference

Mary Jane Sprague

As I walked carefully to keep the dirt out of my sandals, my thoughts raced ahead of my steps. I had seen in the stationer's window my twelve-year-old heart's desire! *The Modern Postage Stamp Album,* a bright red hardbound beauty with an airplane on the cover flying over skyscrapers, symbolized places I'd go—someday. For now, trading stamps with friends and buying from mail-order companies kept me satisfied and fed my dreams. The new album was just what I needed to accommodate my growing collection.

As I neared my house, reality began to cloud my mind. The year was 1936. With an innate talent in money management, my mother creatively prepared meals and ordered school clothes from the Sears catalogue. I never felt that we were poor, but when I visited the home of the banker's daughter I recognized the difference. My father was an independent service station operator in our little desert town. The album was priced at a dollar. And I knew I would not ask for a dollar to buy a stamp album.

I lay in bed that night and tried to think of an answer. I fell asleep knowing I was meant to have that album, but not knowing how.

At school the next day, the teacher announced that in a week she would give a test on capital cities of the United States and the world. As in a spelling bee, class members would line up on opposite sides of the room. She would name a state or country, and we, in turn, would pronounce and spell the capital. "And to the last person left standing I will give a dollar!" she announced.

I was stunned, absolutely giddy with the idea. *A whole dollar!* I knew I *had* to win that dollar; more than that, I knew I *would* win it. At that moment, I caught a glimpse of the heights a human being can reach. Mixed with my elation, I felt a steady, warm calmness as I looked around at my classmates.

At home that night, I carefully wrote on pieces of gray scratch paper the names of every state and world capital, checking and rechecking the spelling of each. *Montgomery*, Alabama. *Juneau*, Alaska. *Charlotte Amalie*, Virgin Islands. Studying took precedence over everything else that week. My list never left me. At the dinner table, in the bathtub, by my bedside, the gray pages were there. *Nairobi*, Kenya. *Vaduz*, Liechtenstein. Mother and Father were pressed into helping. They were instructed to skip around the list, in case I was memorizing in a certain order. *Managua*, Nicaragua. *Canberra*, Australia.

Test day came. I left the gray pages, literally worn out from handling, at home. A kiss from Mother, and I went to claim my victory.

Eyes sparkled, palms sweated, knees shook as we lined up against the blackboard. On the first round, at least half the students went down. The rest of us shifted our feet, cleared our throats. *Copenhagen*, Denmark. *Addis Ababa*, Ethiopia. More went down. The recess bell rang. No one left! Other kids and teachers came to look in our room and stayed to watch. Someone missed *Helsinki*, Finland; another *Des Moines*, Iowa. Four were left, then two. *Valletta*, Malta. *Asunción*, Paraguay. The exhausted runner-up missed *Ottawa*, Canada—and the winner was presented with a brand-new silver dollar!

Restraining myself from rushing to the stationer's right after school, I took the dollar home to savor it for itself a little while. Next day I exchanged it for *The Modern Postage Stamp Album*.

Because I worked, really worked for it, and *knew*, nothing doubting, that I could achieve it, it was the foundation for whatever accomplishments I have made or ever will make. It was running the four-minute mile, breaking the sound barrier, it was discovering electricity!

It was only a dollar—but so much more.

THE SLIME

William Nagel

Near the end of June 1932, during the Great Depression, I roamed the narrow, dark streets of lower Manhattan looking for a place to die.

I felt so depressed that living was an ordeal. So many voices rang in my brain. My teacher: "You, you, William Nagel, will have to gain a good report from summer school if you want to finish the twelfth grade." My stepmother: "You will have to work seven days a week helping your father." My father's business, a small grocery store in a poor neighborhood, was hanging by threads, and I wanted to help him, but that would mean I would have to finish high school at night.

More voices: "He's too skinny for our team." "Get a load of those pimples!" "What makes his hair so red?" As I sat there in a lonely alley watching three stray dogs knock over trash cans to search for food, I felt the grip of poverty and the need to end it all.

It was almost midnight when I finally found a good spot on the East River to jump. I was climbing over the rail when a gentle breeze hit me in the face with a splash of rotten garbage that almost took my breath away. I could not think of a worse death than to be submerged in that filth. "No, no, there must be a better way," I caught myself mumbling.

Glancing to my right, I saw another man about to climb over the rail. "Wait! Wait!" I yelled as I rushed to rescue him from a horrible end. I caught my breath, then blurted, "You better stop and think first."

He climbed down from the rail. "My pappy always told me, 'Look before ya leap,'" he said in a slow Southern drawl. Yawning, he took a good stretch. "Ah been lookin' for a job everywhere." A bright dock light shone on his young shaven face, and from his nice clothes I knew he was not a bum. He was probably about my age. Probably about the same problem.

As we studied the harbor lights across the river, blinking signs of gaiety, I cleared my throat. "All those lights at this hour mean life, activity, employment. All those lights mean people trying to live."

By this time I had convinced myself that life was worth another try, but I wasn't sure I had convinced my friend, so I dug into my pocket for some money. I only had four dollars, and I pulled out two.

"Here, take this. I have plenty more." I left him speechless as I jogged away to find some shelter from a light rain.

My luck had turned. I found an old broken bench in a dark doorway directly across the wide street. It was all I needed for a place to rest and take stock of my thoughts. The flickering glow of the gas lamps on the wet cobblestones and the night air sweetened by summer rain soon put me to sleep. I slept as I never had before. But I also had the worst nightmare of my life: I was drowning in heavy green slime, with hungry, deformed creatures trying to eat me alive. I awoke ready to scream for help, my heart beating wildly.

Suddenly all the ugliness of the dream was gone with the most beautiful sunrise I had ever seen. Broken bits of rain clouds in shades of red and gold covered the entire sky. As I sat there enjoying the quiet of a Sunday morning, I heard a shout coming from across the street. My friend was climbing over the rail again, swinging one arm crazily in the air.

What in the name of hell was he up to? I dashed toward him, knowing that a dog should not drown in that mess. Besides, he still had my two dollars.

When I got to the rail, I saw a garbage barge approaching, with four men on it. My friend was still swinging his arm.

"Hey y'all. Hey! I decided to take that job y'all offered me."

DUST BOWL

Wanda L. Sutton

The Depression years weren't called the Dirty Thirties in western Kansas for nothing. Russian thistles blew across the countryside, lodging themselves against barbed-wire fences along the roads and fields, catching dirt each day as the wind blew. Soon the barbed wire was covered with solid dirt, and we kids could easily walk over a fence as high as our heads.

Every Monday morning my mother would get the old oblong boiler out, placing it across the firebox of the cookstove and building a huge fire. I often collected "cow chips" for the cookstove, and sometimes for the furnace. When feeding a furnace with cow chips you would meet yourself taking out ashes, but it did help to take the chill off the house.

Mother filled the boiler with water that she carried in buckets from the well. After the water was boiling, she cut up a bar of the soap she made from suet and lye, and dropped the pieces in. Then we poured the water into the washing machine, run by a home-made motor. That old motor had a stubborn streak and wouldn't start most of the time. Mother would say, "Run for your father." She knew the clothes had to be washed, rinsed, and hung on the line to dry before eleven o'clock. Otherwise they would be covered with dirt when the wind started to blow.

After eleven you could write your name in the dust on the furniture. Before retiring at night you shook the dirt from your comforter. My parents owned a good frame house, but dust seeped in everywhere. Attempts to clean were futile.

One sunny morning in 1932, when I was eighteen, my parents, my three-year-old brother, and I drove thirty miles to Colby, Kansas, to shop. When we started for home in late afternoon, we noticed a big black cloud, like a huge rolling ball, traveling very fast from the northwest. We drove ten miles east at sixty miles an hour. We turned north for about a mile, until we were caught in dirt and dust so thick we could hardly see. My dad drove another fifteen miles in that awful dirt and wind, and then our 1929 Ford coughed and stopped.

Dad knew where we were. He decided we should walk to a neighbor's house across the field, about a quarter-mile south of the highway. As we got out of the car, we couldn't see our hands before our faces. We linked arms, and Dad carried my little brother, covering his face with his coat.

We walked and walked, getting nowhere. My sinuses were so full of dust I could scarcely breathe. I was ready to give up. If my parents were afraid, I never knew it. They only encouraged me. I'm sure they prayed a lot.

Was that a tiny light? I reached out, and my fingers touched a corner of the house we were looking for. A little farther on we found a door. We knocked, and our neighbors pulled us inside.

Mr. and Mrs. Short had damp white cloths tied over their faces, blackened around the nose and mouth. Mrs. Short immediately tore cloths for us while we thanked her for the light in her window.

"You know," she said, "I was sitting in the kitchen when I felt a strong urge to light a coal-oil lamp and put it in a northwest bedroom I never use. I don't know why, but I did."

That tiny light saved our lives.

The Dirty Thirties made me cautious as well as frugal!

God Was Our Navigator

Lottie Tish

The morning was clear and crisp as my boss and I flew from Charlotte, North Carolina, to Oshawa, Ontario, in the company Aero Commander. After completing our business in Oshawa, we left that afternoon, destination New York City. Below us the Saint Lawrence Seaway was completely covered with snow.

We had planned to refuel at the Boston airport, but the weather closed in around Boston and we were unable to land. Completely on instruments, we headed south to New York, hoping to find an airport and a break in the weather. With zero visibility and our fuel situation fast becoming critical, our pilot lost his composure. Fortunately my boss was a pilot and took over the controls.

As night fell, the fog continued to roll in, and the sky grew even darker and more foreboding. It was impossible to see. Suddenly we came into an opening in the clouds. Looking through, we spotted airport runway lights. We circled and landed.

As we stepped from the plane, a man emerged from a small shack. He seemed amazed to see us. We told him we were out of fuel when we saw the lights break through the sky and landed.

Still looking at us in astonishment, he said, "This is a new airport and hasn't opened yet. We were just testing the lights. I was on my way to the switch to cut them off when I heard you land."

He offered to give us a ride to town, and as we drove into the night we thanked God for being our navigator.

JERUSALEM ENCOUNTER

Bronia Galmitz Gallon

As a member of a kibbutz bent upon building a Jewish homeland, I left my entire family in Poland and arrived in Palestine in the spring of 1936. Before settling in, I wanted to see the country. My first destination was Jerusalem, city of my dreams. For days I walked the narrow streets of the Old City, fascinated by the pageantry of its people, the cacophony of languages, the fragrant, spiced air.

On one of my journeys I ventured out of the city and into the nearby Judean hills, where I stumbled upon an Arab café in an unlikely setting—the rooftop of a Russian convent. The tiny café was hemmed in by a sun-baked clay balustrade with garlands of grapevines running along its edge. Customers sat at low brass tables, sipping coffee and talking in subdued tones.

The sun was glinting on the sparkling brass of the table where I sat down. When I lifted my eyes to look beyond the balustrade, Jerusalem lay stretched out beneath me, from the rectangular buildings, broad boulevards, and blooming gardens of Rehavia, the modern section, to the Old City with its shadowed streets winding in and out of ancient gates.

I could hardly believe my eyes. There in the distance rose the stone walls of the Tower of David. Down to the left stood the Wailing Wall, its stones polished by tears. The Wailing Wall, whose fissures hid a people's heart wrapped in a prayer, held a two-thousand-year history of longing for self-determination. Out of the ruins of the last Temple, out of that Wailing Wall, grew the Mosque of Omar, its graceful splendor consecrated to the worship of Allah. The golden dome shimmered in the sun as my eyes wandered from its mosaic gateway to fall on the Via Dolorosa.

I closed my eyes and let my thoughts sink into the past. The memory of thousands of years of suffering swelled into a sea, engulfing me. When I turned to the present, Nazism and Communism were competing with each other for the degradation of humanity. The world was far from being at peace on that beautiful spring afternoon.

The sun was beginning to set behind the stark hills, and a golden haze embraced Jerusalem. A bell chimed, another answered in a deeper tone, and a third rang out on a higher pitch. The bells intertwined, their silvery tones brushing against the hills and returning in muted echoes. I had the sensation of being suspended between the ages.

Twilight is short in Palestine, and the scenery was changing rapidly. Lights began to glow on the horizon. Up on a minaret balcony, a white figure appeared, turning slowly in all directions. The muezzin was calling his people to worship. Wherever they stood, Moslems rolled out their prayer rugs and knelt, joining the caller in the evening prayer.

The lights went on in a nearby synagogue. The rabbi and a group of students were walking up the steps into the house of prayer.

The Franciscan Brothers turned on the lights in their house of worship, preparing for vespers.

A sweet voice emerged from the Yemenite synagogue. It was the song of the hakam, chanting a prayer.

A lilting soprano floated out of the English church, not far in the distance, and was soon joined by others.

Prayers rang out in Hebrew, Latin, Russian, English, Arabic. The earth stood still in deep meditation. Then, like a whisper, I felt my heart stir. Adding my voice to the chorus, I began to chant my prayer.

"And they shall beat their swords into ploughshares and their spears into pruning hooks. Nation shall not lift up sword against nation, and they shall not learn war any more."

A great calm began to envelop me, and all my bitterness

melted away. A new love was being born in me. I could see the oneness of all people and all religions. I was at peace.

That encounter with Jerusalem sustains my hope for universal peace to this day. Whenever the world is in turmoil, whenever I am about to lose my faith in humanity, I summon the memory of Jerusalem's evening prayer.

War and Remembrance

GROS REDERCHING

Victor B. Geller

You won't find Gros Rederching on any map. This tiny Alsatian hamlet is nevertheless an unforgettable place in my life, for it was there that I met war.

In the clear, frosty December morning, our regiment formed a series of skirmish lines in preparation for our first action against the enemy. The First Battalion was on the left flank, and we were on the right. The Third Battalion was in regimental reserve. The signal was given, the lines began to move forward. By noon, I realized that war in the movies and war in real life differed in three respects.

The first was the pace. In films, our troops always "jumped off." They raced, they sped, they trotted, they leaped toward a visible group of enemy soldiers. Our regiment moved across the barren snow-patched fields in a slow, deliberate stroll toward a strip of woods several hundred yards to the east. Our progress was orderly, even. There was no urging or rushing. There was no enemy to be seen.

The second difference was the sound. In the movies, war was always accompanied by a full orchestra. As events unfolded—the danger, the struggle, the triumph—they all carried the intense impact that only music can evoke. When the noise of shells and the theater-filling shouts of the actors were added, the effect was truly stirring.

In my real war there was no music, not even a bugle. Our line advanced without a sound. There was no conversation, only the soft, methodical tread of hundreds of GI boots on the brittle, cold ground. It was silent. It seemed as if even Mother Nature herself was silent, knowing as only she could what was about to happen. Only many battles later did we begin to understand that this was the silence of utter awareness, of fearful expectation, and that it was totally different from the silence of peace.

Finally, there was the dying. On the screen, the war would pause to allow a soldier to die in the arms of his comrade. There would be time for words of farewell. Death was dramatically sad but temporary. It was soon forgotten in the excitement of the battle being depicted. In my real war, death was lonely and permanent.

That morning Private Isaac Graubart, Private First Class Gerald Feifer, and Private First Class Richard Shankman, among others, waited for the order to go to war. These three young men were in the line that moved from the village they never knew to the objective they never reached. At intervals, they collapsed and lay still. There were no heroics or shouts from close buddies for medics. The advance continued past their bodies. The medics did come, but only to confirm what they already knew.

For these three teenagers the journey was over. There were no more tomorrows. Family tears were yet to be shed, but all their dreams had ended at Gros Rederching.

WHAT WAS SO FUNNY?

Frank Richman

During World War II, Mount Vesuvius erupted. It belched flames high into the air, sending fiery lava down the mountainside like a huge neon sign exposing our location. Creeping forward inch by inch, the lava didn't stop until it covered three towns and damaged millions of dollars' worth of equipment on our medium bombers in the area.

As if that wasn't enough, Axis Sally came on the radio that night with her bull, same as every night. "Hello, Yankee boys. Are you homesick for your wives and sweethearts?" She sounded like a two-bit Bowery prostitute. "While you're tramping around in the mud, your wife is in bed with another man, your sweetheart is whoring it up around town. How does that grab you, GI Joe? We know where you are—you can't hide. We'll be over tonight.... Sweet dreams." After that diatribe, she'd play American jazz records.

If Axis Sally intended to break our morale, she had the opposite effect. She united us, and we cursed her all the more.

Like the lady said, while we were asleep they came over as usual. We were accustomed to the explosions, as frightening as they were. We quickly ran and jumped into our foxholes and waited. While the planes were dropping their bombs, the British who were guarding our airstrip fired up at them. It was 0300 hours before we got to sleep again.

We all had helmets to protect us from shrapnel. Some boys used them for cooking soup or as washbasins. We kept the helmets on the ground near our cots for emergencies.

At 0400 hours on this particular night, the German planes returned unexpectedly, dropping their bombs on our airstrip. The earth quivered under our feet; the British were already firing; the sky lit up like Christmas candles. The four of us in our tent were rushing around in the dark for our gear.

"Son of a bitch," yelled Pat as water poured from his helmet over his head.

"Where are my shoes?" shouted Joe. "Who took my shoes?" A split second later he yelled again. "I'm wearing them. Forgot! Never took 'em off. ... Bastards! Let's go!"

Like schoolchildren at recess, we were laughing hysterically as we ran toward our foxholes.

When it was all over, we asked ourselves, "What the hell was so funny?"

COME FLY WITH ME

Donald L. Huron

The tail gunner of a B-24 has an awkward view of things. None of the crew could see the whole picture, but I had the added disadvantage of never knowing where we were going—only where we had been. When I look back to the bombing mission of May 10, 1944, I realize that the best perspective on such an event is from the safe distance of many, many years.

We were with the Fifteenth Air Force, flying out of southern Italy. The day was typical. We stumbled off in the predawn gloom to the mess tent, where we picked at an uninspired breakfast. Then the flight crews were herded off to a briefing and told that the target was to be a ball-bearing factory in Wiener Neustadt, Austria. The tone was grim, casting a pall over the assembled airmen. The briefer assured us that we could expect swarm after swarm of assorted Focke-Wulfs and Messerschmitts to harass us coming and going, and that the antiaircraft fire in and around the target would surpass anything we had ever seen. It was still dark when we headed for the flight line.

We were all quiet. The customary fear now had company, an uneasy sense of foreboding. We crawled into the plane, took our positions, and queued up with the rest of the group to wait for takeoff. At last it was our turn, and the muted rumble of the engines switched to a vibrating roar as we blundered down the runway in an all-out stretch for flight speed. What with the extra fuel and bombs, it seemed that we would never get airborne. The pilot seemed to will the plane off the ground. As soon as we began our climb we were wrapped in clouds. After an interminable time—maybe ten minutes—we burst out in bright sunlight at about ten thousand feet and still climbing. More and more bomb groups joined the formation until there were about six hundred bombers at twenty thousand feet headed north-northeast to the target. Time droned on.

There was nothing much to look at but the lone group behind us bringing up the rear of the procession. I didn't pay much attention to them, being too busy scanning my limited area of sky for trouble. Where were all those enemy fighters? For that matter, where were our friendly escorts? Maybe they were off somewhere chasing each other.

The pilot came on the intercom to report that we were about seven minutes away from the final leg prior to the bomb run. Abruptly the trailing bomb group turned tail and left. Why did they all abort? What did they know that we didn't?

The first bursts of flak exploded off to my right and low. As we got closer to the target the antiaircraft shelling became more and more intense, until it reached a level of firepower that was unbelievable. I remember hearing "Bombs away" on the intercom, followed shortly by "Bomb bay door closed," which proved to be the final message. The flak was thick enough to walk on, with occasional reddish shells that exploded like fast-blooming American Beauty roses. I wondered how I could be so scared and see beauty in something so deadly. I always tried to take comfort in the thought that any flak I saw had already exploded and could do me no harm.

By now the plane was beginning to pitch and buck, responding to the ever-closer concussions. My turret felt like the inside of a vigorously beaten drum. I smelled a strange odor and called out on the intercom, "Something's burning. I hope it's just flak smoke." It was then that I realized my mike was dead and we were in big trouble.

I swung around and looked back over my shoulder, and my fears were confirmed. Wells was coming toward me making a sweeping motion with his right arm. He didn't say anything, but I knew "Let's get out of here!" when I saw it. Andy was on the left, as usual, but he had moved toward the camera hatch, our jumping-out place. Blackie was beginning to crank up the ball turret. Farther back I saw the reason for all the concern. Ominous red-black flames were pouring out of the bomb bays. Now there was no chance to communicate with those up front, and every possibility that we could all disappear in an explosive instant. Andy stepped forward, closed his eyes, and jumped. Then Wells approached the hatch, hesitated, and dropped through. While all this was going on I realized that I was saying the Twenty-third Psalm. I don't think I got much beyond "the valley of the shadow," but it seemed appropriate and helped me to work around the fear and do all the things that had to be done. By now Blackie was up and out of the ball. I gave him a half-wave and jumped.

The chute seemed to open up in another world, noiseless and serene. No antiaircraft; no aircraft, for that matter, just a great big beautiful sky with me hanging in the middle of it. I felt wonderful. My chute was so stable that I flipped back, hooked my feet in the shrouds, and hung upside down for a while. That's when I saw the two fighter planes circling the area. They were close enough to be recognized as our P-51s. I could have cheered. I was still riding an outrageous high, sticking out my best hitchhiker's thumb. I would always savor those moments, but they couldn't last forever. I would finally come down to earth. There would be a year of prison camp to endure. I would have to come to terms with feelings of guilt that I was alive and better men were dead.

From this whole experience, I hold fast to one unwavering certainty. Life ought to be lived, not just put up with. I am eternally grateful for my second chance at it.

PILGRIMAGE

David Weixel

      In attack and counterattack our battalions withered. We faced the shattering onslaughts, hurled back the charging Panzers' deadly thrusts on the Anzio beachhead.

      Once, after sunset, I crawled into my dugout to rest. Machine guns chattered, artillery boomed and echoed, shells ripped the night apart. I tucked my GI blankets up to my chin to cover my weariness, and with my helmet and carbine by my side fell into a worried sleep.

      (I was riding a Brooklyn trolley homeward bound. Day had vanished, streets were empty and dark, and I was the only passenger. The motorman clanged a muffled bell. No sound came from the wheels; we floated like a ship as we turned down Fulton Street past the RKO Albee, the Brooklyn Paramount, and other places I knew. Corner after corner I sat there alone with the motorman. He never stopped, he looked straight into the night where streets were empty and dark. I saw my block. Soon, I thought, soon I'll be home. "Mama," I'll say, "I came back." I pulled the stop cord. No signal sounded. The motorman clanged the muffled bell and rode on. I panicked and yelled, "Hey, let me off! This is my stop, here's where I get off!" And the silent motorman turned and spoke: "I'll tell you where to get off!" His face was a death's head!)

      Machine guns chattered, artillery boomed and echoed, shells ripped the night apart. Drenched with fear, I said, "I will die on the Anzio beachhead." I tucked my GI blankets up to my chin to cover my goose pimples, and with my helmet and carbine by my side fell back into my worried sleep.

      In the springtime Pop Lardell got his. Brainard got his too, never knew what hit him. Chris Keegan stopped a slug from an S-mine and died. Private Rossi went out on patrol, never came back: missing in action.

      Twenty-five springs later, I came back to the beachhead. I visited the graves of Pop Lardell and Brainard, I stood by the grave of Chris Keegan. Private Rossi was still "missing in action."

I found the site of the old front line and climbed to the highest place. Knee-high in swaying flowers, I faced the enemy again.

"Hey you," I called. "You never got me. I'm here! You Nazi bastards tried to kill me! You tried with bullets, you tried with cannons, you tried with bombers. See, I'm still around. Here's one Jew you couldn't murder!"

The faces of the fallen still appear to me. Sometimes I hear the sounds of a very distant battle. Why that motorman spared me then, I don't know.

He hasn't told me where to get off yet.

BRESLAU, MY CAMELOT

Eva-Maria Robinson

I'm an ordinary person, but I have my very own Camelot. In a book I read, it said that Camelot is a place, time, or circumstance marked by idealized beauty, peacefulness, and enlightenment. Breslau, the city in the east of Germany where I was born, was all of that to me.

I was born in 1930, at the beginning of those crazy, terrible Hitler years. My parents managed, for the most part, to keep me isolated, away from the ugliness of Nazism. I went to a Catholic kindergarten and spent the summers with my grandparents in a little village surrounded by beautiful woods. I played with the village children, picked huckleberries, and found wonderfully fragrant lilies of the valley.

When I was a teenager it was harder to stay away from the Hitler craze. We were ordered to join the Hitler Youth, and I hated to go to their weekly meetings. In the fall of 1944 our schools were shut down, and we were ordered into the "war effort." I was among a group of girls who were bused to a huge farm where we picked potatos all day for weeks. They closed our grocery store and sent my father to a sanatorium because he had TB. My grandfather died, and my mother went to the little village about fifty miles away for his funeral. It was winter by then, and while she was gone loudspeakers in Breslau started blaring.

"The city is being evacuated! Take warm clothing and food and start walking west."

Over and over they told us to get out of Breslau. My brother, Hans, also had TB and was weak from his illness, but we took a crowded streetcar to the railway station. We waited for hours in the cold, but no trains came. Confused and scared, we went back to our apartment and waited for Mama to return. She got back long after midnight because the train had stopped outside the city, which was being bombed. She walked all the way home to us.

Mama decided there was no choice but to walk to my grandparents' village. We were hoping Papa would assume that's where we'd gone and try to get to us. The next day, one of the saddest, hardest of my life, we left our home, our Breslau, my Camelot.

It had snowed, and we trudged through the streets, wondering if we would ever come back. We joined one of the wagon trains outside the city. My mother managed to get Hans a sleigh ride part of the way, and we were so thankful. He was only sixteen, but he almost didn't get out of Breslau. All "men" were held back to defend the city, but luckily he had a paper stating that he had TB. When we finally got to the village, half frozen and ready to drop, my father wasn't there. For three days we worried and prayed. We could hear the sounds of battle, not far away, and the villagers decided to leave in a wagon train. Somehow Papa finally made his way to us. We had lost almost everything, but we were together as a family.

It was a cold day in February when the wagon train pulled out of the little village. Even now I can't let myself think about the poor domestic animals left behind. We headed west and eventually got to Czechoslovakia. Both Papa and Hans were very sick, and Mama's feet were swollen and painful. "We can't go on like this any longer," Papa said. "We will have to take a chance, go to the railway station, and hope to get on a train to the west."

I was scared to death. If we separated from the people we knew and then we couldn't find a train, we'd be left alone in a country where the people hated us because we were German. What would happen to us? But Papa prevailed. "We have to take this chance."

We said a tearful goodbye to the village people and pulled our little wagon with our few belongings through the town of Nachod.

We waited at the train station for at least six hours. I was still frozen with fear when Papa came running into the waiting room. "Quick," he shouted. "There's a German train. They are just taking on water. They said we could try to get on. Hurry, hurry."

We raced across the tracks and started throwing our things into an open train door. Mama, Hans, and I boarded while Papa tried to secure our little wagon between two railway cars. I was hysterical, sure the train would pull out and leave Papa behind, but he managed to jump aboard as the wheels began to turn. We didn't even know where we were going, just west.

The train was crowded, and we stood most of the time. It was a ride full of fear of the unknown. The train would stop abruptly, trying to hide from planes that had strafed other refugee trains, we were told. We were lucky. We made it into Germany without being shot at. But when we got off the train in a little town called Furth im Wald, I didn't really think I was in Germany. The people spoke a dialect that seemed anything but German. They resented us heartily and told us that if the Russian troops came they would fight them with pitchforks. I thought about that later when those brave big-mouths ran to hide in the woods while the friendly Americans "invaded" their homes. Their Nazi mayor was still in power, and he forced them to take us in.

My family ended up in a tiny room where nobody had lived for years. The worst things were the bedbugs and other insects I encountered for the first time in my life. Later the American DDT powder helped a lot. We tried to make the best of things, thankful that we had escaped the Russian army. The people from my grandparents' village were not so lucky. Their wagon train had to turn around and go back. My favorite cousin, thirteen years old, was raped and died, and so did my uncle and grandmother. We were the only family from that wagon train who escaped, only because Papa trusted his instinct and took a stand against odds.

My family and I lived for the day when we could go back home to Breslau. One day I saw a newspaper that said Silesia and other eastern provinces were going to Poland. I raced home. "They can't do that, Papa. They can't just cut out a piece of Germany, our Silesia and our Breslau, and give it to another country." Papa gave me a sad smile. "They can do anything they want to. They won the war."

My brother died in November 1945, seventeen years of age. My mother cried for him every night. Eventually I took a job as a maid so I could move to the city. It was the only way, since you could get no rooms because of the bombing. I managed to buy an old typewriter and taught myself to type. I even managed to find a room for rent in a suburb of Munich. Without much hope I went to the nearby American air force base and applied for a job. After two tries I was hired as clerk-typist. I was so proud and happy. So were my parents. Papa was sick with TB again. I went to visit as often as I could. In 1955 I started dating one of the airmen in our office, and in 1957 we got married. I hated the thought of leaving my parents, but Papa said, "Ever since my uncle emigrated to America I have wanted to see it. Now you can see it for me."

Papa was always good at making decisions. He got us on that train in Nachod and saved us from a lot of harm. He accepted the loss of our home and everything he ever worked for. And now he was urging me to fly across the "big pond" to make a new home. He was right. I found a good, safe home in Kansas, where the people are mostly welcoming and kind.

Papa died only three months after I left, and Mama in 1980. I still have a cousin in Germany, and for the past two years he has driven to Silesia on vacation. He sent me a postcard of the city hall in Breslau, and I ask myself, If I had the money, would I go back?

No, I don't think so. You can't go home again. My beloved Breslau disappeared in the rubble of total war in 1945, and later in the judgment that it was not my home after all. But in my dreams it lives on as my Camelot.

The Book

Lotte Schiller

Berlin, 1934. The preparations for leaving Germany were fraught with excitement and anxiety. At age fourteen I did not feel much burdened by the responsibilities of my parents. The decision to uproot our family, the initial planning, the financial worries, and the endless chores of dissolving our household were still far beyond the horizon of my consciousness.

That did not prevent us children, my eleven-year-old brother and myself, from feeling suddenly a grave responsibility for the state of the world. Something was very, very wrong with the world: terrifying sounds, night after night, of Nazi boots pounding the pavement outside our darkened windows; ominous whispers among the adults about dire fates to befall us; talk of oppression and social injustice. We, the children, needed to put things right again and fix the world!

We had been rudely awakened from our childhood dreams. No longer were we fascinated by tales of fantasy, by sagas of slain dragons or perilous journeys on stormy seas. Instead we were drawn to the real-world drama of the human condition. Some of our teachers, courageously and in defiance of the new regime, inspired us to read poetry, philosophy, ancient and modern history, always seeking out themes of struggle for freedom and independent thinking. We reveled in the spiritual liberation of the French Revolution, we adored Gandhi, and we worshiped the early Zionist pioneers who turned the barren hills of the Holy Land into green orchards. We were particularly fascinated by the Bolshevik revolution—so recent and so close to our borders. The struggle for a totally restructured society, the abolition of religion, which seemed to promise an end to anti-Semitism, and the wild stories of heroic deeds, courage, and suffering inspired great curiosity in our young minds.

We read whatever we could lay our hands on, and soon we learned about Hitler's latest threat: book burning! What greater challenge than to defy authority by making a special effort to discover just these forbidden books. We admired any classmate who surreptitiously smuggled one out of a grandfather's library or from heaven knows where else. At our weekly school outings we would eagerly gather around the campfire and discuss our acquisitions late into the night. We felt very mature and serious about it, but there also was the thrill of adventure.

I possessed one such book, a Russian novel. How it fell into my hands I do not recall. I was very fond of it. Unlike many of the materials we read and discussed, often well above my level of comprehension, this was a story, a simple, sad story about love and a mother's devotion and sacrifice to the cause of a desperate revolution.

When we left Germany at last, there was little we were permitted to take with us. My parents applied the same standard to themselves as to us: one single suitcase, no bigger than we ourselves were capable of carrying. There were tearful goodbyes to the treasures of our childhood—all the trappings of a comfortable home, books, toys, and bicycles. We outdid each other in packing and repacking our scant belongings until they fit comfortably into our designated bags. But there was one item I was not willing to part with: my beloved little book. Its size and weight were not the problem. It was forbidden, and would mean grave danger if discovered. My imagination went wild trying to picture what might happen to me, or worse, to my innocent parents, if the book was found.

Overnight we stayed in Munich. Here was my last chance to dispose of the dangerous item, but where could I do it? Wasn't Munich more treacherous a place than I had ever been to? Armed with a flashlight, I hid in the huge closet in our hotel room with my little brother, the only person who shared my deep, dark secret, for one last look at the contents of my suitcase. There was my treasure, well hidden among the carefully folded underwear that no border guard would want to examine. Together we decided that in my suitcase it would stay.

A wave of terror gripped me every time the train came to a stop. Another and yet another ticket check, another "Heil Hitler, passports please!" to tremble through. There seemed to be no end to the clickety-click of the wheels or the constantly changing landscape whizzing by.

Only vaguely do I remember the moment we crossed the border into Yugoslavia, but I do remember an unfamiliar feeling of freedom, and how I suddenly began to enjoy looking out the window, awed by a spectacle I had never seen before—tall, snow-covered mountains, their peaks hidden in the clouds.

More than fifty years have passed. Holding the book in my hands and reading it again, I find it still a moving story. Yet gone from its faded pages is my excitement. It no longer evokes in me the challenge to defy authority, to have the courage, in the face of real danger, to rescue but one little book from the flames of Hitler's inferno.

PROLOGUE TO
THE HOLOCAUST

Abner P. Grunauer

At age thirty-six, I, Abner Grunauer, a Manhattan-born Jew, marched with the chancellor of Austria in his historic open defiance of Adolf Hitler. Today, within five weeks of my ninetieth birthday, the events of those months in Vienna are as vivid in my memory as when I was there with a correspondent's press accreditation card in my pocket, serving 186 U.S. newspapers and magazines.

That February afternoon in 1938 I stood outside the Austrian Parliament building, along with thousands of anxious Viennese, to hear Dr. Kurt Schuschnigg's report on his visit to Hitler at Berchtesgaden a few days before. Hitler had summoned Dr. Schuschnigg and had handed him an ultimatum—surrender Austrian independence and become part of "Greater Germany," under the slogan "Ein Reich, Ein Volk, Ein Führer."

We listened to the loudspeakers carrying the chancellor's address to Parliament. The fate of a nation depended on his reply to Hitler. Would Austria capitulate? No, declared Schuschnigg. Austria would resist.

When people heard the news, they came by bicycle, by car, and on foot from all over the city. Eventually the chancellor came out of the Parliament building and walked down a long, curbing ramp, right into the middle of the crowd. He continued down the Ringstrasse, Vienna's magnificent main boulevard, followed by tens and tens of thousands, cheering and singing in an impromptu parade of defiance to Hitlerism. And up front, marching alongside Dr. Schuschnigg himself, was this young man from Manhattan.

In March I went to Czechoslovakia for a few days. In Prague, on the evening of March 12, I heard on the radio that the German army had broken across the Austrian border about two hundred miles west of Vienna at a town called Linz. I went straight to the railroad station and took the first available train back to Vienna. It was a sort of milk train that picked up and deposited freight and farm products every few miles. It left about 2:30 a.m. I was the only passenger. I wanted to be in Vienna from the beginning, to cover the whole story of the first rape of a nation by the "Master Race."

The way south was tedious as I sat alone in the one rickety old passenger car. About halfway to Vienna we passed our train's twin, headed north to Prague. But what a difference! Its single passenger car was bursting with human beings, jammed inside and standing on the front and rear platforms—obviously Jews and anti-Nazis fleeing to what they hoped would be safety!

I got in about dawn. When the stores opened, I went into a novelty shop and bought two little tin American flag pins and put one on each lapel of my overcoat. I wore those pins for months.

In the late afternoon, half starved, I headed for my favorite café, the Café Europa, for a bite to eat. This large, elegant coffeehouse was dark and almost empty. The headwaiter said that there were hardly any customers and only 10 percent of the staff had showed up. "But there's a group upstairs in a private room," he said. "If you're hungry, we're serving food and drink up there."

I went up and walked in. There were about twenty or thirty people in the room, all wearing swastika armbands. These were Austrian Germans. They had just been released from jail by the Germans. They weren't in jail because they were Nazis—the Schuschnigg government didn't imprison Nazis. They were in jail because they were criminals. These were guys who had murdered or assaulted people, smashed and looted Jewish stores. They had been convicted by the Austrian courts. Now they were free, celebrating and drinking beer and singing raucously.

I decided to play innocent, a tourist who knew from nothing. I wanted to find out what was on their minds, what their plans were. I sat down next to the biggest one of the bunch and spread out the *London Times* in front of me, looking bewildered. The Austrian Nazi spoke English well and was very anxious to tell me all about this "moment of liberation"—that now they were able to breathe in Viennese air that no Jew had ever breathed out. This while I was breathing directly into his face!

I kept on eating my sandwiches and asking questions, getting replies full of boastful plans and intentions, freely revealed, stimulated by liter after liter of good Austrian beer. Under no circumstances would a Jew ever dream of walking blithely into a Nazi meeting or victory celebration unless he was insane. So when this "politically ignorant" foreigner walked in, he was automatically assumed to be a fellow "Aryan."

A couple of days after Hitler's triumphal entry into Vienna I realized I had not gone for my mail and it must be piling up. I received it care of American Express, which was located in a street-front store in the Hotel Imperial, Vienna's most elegant, now commandeered as the residence of officers of the German General Staff.

I collected my mail and came out into the Ringstrasse. Though it was a beautiful morning, there was practically nobody out on the sidewalks, and very little automobile traffic. I was clutching a section of the *New York Times* that my brother had sent me, walking slowly toward the hotel as I examined my armful of accumulated letters—totally unaware of two men talking and laughing at the red-carpeted hotel entrance. One man was short, the other over six feet tall, both beribboned in military top-brass splendor.

Suddenly my mind became conscious of what my body was doing! A "nice Jewish boy" from Manhattan was marching directly toward and about to bump into Adolf Hitler on a bright sunny street in Vienna! I did an instant about-face. Later I asked myself what those two men could have been laughing about. How easy it was to conquer a whole country without firing a shot?

Back in the U.S.A., I spent a good part of two years speaking to American audiences at colleges, churches, synagogues, clubs, any organization that wanted to hear from a newsman just back from witnessing historic events in Europe. I got serious attention from some, skepticism from others, and bland indifference from many. During discussion periods, I often heard the word "propaganda." So many didn't believe in 1938. The owner of a large, popular, strictly kosher Catskills hotel hesitated ten days before letting me deliver a talk entitled "The Plight of the Jews in Europe Today." It was too controversial, he said.

They believed three years later—Pearl Harbor, "the day that will live in infamy." Infamy had finally struck home. Yet how many days had untold millions suffered in infamy since the Nazis first came to power?

And I had witnessed infamy brought down on a land of great music—another prologue to the Holocaust.

THE CRYSTAL NIGHT

Lore Metzger

When Adolf Hitler became chancellor of Germany in January 1933, I had just celebrated my twelfth birthday. I was a student in the all-girl high school of Landau, Rhineland-Palatinate. My thoughts and hobbies were typical of any budding teenager's, and my biggest worries were to get perfect grades and to be noticed just for a moment by one of the students of the all-male high school.

My childhood was an abundance of happy occasions: birthday parties, the annual children's masquerade at the city theater, long walks through Landau's beautiful parks, visits to the zoo, skating and sledding in winter, swimming, biking, and hiking in summer. I loved to climb high in the mountains, each crowned by romantic ruins, castles of kings and emperors of long ago. Life was joyous, carefree, safe.

Shortly after Hitler's rise to power, menacing signs sprang up everywhere, at the swimming pool, the zoo, the parks, the theaters, the restaurants: "Jews forbidden." Jewish homes were soiled with swastikas and hate slogans, Jewish stores were boycotted, Jewish men and even children were beaten in the streets. In school, Jewish students, now "non-Aryans," were segregated from their fellow students. To have to sit in the so-called Jew corner, to have to listen to the most degrading remarks and avoid all contact with class-mates who until then had been my friends, made those years agony for me. More and more of my Jewish classmates left Germany with their families.

For the longest time my parents refused to think about emigration, but in 1938 they finally made the decision to go to America. The German government no longer allowed Jews to take money out of the country, but we could take what we wanted of our household possessions as long as we paid a special tax. By November all the plans for the big move had been made. We were to set sail for America on the S.S. *Washington* on November 28.

During the dreary days of early November, the damp, cold mood of Mother Nature reflected our own only too well. Through the terrible years of the Nazi regime, our home, with its beautifully furnished rooms and magnificent garden, had always been a center of peace and comfort. Now my brother and I could read the sadness and fear in our parents' eyes. They had both been born in Landau, as had my grandparents. They had both served in the military during World War I, and they were deeply involved in the social, cultural, and economic life of Landau. My father didn't know how he would support his family in a strange land, with no knowledge of English and few resources. My mother couldn't sleep for worrying about her aged father, who would have to be left behind because the American consulate wouldn't issue a visa to anyone over seventy. We were all so preoccupied with the emotions of leaving our home and the preparations for the move that we hardly noticed the news item that was to carry such enormous consequences. In Paris, an enraged Polish Jew shot and killed an employee of the German embassy when he learned that his parents had been deported from Germany back to Poland.

At seven o'clock on the morning of November 10, one of our maids came into my bedroom and awakened me with soft, halting words: "Honey, if you want to see the temple again get up now, because it's on fire." Shaking all over, I dressed and ran outside, without stopping for a coat. As soon as I left the house, I could detect a burning odor in the foggy air. I stopped in front of the hotel about a block from the temple and stood there paralyzed by shock and disbelief. Flames were shooting out of the stained-glass rose window, and a second later more flames engulfed the beautiful five-domed sanctuary. How long I remained there I cannot remember.

In tears, I ran back home. My parents were sitting down to breakfast, and I was just about to tell them of the dreadful thing I had witnessed when I heard loud male voices in the hall. In my confusion, I had left the front door open. Suddenly six or eight men pushed their way in, and without so much as a word, one of them yanked the tablecloth off the table, sending the breakfast dishes crashing to the floor. Another grabbed my father by the arm and barked, "You are under arrest!" When my father asked why, he was told, "Today we get all the Jews." We watched, stunned, as they led him away.

Moments later a dozen storm troopers burst into the room brandishing axes, crowbars, hammers, and revolvers. Like beasts of prey fallen upon their victims, they went from room to room, systematically smashing furniture and dishes, cutting up oriental rugs, tearing open feather pillows, even slashing canvases in their frames—my mother's own paintings. As they were about to destroy a recently completed picture, my mother found the courage to say, "What do you want from us? We have served Germany faithfully both in peace and in war," and with that she pointed to the china cabinet, where the military decorations bestowed upon her and my father lay on a black velvet pillow, along with my grandfather's medals from the Franco-Prussian War. When the men saw these, one of them immediately gave the command to stop, but it was too late.

No sooner had they gone than one of our faithful servants arrived and broke down at the sight of the devastation. Struggling to compose herself, she told us she had heard that during the coming night all Jewish houses were to be set afire and all Jewish boys killed. She wanted to take my brother and hide him in the forest, but my mother declined her courageous offer and tearfully sent her away, not wanting to endanger her life as well.

Darkness fell early that November afternoon. My mother dressed us in extra-warm clothes, and we left our home and went through the desolate park in the direction of the Jewish cemetery. There we spent the night, wandering around in a daze or sitting on the tombstones of my grandparents' graves.

At daybreak we returned to the park, where we had a perfect view of our home through the leafless trees. It had not been burned. We saw a large car pull up in front of the house. Two SS men got out and went inside. I was terrified and wanted to run back to the safety of the cemetery, but my mother thought they might have news of my father, so we hurried across the park. As we entered the house, the two men were voicing their disgust at the destruction all around them. Oddly enough, they were the same two officers who had inspected our belongings several weeks before to determine the exit tax. They assured my mother that they themselves would see to it that the government paid for repairs. "We would not want you to go to America and talk about us Germans as barbarians," they told her.

After they left, my mother sent my brother and me to bed. I dreamed of the telephone, which rang and rang and rang, until I finally realized that this was no dream. The phone—miraculously undamaged—was indeed ringing. I stumbled to the den through the debris and picked it up. A harsh male voice said, "Pack your bags and be at the railroad station by noon. Be sure to take all your money and jewelry with you." My mother, who had been out when the call came, returned to this dreadful news and began packing. Shortly before noon on November 11, the three of us left our home for the last time.

Lugging our heavy suitcases, we walked past the temple, which was still burning, and past the ransacked homes of our friends. Worst of all, we walked past the people of Landau, our former neighbors, who stared at us with wordless hostility. Some of them forced us off the sidewalk into the busy street.

A cold drizzle was falling as we reached the plaza in front of the station. There about two hundred women and children were huddled together, trembling and scared, knowing nothing of the fate of their husbands and fathers, or of their own. True to her greatness, my mother made it her business to go around and speak to everyone encouragingly, especially the children.

One by one, the women and children were taken to a small room in the station, ordered to disrobe, and examined by members of the Nazi women's group, who wanted to be sure that no money or jewelry was hidden on their bodies. All the valuables we brought with us had already been confiscated, except wedding bands. A little after eight o'clock, we boarded a train that took us to Mannheim, on the other side of the Rhine River. That day the Palatinate was to be made *judenfrei*—free of Jews.

We were fortunate to have distant relatives who ran a small hotel in Mannheim. These good people sent a taxi and umbrellas and money to the station. By a miracle, their place had not been touched the day before, and I could hardly believe my eyes when we stepped into the warmly lit foyer. It was difficult to comprehend that such things as unbroken furniture still existed. The dining room table was set, awaiting us, and on it was the most beautiful sight of all: two burning Sabbath candles. It was Friday night, and the Sabbath had begun. After the events of the past two days, the radiance of their flickering light gave me an indescribable feeling of peace. Suddenly I discovered a new pride in being a Jew, and in my heart I knew that God would never forsake us.

The next day my father was released from the Dachau concentration camp. He traced us to Mannheim with the help of our former chauffeur, and we were reunited at last. The two SS men kept their word, and my mother was allowed to return to Landau to pack our repaired furniture.

Twenty-three years later, in 1961, my husband and I went back to Landau. For the first time in my life I saw bombed-out houses, whole blocks leveled by air strikes, and I was grateful—yes, grateful—for I realized that the events that drove us from home, the horrors of the Hitler years, of that Crystal Night, had spared my family the horrors of war.

How My Name Saved My Life

Masha Leon

"It's Masha, *not* Marsha," I have to tell people who insist I should Americanize the spelling of my name. How can I explain that to change the spelling would be to tamper with a part of the past?

Masha is the Russian for Mary—but I was named after my paternal grandfather, Moyshe. In prewar Warsaw it would have been more prudent to be called Maria, Marisia, Marusia. Masha was a giveaway that I was not Polish and might be Jewish.

When the Nazis occupied Poland in September 1939, my parents agreed that they would meet at their hometown, Bytom, then under Soviet occupation as a result of the Stalin-Hitler pact. My father left Warsaw in the first week of the war, as did many intellectuals and journalists, assuming they would return a few weeks later. My mother and I left Warsaw in the winter of 1939–40 and headed for the German-Russian border. En route we were taken direct to Gestapo headquarters by our Polish peasant driver and lined up to be shot, but because my mother and I had even-numbered tags (6 and 8) and they shot the odd-numbered refugees, we survived.

My mother had warned me never to cry in front of a German and never to call her Mamma. (I was blond and blue-eyed, and she had black hair and dark-brown eyes, so calling her Mamma might condemn me as a Jewish child. She passed herself off as my Italian nanny, since she spoke Polish with a Russian accent.) However, should we be stopped by the Russians, then cry a river, for Russians were reputed to have good hearts. My being able to blend with peasant children, my mother's willingness to live in a barn, to milk cows, to dig potatoes, was a passport to a night's lodging or a glass of milk. Our currency was salt, needles, thread, matches, all prized by dirt-poor peasants.

After a number of life-threatening encounters we finally reached the border, where the Germans willingly, smilingly let us through, along with hundreds, thousands of refugees. But once we crossed, Russians on horseback with peaked hats and bandoliers told us to go back to the Germans. "We don't want any *pans* [misters] here—we are all *tovarischi* [comrades]." And so for three days we shuttled between Russians with poised bayonets and Germans who laughed and taunted, "Go back to your Bolshevik friends." Eventually people began to die from cold and hunger, and trucks would appear to cart off the bodies.

I left Warsaw with a case of the mumps (the fever kept me warm) and a malnutrition rash in my mouth. My mother decided on the third day that we would leave the other refugees and walk parallel with the tree line in hopes of breaking through to the Russian side. No luck. Miraculously, a Polish peasant woman who had fields on the Russian side and a house on the German side came by with a hay wagon and offered to help us. She fed us, hid us in her cellar for several days until we recovered, and had her son get us past the Germans. Then we were on our own in the middle of no-man's land.

We had just entered the forest on the Russian side when a lone Russian soldier appeared with bayonet fixed and ordered us back. As my mother put down her bundles and I removed my knapsack, I heard her say in perfect Russian, "I'd rather a Russian shot me than a German." On cue, I began to cry, to weep, to howl. But the soldier was adamant. "Go back or I shoot you," he repeated. My mother showed him her papers, indicating that she had been born under Russian rule. He threw them in the mud. Obviously nothing was working. I kept on wailing.

"Don't cry, Mashinka," she said. The Russian suddenly turned to look at me: "Since when do Poles give their children Russian names?" My mother gave me a *zetz* in the ribs—"Sing! Sing!"—and I sang the only Russian song I knew, *"Pod samovarem, ja i moya Masha"* ("Beneath the samovar I and Masha...") I kept repeating the same phrase, over and over.

"Enough!" shouted the Russian. "Why Masha?" he asked again. Go tell a soldier that I was named after Moses-Moyshe. My mother wove a fable about having been inspired by Chekhov's *Three Sisters*, Masha in *Brothers Karamazov*, Tolstoy. ... The soldier was a peasant kid who had probably only dimly heard of any of these literary giants and waved at us just to stop!

He looked at me and shook his head, put his hand in his inner pocket, and pulled out a family photograph, pointing to a little girl about eight, the same age I was, with the identical long braids and bows. "My sister Masha," he told my mother. "How can I shoot your daughter? It would be like shooting my sister." He led us to headquarters, and when the local commander and troops heard my name—Masha, Mashinka—out came the black bread, butter, tea, apples. They took us by truck to the train station, where the soldiers, again hearing my Russian name, serenaded us and fed us.

Marcia, Marsha—it's not the same. I often wonder, of all the miracles—surviving the bombing, leaving Warsaw on the right route on the right day, going left or right on a road, finding a peasant willing to hide us, not being shot, the Gestapo believing that the dark-haired woman was indeed my nanny, an elderly German at one of our stops telling us how to avoid being caught by a German patrol, etc., etc., etc.—if that encounter was not the most pivotal in our survival.

Masha it is, and Masha it shall remain.

My Nazi Inheritance

Henrietta Mayer

From 1942 to 1945 I lived in Vienna under a false name and false identification papers. I fled there with my daughter in order to escape the persecution of the Jews in Yugoslavia.

Since my status was "forced laborer," I had to live in a camp. The head of the camp noticed that I spoke fluent German, so he decided to keep me as a translator in his office and the doctor's office. Every morning sick men came to Dr. Kronberger with all kinds of aches and pains. I could very much identify with these people, taken by force from their homes and transported all over Germany and Austria to work in war factories, and I tried to help as much as I could by explaining their problems to the doctor.

The first few days I worked for him, Dr. Kronberger told me that he had also been drafted for his job and was not at all happy with the whole situation. "It won't be long before Austria will be free from that lunatic," he said. I was surprised that he talked so openly and afraid that he suspected something, so I was very evasive.

There was in the camp another young woman, Helen, also a forced laborer. She worked in the kitchen and distributed food rations in the morning and evening. I became friendly with her since we were the only women there. She always gave me a little more than my ration, "for your child," she said. Helen did not live in the camp; she had a rented room nearby. She and the doctor encouraged me to ask for permission to move out and just come to work from 6:30 a.m. to 8:00 p.m. It took me a few days to gather my courage—I should not "rock the boat," they should not start asking me too many questions. But the circumstances and the cold weather forced me to act.

To my surprise, permission was granted, and I moved to the house of Frau Brueckner, a seamstress. Every day I brought my food ration home and gave it to Frau B., since Helen and my daughter and I had our evening meal in the camp. Frau B. was naturally very happy with all this extra food and thanked me for it. To show her appreciation she even made my daughter a winter coat and hat from her extra materials.

One day I came home earlier than usual. Already in the hall-way I heard Hitler's screaming voice. I opened the door to the apartment and saw the radio on the windowsill. When I asked Frau B. why she had the radio in the window full-blast, she said, "So everybody in the house can hear our Führer speaking." To myself I thought, Now I got myself into a real pickle. In the morning Frau B. said to me, "If our Führer could get rid of all the Jews in the world, we would have paradise on earth." Between two evils, I thought, which is worse? Living in the camp or living with this crazy woman?

Frau B. was always waiting for me when I came home in the evening. She had a glass of milk ready for my little girl and a cup of tea for me. She treated me like a daughter, and my child like a grandchild. She told me she had no family at all, except for a brother in upper Austria, and they were not on good terms.

"I have a surprise for you," said Frau B. one evening in early spring. Surprises in those years were very scary for me. "I made pancakes with jam out of all the goodies you're bringing home, and you have to have some." We sat down at a nicely set table, and I have to say the pancakes tasted delicious. All of a sudden, Frau B. leaned back in her chair, very pale, and blood started spurting from her mouth like water from a faucet. I was beside myself. I couldn't carry her to bed, so I put her on two chairs in a horizontal position to stop the bleeding. Luckily she had a phone. Now I really needed help from my doctor friend.

When Dr. Kronberger arrived half an hour later, he just shook his head and gave Frau B. an injection. He immediately called an ambulance. The hospital was on the outskirts of Vienna. We were directed to the emergency room, where a doctor was waiting to take her vital signs. The admissions office asked me a lot of questions, but I could only tell them about the brother in upper Austria.

The next day, through Dr. Kronberger, I found out that Frau B. had cancer all over her body and had one or two weeks to live. All kinds of thoughts went through my mind. What should I do now? Who is going to make her funeral arrangements? And where will I live?

When I visited Frau B., she had changed overnight into an old woman with gray hair and no teeth. I stood at the foot of her bed and she opened her eyes, a trace of a smile on her face. I knew she recognized me. She motioned me closer, grabbed my hand, and kissed it, whispering, "You are my guardian angel. Without you I would be already dead." Tears were running down her face as she told me to write down what she said. I asked the nurse for a sheet of paper, and she began. She explained that she didn't have long to live and since she had no family she wanted to leave me her money and all her belongings. She took the paper from my hand and slowly signed it.

Four days later I received a telegram from the hospital saying that Frau B. had died that morning and I should come to make arrangements for her funeral. I was at my wits' end. If she had known my real identity, I would probably be in Auschwitz now. When she talked of Hitler, she became a different person. She definitely had two personalities. She treated me as a daughter and my child as a granddaughter. She was good to me and happy that I was there. But if she only knew?

That evening when I came home I broke down and cried. When my little girl tried to console me, I realized how upset and frightened she was. I could not give up now. I had to go on and put this episode behind us.

The next day I went to the hospital and explained that I had only lived with Frau B. for a few months in a rented room. It just so happened that I was at home that evening and tried to help her out of human compassion. They understood and said they would take care of her.

I never told anybody about the will. A few days later I disposed of it.

THE WATCH

Mira Kimmelman

First came the shrilling shout: "Du verfluchtes Schwein!" ("You damned swine!") Then I felt a cutting pain on my back, my shoulders, my head. The soldier caught me as I ran down the stairs of the empty factory on Stolarsta Street where the SS had taken us.

It was November 1, 1942, the day the liquidation of the Polish Tomaszow Mazowiecki ghetto began. About three hundred of us, mostly young men and women, had been pulled out of the marching columns as the other Jews from our ghetto walked to the railroad station. We were told we were all being sent east to work. The true destination was Treblinka, the death camp. The day before, my parents, my brother and I, and all the families of the slave workers for OT (Organization Todt) had been moved to the factory. Early the next morning, all the men left for work. Only women and children remained. About 8:00 a.m. we heard the dreaded loud knock at the door. The SS ordered everyone to assemble outside in ten minutes. "Wear your heavy working shoes and warm clothing. Pack all valuables in a small satchel."

Upstairs my mother and I dressed hurriedly in layers of clothing, took our rucksack, and ran downstairs. In the rush I left my wristwatch, a thirteenth birthday gift from my father, forgotten as we were confronted by the brutality of the SS. We were marched five in a row toward the railroad station. From every corner, from every street, Jews were marching: old ones, young ones, mothers with babies in their arms, children holding on to parents. Now and then a shot was heard, but we were too scared to look back. As we passed an SS officer in front of the small church, he pointed to me and ordered me to step out. It happened so quickly I had no time to say goodbye to my dear mother. She went on with the column, and I never saw her again.

Time passed slowly as we, the selected three hundred Jews, stood for hours in the churchyard. At evening we were taken back to the factory on Stolarsta Street where my family and I had spent our last night together. The SS ordered us to stay downstairs. Then I remembered the watch. I have to get upstairs and retrieve it, I thought. Why did I risk my life for a watch? An inner voice told me to get it. I found the chrome-plated Optima and hid it in my clothing. Then came the encounter with the SS officer who caught me on my way downstairs. Sore from his brutal blows, I could not stop thinking of my family. My mother, grandparents, aunts, uncles, cousins were gone. Only my father and brother remained. Sitting on the cement floor of the factory, we grieved for our dear ones.

Suddenly the front door opened. A drunken Ukrainian SS soldier entered the factory. Rifle in hand, he grabbed our gentle Jewish ghetto policeman. The Ukrainian shouted in a slurred voice,

"Give me a watch or I shoot him." Not a sound could be heard. I reached for my watch and handed it to the Ukrainian, who left the factory satisfied. The watch my father gave me in Danzig in 1936 saved the life of a friend, the life of a kind person.

I Am Not
a Corpse Yet

Anna Grun

One afternoon in November 1942, my sister and I left our parents and our little brother. I didn't know then that I would never see them again.

Shortly before the final action we left town. My parents had a hiding place where they thought they could evade deportation. I shall never know whether they hid and were discovered by the Germans or were denounced by our Polish neighbors. All I know is that they were caught and murdered in a German camp.

I never wanted to leave my family, but my mother insisted. She hoped that this way my sister and I might survive. So that dark afternoon at the end of autumn we left our home for a life full of fear and anxiety, exposed to constant danger from hostile Poles and vicious blackmailers. Whether in hiding or in the open, we were all the time faced with death; we became two hunted animals.

After weeks of wandering through field and forest, suffering from hunger, we came across a Jewish settlement. We entered a small hut and collapsed on the floor among other Jews who sat hunched and tired, heads lowered, faces in their hands. They sat in silence. Overwhelmed by exhaustion, I fell asleep.

I don't know how long I'd slept when I was suddenly awakened by the sound of blows and screaming. The hut was full of German SS. They had long whips in their hands and seemed to be drunk. With animal excitement on their faces, they swished their whips and yelled, "Los, los, aber schnell," pushing the people out of the hut. A crowd of Jews was already herded together. The old and the sick were taken to the Jewish cemetery, where a death brigade was waiting for its victims.

The search for more Jews lasted the whole night. In the morning, guarded on all sides by SS, Ukrainians, and Polish police, we were marched across the fields until we arrived at our destination, a cattle train. Amid screams and beatings, we were ordered to enter the wagons. The heavy metal doors slammed shut and the train began to move, first slowly, then faster and faster.

The cattle train was full of children, women, and men. I don't remember how long we'd been inside when my sister started to talk about escaping. Elka, my girlfriend, cried. Her whole family was dead, and we tried to convince her that she should escape with us, but she was paralyzed with terror. People in the wagon took sides. Some encouraged us to save ourselves, others shouted hysterically, afraid that they would be killed because of us.

I decided to jump first. It was impossible to reach the small opening in the ceiling, even for a tall man. Somebody lifted me. I looked through the tiny window. It was very dark. Not a single light could be seen—a precaution against air raids. I listened to the sound of the wheels and waited. After a while I jumped and fell on a pile of stones. I managed to stand up and started running alongside the train, calling out my sister's name. The sudden sound of shooting told me that I was the target of German machine guns. I ran in the opposite direction. My sister was supposed to jump after me, but in the dense darkness I couldn't see her.

We found each other three weeks later. After many days of wandering, I managed to slip into the Kraków ghetto one evening. I learned from a friend whom I met by accident in the street that my sister was alive and was staying with three of her schoolmates. It took me only a few minutes to reach my sister's lodging. I knocked at the door. In a few moments she stood in front of me, shrinking in terror.

"They told me you were dead," she said.

"Don't be afraid," I replied. "I am not a corpse yet."

I Never Cried
for My Mother

Erika Brodsky

I am young and strong and blond and pretty and the lines form on the right and on the left. I am sent to the left and to the sauna, and now we stand naked, a hundred or so, and we laugh at the size and shape of our bodies, at our shaved heads, and we are transported into unreality, which allows us to be totally detached from the moment, the fear and the unknown. Showered and dressed in rags—shoeless, cold, freezing cold—we line up to be tattooed, numbered, wondering what happened to the line on the right, wondering too why the air is filled with a dense odor of burning chicken feathers, the same odor that haunted us for days in the boxcars. The ground is frozen, we have no underwear, and my French friends bemoan the fate of their breasts, doomed to sag without bras, so that any future bare sunbathing will be impossible. Droll, the mind is surely an odd instrument.

I ask a guard, a female—tough—what happened to the line on the right where I last saw my blind mother, whom I had refused to leave, turning myself in so I could take care of her. She was being held by the hand, by a new friend—a friendship formed in Drancy, the gateway camp, last stop before Auschwitz. A lovely lady she was, this friend; she and her sister, both professors at the University of Berlin, had escaped to France, as had we, and been interned there. Both had been infested with lice and were shaved in the courtyard for all to see and laugh at. Both, like my mother, had been sent to the line on the right.

The guard bursts into roaring laughter, and pointing her ersatz rubber whip toward the smoking chimney high above us, yells, "There is your mother, there in the smoke."

I never cried for my mother. The truth, the reality of the horror, was too much for me to comprehend or absorb, and so I never cried for my mother, nor for myself ever again.

Over the years, there was so much that made living less and less possible, or even desirable. The digging of ditches to bury the cadavers when gas was short, the attacks by biting dogs at the mere drop of a shovel, the untended diseases, the recurring diarrhea, the fevers and coughing of blood. Truckloads to the crematoria, that was our future, our only future. The only thing that seemed to matter was that someone survive to tell the world. That became an obsession. Someone to tell the world. Imagine the pain, the pain that has never left me to this day, to learn that the world knew and did nothing—no one cared enough at least to bomb the train tracks. Jewish life was always cheap, but *that* cheap? Where were you, world? When your mothers die, you cry—I never did, you did not let me.

Toward the end of the war we were marched to Bergen-Belsen, a march that seems humanly impossible when I look at a map today. We were all too sick to work, and death piles became the everyday norm. I dragged my best friend to the pile and was shortly dragged there myself. Liberation came, the British found me still alive on the pile, and I was sent back to France, where a kindly doctor performed lung surgery, surgery with not one human being in the world who cared if it succeeded or not, if I awoke or not, no one to wait outside. Eventually I arrived in Marseilles, where I met my Ben, an American soldier, who sent me to a tuberculosis sanatorium in the Alps.

One year later, cured, fed, fattened, married, and pregnant, I arrived in the United States to begin a new life amid new difficulties, wonderments, and a whole new set of problems. People asked what those numbers on our arms meant. Some of us wore the tattoos proudly, some covered them up, and some, like me, had them surgically removed so that our children would not feel different.

The years have passed, my two children are grown, and if I don't look in the mirror, my youth has never gone, my hopes and dreams have never gone, tomorrow is still ahead. Fifty years is such a long time. Regrets? Of course. I should have found a way to immortalize the names of my parents. I should have had more children, at least as many as were killed in our family, they needed to be replaced. And I should have learned to cry for my mother.

ENOUGH

Frieda Friedman

It was near the end of the war, maybe late 1944 or early 1945. After all the time in the concentration camps, I couldn't tell you what year it was, let alone what day or month. But it was near the end, and I was in Bergen-Belsen. I had also been in Auschwitz for a short while. I had spent the first two years of the war making uniforms and clothes for the Germans in Plaszow, the labor camp near Kraków, where I grew up. I was young and in good physical shape then. Otherwise I would have been killed.

In Bergen-Belsen I got very weak and was put in a typhus block with about two thousand other girls. All around me everyone was sick. We slept on the cold, hard floors, we ran high fevers, and we were dying. The Germans hadn't fed us for a long time, and everyone was starving.

But I never felt hungry. My mother, who was a holy woman, I always thought, had been killed by the Germans earlier in the war, along with my father, my first husband, and my eight brothers. She was dead, but she was still able to help me, the way she always did. At night, maybe because I had such a high fever, maybe not, I would dream that my mother came to me and fed me. She gave me all the wonderful foods I loved. I ate and ate till I was full. In the dream, she even told me to give some of the extra food to my youngest brother. There was so much. Those dreams kept me alive.

The Germans finally began feeding people. They gave everyone a soup of carrots, potatoes, and ground glass, which they made to seem like flour. I think by then they knew they were going to lose the war and they wanted to destroy the evidence of what they had done before the Allies came.

You needed a cup to put your soup in. I didn't have a cup. A friend of mine said she would get one for both of us. I told her, "No, thank you, my mother gives me enough food."

My friend died the next day. So did most of the other girls in the block. After one cup, they suffered great pains. With two cups, they dropped dead.

I was lucky. I didn't eat. I survived. My mother gave me enough.

THE MAKING
OF A PHYSICIAN

Judita Hruza

The last year of World War II was
the year the war reached my family.

In March 1944 the Germans occupied Hungary, causing an
endless series of earthquakes in Jewish lives all over the country. I
was nineteen. Just two hours after the news of the occupation, my
fifteen-year-old brother and I were turned back at the railway station: Jews were not permitted to use the train or leave the city by
any means. We were living with family friends in Budapest, going
to school. In this frightening situation all we wanted was to go
home to our parents to face whatever would come. It never happened. We exchanged letters full of love, anguish, and hope,
promising each other to survive and meet again "when it was all
over." We never saw our parents again. They were killed in the gas
chambers of Auschwitz.

My personal Holocaust started when all Jewish women
between sixteen and forty were ordered to report to work. We were
to bring sturdy shoes and warm clothes and food for three days.
The huge crowd of young women looked like a summer camp gathering. As we set out for the march to our first destination, I felt
tough, strong, and determined to take any hardship and survive.

The awakening came in brutal shocks. Everything was a shock
the first time. The first night, crowded in a building with a bombed-
out roof, standing room only, the October rain pouring on our
heads, running down our backs, collecting at our feet up to our
knees. The first body, a girl beaten to death, paraded in front of us
in a wheelbarrow for enlightenment. The first of thousands of lice
in my clothes. The first shooting spree by the guards, just for fun.

The march toward Germany showed more and more evidence
of its real purpose, and it was not to get workers. They did not
want us to work. They wanted us dead. Some of us gave up. All
you had to do was sit down by the roadside and you were shot to
death. We got no food, we all had dysentery; we were hopeless and
confused. We spent our nights in the open in a softball field, in the

hold of a cargo ship, in pigsties where the pigs had just been evicted. The inventiveness of our captors was inexhaustible.

Whenever we arrived at our night place, there was one single solid semblance of normalcy, of purpose, order, and hope: a Red Cross flag and a makeshift tent and two or three doctors with their bags. They were prisoners like the rest of us, they got here by the same painful marching, but somehow they still had the energy to help others. They cleaned wounds, gave advice, comforted. I felt they must know a secret hidden from us ordinary people that gave them strength in this desperation.

One day a young doctor was removing a bullet from a prisoner when the order came for a head count. The guards rounded everybody up, but the surgeon just kept operating. The commandant walked over to him and ordered him to join the roundup. "I am almost done," he replied. "I must stop the bleeding first." The commandant said jokingly, "I'll give you a choice. You can do as I say and I'll let you live, or you can finish and then I'll shoot you." The doctor finished the suturing, dressed the wound, and was shot dead on the spot.

I didn't think I would ever have the courage to behave like that, but I made myself a promise: If I survive, I will become a doctor. This dream faded through the coming months. The starvation, the cold, the lice, the beatings, and the shootings killed some two hundred people each day. My mind was reduced to a simple thought: to survive, one hour at a time.

And I did survive, one of sixty of the original five thousand women sent to "work" nine months earlier. I went to Budapest and found my brother, who had also survived; the rest of our family had been killed. Strangers were living in our home. We stayed in a shelter for returned prisoners. I was planning to find a job to support the two of us after I recovered from some wounds.

One day my brother brought home my papers for medical school. He had enrolled me secretly. After the war everybody who wanted to study was accepted. My dear little brother beamed at me. "Isn't this what you wanted to do? We'll survive, don't worry. We've survived harder times!"

Five years later I received my M.D. Did I learn the secret of the doctors in the camp? I don't know. I learned patience, curiosity, self-discipline, and compassion. I have been a physician for forty years now.

So My Grandchildren Will Know

Henry Williamson

I was a captain in the Fourteenth Cavalry Group attached to the Third Army in April 1945, when two enlisted men and I drove through the quiet countryside to Dachau, a typical, clean German village, undamaged by shells or bombs. One side of the paved road was lined by neat houses with perfectly kept yards, the other by a long wall of masonry and rock, about eight feet high, with big steel gates. Behind this wall was the infamous German concentration camp that had been liberated thirty-six hours earlier by American troops.

As we were not allowed to enter at the main gate, we turned left and drove between an electrically charged barbed-wire fence and a beautifully landscaped nursery. We learned later that this was where the ashes of the victims of the Holocaust had been scattered. There were also grass-covered mounds where partially cremated bodies were buried in mass graves.

We entered the camp afoot by a small gate on the north side. The crematorium was at the back, and there we saw bodies that had not been cremated or were only partially cremated. As the end of the war became imminent, the Germans had overcrowded the crematorium and stacked the bodies in orderly piles. Many other people had died in the barracks, and the Americans made the German villagers and guards remove them so they could be identified and buried. But the Germans had destroyed the records, and in spite of the tattoos on each body, it was impossible to identify most of them.

I thought I'd become hardened to the sight of dead bodies as we fought our way across Europe—enemy soldiers, civilians, too many American soldiers—and it was not the deadness of these victims that got to me, it was the piteous condition they had reached before death mercifully released them. They were literally skin and bones, with arms and legs like broomsticks. I wondered how many hours and days of starvation had been required to bring them to this state.

We saw medical corpsmen feeding broth a spoonful at a time to emaciated survivors. We looked inside the long single-story barracks with bunks stacked end to end and saw the stark, dirty bathhouse with cold-water spigots and chemical toilets. We saw the gate that had admitted trainloads of prisoners tightly packed in boxcars, who would load ammunition and shells to be shipped to other parts of Germany.

We spent about an hour in the camp, looking around and smelling the odor of death, disinfectant, and despair. As we made our way back to the gate where we left our jeep, we were stopped by a lieutenant who sprayed us with DDT because of the lice and typhus in the place.

We drove past the well-fertilized nursery back to the paved road in front of the pretty German houses with sweet flowers blooming in the yards. I thought how appearances can be so very deceiving, and I couldn't help but wonder at the ability of mankind to ignore the needs and sufferings of our fellow man across the street.

I HAVE A STORY TO TELL

Wilson Alonso

I was born in Barcelona in 1920. When I was seventeen years old, I was "requested" to join one of General Franco's labor battalions and was sent to Leon, where the Condor Legion had established an air base. We were commanded by a German officer named Milch. Our orders were to dig a trench around the perimeter of the base to protect it from a reported invasion from the province of Asturias, some eighty kilometers away.

One day a car flying two small American flags drove into the compound. A man inquired for a Wilson Alonso, American citizen. I was produced and told to get my gear and go with him. It turned out that my father, who was in Paris, had asked the American consul in Bilbao to find me and get me out. My dad had been born in Cuero, Texas, in 1888, and had had me properly registered with the American consulate in Barcelona.

I came to the United States on the S.S. *Excalibur*, Marseilles to New York, and landed at Pier F in Jersey City. Five years later I was in the United States Army and eventually joined the Military Intelligence Service. Our team made the landing on Utah Beach on D-Day and became attached to HQ VII Corps commanded by General J. Lawton Collins, "Lightnin' Joe." The corps saw action all over Europe and was part of the offensive that brought an end to the war. We crossed the Rhine, Cologne fell, and in the general advance from Kassel to the Elbe our forward elements came upon the first shocking evidence of Nazi atrocities.

One of the members of my team was Master Sergeant Maurice Werblird, who was from New York City. We were driving one day in my jeep, nicknamed Jo-Jo, when we encountered a French prisoner of war who directed us to "un endroit terrible"—a terrible place. We found ourselves at the entrance of a tunnel that led to a vast area several hundred feet in height, with railroad tracks on either side and hundreds of rail cars loaded with V-2 rockets that only needed engines. There were German technicians in white lab coats all over, unaware that they were about to be occupied by the American army.

We had stumbled on the notorious underground factory that produced the V-2s that had bombarded London and Antwerp. And surrounding it all was the slave labor camp at Nordhausen.

Row upon row of skin-covered skeletons met our eyes. Maurice threw up. Men and women lay as they had starved, discolored, in indescribable human filth. Their striped coats and prison numbers hung on their frames, a last token of those who had enslaved and killed them. It was obvious that we had moved so fast that no one had time to bury them. No attempt had been made even to hide them. There were so many.

We went downstairs to one of the barracks, assailed by a horrible dead-animal smell. There, in bunks of the crudest wood, we saw men and women consumed by diarrhea and starvation, too weak to move dead comrades from their side. To add to the horror, Allied bombers had recently—unknowingly—hit some of the barracks where the slaves were held. We found about three thousand bodies in the buildings. Some eight hundred people were still alive, but many of them died in spite of the intense efforts of our medics.

General Collins was called immediately and was so appalled that he ordered the mayor of Nordhausen to make the entire population of the town—men, women, and children—carry the emaciated victims, one by one, to a burial plot that had been dug by our bulldozers in a nearby cemetery. There the bodies were interred in a service conducted by chaplains of the three main faiths. Next day the mayor hanged himself in the attic of his house. All we heard from the rest of the population was, "We knew nothing."

Through the years I have heard it said more than once that the Holocaust is a fraud, a hoax, a fairy tale—in other words, that it never happened. To all who say that, I say no. We who witnessed it will carry this message to our final resting place. *It happened. We saw it.*

OKINAWA, 1945

Sophia Strong

That first night on Okinawa was a disaster. Just a few days before, an especially virulent typhoon had leveled every structure above ground. When I alit after a long day's flight, night had set in, cold, damp, windy. My unheralded arrival at Red Cross Headquarters evoked consternation. Where could they put me that night? There were no empty cots at the makeshift women's lodgings. However, they did locate one in the torn tent housing the army nurses of the General Field Hospital. By the time we arrived there, the wind had strengthened. It was now a howling gale with drenching rain. To add to the general homeyness of the scene, the tent joined in the noisy chorus with loud flappings from numerous tears.

My cot was crowded into the only available space, immediately beneath a large gash in the canvas. Two ponchos took care of the rain that poured down on my cozy boudoir. In the dark, the nurses were disembodied voices issuing from equally damp cots, greeting me with friendly conversation. These women were waiting to return home after years of horrifying duties, but they all assured me that Okinawa had been the worst, for here flamethrowers had been the hand-to-hand weapon of choice. I heard of men burned to a crisp, requesting a last cigarette before dying. The nurses tried to describe the effect on them of the nauseating smell of roasted human flesh.

After a while, quiet reigned. Weeping silently, I pulled an extra poncho over my head, listened to the rivulet musically falling from my ponchoed blanket onto the dirt floor, and so, to sleep.

Sometime later, I awoke with a start. Something heavy had plopped onto my bed with a thump, then off; a pause, and then a repeat. What could it be? The nurses were all awake, laughing and cursing. By their flashlights, I could see what was causing the commotion. Large fat rats were enjoying a kind of rodent leapfrog, jumping from bed to bed. The nurses were throwing shoes at them. Though terrified, I managed to control my horror. How could I *dare* let out even a small squeak when to these women this was just a minor nuisance? The next day I learned that these were playful mongeese, but that night they were rats to me! Despite my fear, I had to join in the laughter when the last small beast, routed by the flying shoes, was seen in the beam of a flashlight backing out the door flap. With jeweled eyes gleaming, it dragged a pair of pink panties clamped in its jaws slowly and inexorably through the mud. "Come back here! You come back this minute!" yelled the outraged owner. But the panties continued their exit till lost in the dark outside.

Somehow I fell asleep again. When I awoke the wind had died down, the sun shone. Where was I? Still confused, I swung my feet off the bed, to sink into mud up to my ankles. Thus, auspiciously, began my seven months' stay on the war-devastated island of Okinawa.

It was a dead world. The autumn day lacked even the grace of fallen leaves. The numberless bombs, tanks, and flamethrowers had decimated men, blasted trees, erased the small chirpers in the grass. Even the birds had fled. Involuntarily, my mind intoned over and over, "The sedge has withered from the lake, and no birds sing!" An awesome soundlessness prevailed.

After a month on Okinawa, when a friend said he'd be visiting a small neighboring island where life had gone on sans war, and would I care to see some green again, I jumped at the chance.

Our amphibian "duck" rode along the beach till a surfless shallow presented itself; then into the water it rolled. The sea was green-blue, the sky blue-blue. Nowhere did I see the endless rusting cadavers of war machines lying disconsolately about. That in itself was enough to elate me.

Finally, the small island: green waving grass, ripening rice bowing in the breeze. A village lay ahead at the foot of a steep hill. "You go ahead," I said to my friend. I wanted to drink in the blessed peace.

And then—piping voices! Could it be? Children? It was, a small group of them rounding the hill. I was overwhelmed. How beautiful, how natural. What an affirmation of joy—of life—after weeks and weeks of nothing but death.

Unconsciously, yearningly, I raised my arms as if to embrace them. The children saw me. A foreign devil! They stopped in their tracks, horror-struck. Shrieking, they turned and fled. The smallest child, a little boy, looked over his shoulder as he ran. He must have sensed my love, which was enveloping me in waves, for he stopped and took a few uncertain steps toward me. Then he said the first Japanese word I had ever heard. "Otamadachi?" I knew exactly what it meant. "Friend?" With streaming eyes I nodded my head. Yes!

Grinning, all fear allayed, he skipped toward me, searching in his pocket. He found a small snail shell, gave it to me gravely. I found a small coin in my pocket, gave it to him with a smile. Then, his small hand in mine, we went down the hill to the village together.

AUGUST 15, 1945

Katsuko Ketchum

I was still in bed. The sun was already high. Another warm summer day. The clock on the wall showed 8:10 a.m. Ordinarily I would be at work by this time. Ordinarily the first air raid of the day would be under way. I waited. I had no feelings. I felt numb. Imminent death hovering.

The date was August 15, 1945—the day the atomic bomb would be dropped on Kokura, our city of 350,000 on the northern tip of Kyushu Island, with its arsenal and steel mill. We had been warned a few days ago by handbills dropped from enemy planes. We were stunned. We faced death daily and assumed it was just a matter of time before we were hit in the raids ... but atomic bomb? We had heard what happened in Hiroshima and Nagasaki within the last two weeks. The devastation and the destruction, the intensity of a kind unheard of before. Well, the bomb would take care of all the waiting. It was final.

Until now the air raids had followed a pretty regular schedule: one in the morning, one at midday, and one late at night, each lasting about twenty minutes. Now we wouldn't have to run to the bomb shelter when we heard the alarm. No more fire-fighting drills either, with everybody, mostly women (all the young men were in the army, and the very old and very young had been evacuated whenever possible), lining up to pass buckets of water from hand to hand. How comical to think we could put out the massive fires caused by bombing with pails of water. One day I decided to skip the drill. When the call came I hid in the bathroom. At the end of the drill I heard a banging on the door. There stood our block honcho, raving mad, and he reprimanded me in front of all my neighbors. "You unpatriotic good-for-nothing!" he shouted. Well, I didn't have to worry about him anymore. I was barely out of college, and my life would be blown away today.

Toward the end of the war, most high school and college boys were either drafted or volunteered to go to the war. These young boys were the so-called kamikaze pilots. It was their only and yet their highest contribution to the country and to the emperor. The doctrine that the highest honor bestowed upon a man is to die for the country and the emperor—the two were almost synonymous in those days—was hammered into Japanese children from a very early age. In the meantime, high school and college girls were put to work in various defense factories. I was living in a rooming house near the steel mill where I worked. My home was about four miles away. No matter. We would all be blown away today. My parents, my sisters and brothers.

It was now 8:45 a.m. Still no alarm. Why, they're taking their time today, I thought. I noticed a kind of eerie quietness. Of course I knew nobody had gone to work on this day. No sound of traffic.

No footsteps or hustle and bustle. And no food. We'd eaten up all of what little rations we were given weekly. But no sense in leaving any. I suppose by alerting civilians the Americans thought people could flee to safety. At least they warned us. But it was not possible for us to get away. Nobody owned a car in those days; the train station issued only a few tickets a day; the streetcar did not go far enough. We were simply stuck.

Nine o'clock came and went. An hour or so later the word got around to me that there would be a very important broadcast at noon. Everybody was up now. Reluctantly. What do they want? Something to remember before we die? Finally noon came, and we all gathered around the radio, my landlord and his wife with a baby feeding on her breast, the next-door lady with her soldier boyfriend, an army captain who was on leave, and me. Soon an unfamiliar voice came through the radio. I did not understand what he was saying. I listened more carefully. Halfway through I vaguely caught something like "bear the unbearable..." I still didn't know what it was all about. The speech lasted around ten minutes. It turned out that it was the emperor. I was flabbergasted. It was the first time the public had ever heard his voice. To the Japanese people the emperor was almost like God, and when he or his relatives happened to pass through town we had to line up along the side of the street and bow our heads to the ground and never look up until they were two blocks away. We couldn't even look at the face let alone hear the voice. The emperor did not speak ordinary Japanese language, and I had a hard time understanding him.

"The war has ended," said the landlord. He looked somber.

"What? You mean no more air raid?" I asked.

"No more air raid."

"You mean no atomic bomb?"

"I guess not."

I was dumbfounded. We are going to live? Suddenly I heard a choking sound. I looked around and saw the captain sobbing, covering his eyes with one arm, his body twisting. It took some more time before I fully understood that we had lost the war. Somehow I did not feel sad. I just felt relieved.

Forty-five years have passed since that fateful day. Yes, I escaped death by the skin of the teeth. I keep reminding myself how lucky I am, and that every day I have lived since then has been a God-given bonus. And it is incredible that I should be living in this country with which we fought the war and lost, which I now call my country, the United States, the land that I love.

GAMBARE

George Omi

I studied my face in the mirror. I asked myself: Why?

I looked around the room, at the wallpaper green and faded; at the floors, sheet linoleum, gray, chipped at the edges; at the Murphy bed gone into the wall; at the table, shiny with varnish, scratched all over, moved to where the bed was last night. I climbed on the green sofa, spotted with brownish stains, and stood there with my shoes on, as I had been told not to do. I could hear the vacuum sucking steam. Papa was out front, in the store, pressing another pair of pants.

Mama was in back, in the kitchen, cooking. There was no mistaking the smell, burning sugar and *shoyu*, teriyaki chicken, marinated. She had the flame up high; the smoke left the kitchen and filled the room. We were going to eat Japanese again, I thought. Why couldn't we eat roast beef, mashed potatoes, and gravy, with silverware, like my friends? I was eight years old, and Franklin Roosevelt was president.

Papa called out my name from the front of the store. He had to shout so that I could hear him. "Minoru!"

Why doesn't he call me George, like the teacher and the kids at school? What a stupid-sounding name, Minoru.

"Minoru, *chotto*, come-u here-a."

Why do we have to speak so much Japanese? Why can't Papa learn to speak better English?

Mama and Papa were both Japanese immigrants. I was *nisei*, a second-generation Japanese born in America.

• • •

"Hey you, Chink! Yeah, you, c'mere!"

"I'm not Chinese, I'm Japanese. Don't call me Chink."

"Then c'mere, Jap."

My mother said, "If anyone calls you Jap, don't pay any attention. Just walk away. *Gambare.*" Bear the pain.

My father said, "If anyone calls you Jap, come and tell me. I will teach him a lesson." Papa hated the word.

"Hey, kid, where you going? Don't you wanna play?" He was a fat redheaded boy with large freckles.

I walked away. He didn't call me anymore.

"Hey, George, wanna come over to my house? My father just got me a pool table."

It was Sonny Selleck. He lived two blocks from the cleaners. It was an all-white neighborhood except for us. Sonny wore a heavy metal brace that fastened above his right knee. When he walked, his right leg swung stiffly from his hip. Whenever kids made fun of him in school, he would try to clip them hard with his leg brace. His father said that Sonny had infantile paralysis when he was three years old. Sonny and I played a lot together. I always ended up at his house. Sometimes his father would invite me to dinner. Sonny had no mother.

Mama would say, "No, no, no, maybe next time. Tell your friend's father thank you, okay?"

I couldn't invite Sonny or any of my *hakujin* (white) friends into our makeshift quarters. Papa would say, "Play outside. I don't want you and your friends inside."

"Why?"

"*Ammari mucha kucha.*" Too messy. "Play outside."

When the war began, we were herded into prisoner of war camps. Wearing helmets, soldiers stood by with rifles as Papa and Mama sold or gave away most of our possessions.

They sold my bike.

We boarded a Greyhound bus that took us to the racetrack, except there weren't any horses at the track when we got there, just a lot of tar paper buildings.

The newspapers and the radio said it was for our own good. The army was afraid that we were going to blow up California with bombs and hand grenades. Even the FBI came to our cleaners.

Two men stuck around for about a week. They thought we were Japanese spies. When one of them asked Mama if we had any dangerous weapons in the house, she took him into the kitchen, opened a drawer, pulled out a carving knife, and pointed the blade toward him.

"Hey, be careful with that," he said, backing away.

"You ask me, so I show you." She smiled, put the knife back in the drawer, and closed it. Mama was not afraid of the FBI.

Toward the end of the war we were in a camp in Arkansas. They let us out, but we couldn't return to California right away because Californians were still afraid, so we went to Denver instead. I was fifteen. I didn't have any *hakujin* friends, only Japanese. *Hakujins* still called me Jap or Chink. It was harder to walk away.

I often reflected upon my childhood, on my nationality, on our difficult life. Why had it been so painful? It wasn't only the overt hostility; there was a deeper problem. As a child, I went to the movies with Papa, and we listened to the radio at home and in the car. The villains and dolts were often men and women of color. I didn't consider the message; ironically, I derived vicarious pleasure in pretending to be John Wayne, Errol Flynn, Stewart Granger. ... I had been lulled by the spell.

When I went to Japan as an American soldier and met my relatives for the first time, I felt at home. Even though I spoke their language poorly, I felt comfortable talking to them. I enjoyed walking through the department stores and down the streets, seeing around me Japanese people who had dark hair and facial features similar to mine. It was wonderful to be Japanese. I was the ugly duckling who discovered swans.

After a while, the novelty wore off. I yearned to be home in America with my family and friends.

Upon my return from overseas, the people of America were beginning to appreciate the beauty and culture of Japan. Tensions were easing. Papa and Mama were back in the dry cleaning business and doing well. They bought a house, but in my name, because aliens ineligible for citizenship were still unable to take title to property in California.

Soon after the passage of the McCarran-Walter Act in 1952, Papa and Mama took their tests and became naturalized U.S. citizens. The new law permitted me to transfer title to them. It was their first house in America. I felt proud. It took nearly fifty years, but they had made it.

It was Papa and Mama who taught me, by example, the value of *gaman* (perseverance), *shikkari* (resoluteness), and *omoiyari* (compassion). I began to understand that my uniqueness was my heritage, my redemption. I had secretly scorned it as a child because it brought me pain, but it also gave me *chikara* (strength) and *nagasume* (comfort) in times of adversity.

The wounds were healing, the pain subsiding. I began to feel like a whole person. Not Japanese, not American. Japanese American.

HAVE YOU FORGIVEN ME, SOOK?

Bill Pearson

Forty-eight years since you disappeared. I know how old you are because you were seventeen then, same as I was. Remember? We were born one day apart in the same hospital, and when we were five we sat together in kindergarten at the Sespe Avenue School. That's when we started calling you Sook, which was easier than Masayuki. You wore a blue-and-red plaid sweater and a shy grin in the class picture. It's in my album. Would you believe that was in 1930? Then we went all the way up to being proud and mighty seniors at Fillmore High, with all the attendant privileges, like initiating the lowly freshmen and wearing our new class rings.

Remember the special assembly to announce the bombing of Pearl Harbor and that our country was at war with Japan, Germany, Italy, and the other Axis countries? And soon after that, very soon, you said an angry and bewildered goodbye. They wouldn't even let you stay for graduation. It was like you had done something horrible, committed some unspeakable crime, and were condemned to a mysterious punishment in a secret, far-off place. It was confusing and unreal.

On your last day at school I asked, "Sook, how do you feel about leaving?" A stupid question.

You answered in a soft voice, bitter and mature. "How do you think I feel? How the hell would you feel if you had to go?"

I didn't know. It was impossible to imagine that happening to me. And your voice was so different, none of the usual laughing tones. You sounded old and disgusted. You looked different too, lifeless and sad.

And then you were gone, along with your family. And Ben Hamamoto, number two on the tennis team. And Yosh and Inadomi were gone, along with their parents.

I was sad about all those who had to leave, but most of all I missed you, Sook. I missed you in class, where we sat in the back row by the window and got away with whispering and passing notes; and at lunch on the grass in front of the school in the shade of the redwood tree, where most of the pretty girls were; and on the basketball court, where you were so quick and everybody wanted you on their team.

We talked a lot about you, but we did nothing to help you. We wrote no letters of protest to our congressmen, much less to President Franklin D. Roosevelt, who stripped you of all your rights with a stroke of his gold pen on Executive Order 9066. We didn't even complain to Mr. Hawley, the high school principal. We were so naive and inexperienced. Wonderful excuses. We wrote no letters to you, didn't have your address. Didn't try to get it.

We soon forgot about you, Sook. Too many things going on: finals, senior prom, graduation, college, gas rationing, dimouts, war news on the radio and in the papers all the time, someone enlisting, someone drafted, someone home on leave, someone getting married, someone having to get married (in Fillmore everybody knew), someone going overseas, someone dying.

Years went by and I never said your name. I never thought of you behind the barbed wire, or your mother and father behind the barbed wire, or your little brother and sister behind the barbed wire. I never thought of your family losing their home, losing their store, losing their identity, losing their freedom, losing their native-born constitutional rights when our frightened, hysterical, beloved president signed that executive order with his gold pen.

Did you wonder why American-born Germans and Italians didn't have to go into custody? Or why even foreign-born immigrants from Germany and Italy didn't have to go to internment camps? We were at war with their countries too, weren't we? Why just Japanese-Americans? Even if they were born here? Even if their fathers and mothers were born here? Even if their grandparents were born here? How could this have happened in America? Where was the fairness? Where in the name of our Constitution was the legality of it? Where in the name of the Supreme Court was the justice of it?

Our president, the commander in chief of our armed forces, destroyed you, Sook, to get even with the Japanese for the attack on Pearl Harbor. You also took the blame for our admirals and Joint Chiefs of Staff, who with their smug World War I mentality put most of their battleships and navy in one basket and neglected to watch the basket.

Thirty-four years later President Gerald Ford admitted in a proclamation that our country had wronged you. And then, eleven years after that, Congress passed a bill to pay you for the wrong. A wrong that can never be redressed. A magical moment stolen from your youth, Sook, that can never be restored. And dignity and self-esteem that can't be returned, even with a government check in five figures.

But I hope you got your check, Sook. So many didn't. They couldn't wait forty-five years. But you're one of the young ones, Sook. You're only sixty-six. I know because your birthday is one day after mine.

Have you ever been back to Fillmore? Have you ever forgiven our country? Have you ever forgiven your classmates? Have you forgiven me, Sook?

THE SOLDIER LAVINE

Dorothy W. Lavine

When the Persian Gulf War broke out, it brought back sharp memories of World War II. My husband, Sergeant Sanford S. Lavine, was killed in action on November 3, 1944, while serving with the 104th Infantry Division ("Timberwolves") in Holland. While his division was in Belgium a few weeks earlier, he had written me—on toilet tissue—of an experience he had after meeting a stranger in a book shop. This gentleman invited Sandy home with him to meet his family and have supper and spend the night, in a bed instead of on the ground. They lived in Mechelen, and Sandy wrote me about the family, and particularly about their pretty little daughter. He visited again, before he was sent to Holland and the terrible battle on the dikes, and brought them food rations from him and his buddies. They became friends.

Many years later, in 1960, the War Department permitted me to visit Sandy's grave at the Henri Chappelle Cemetery in Liège, Belgium, where there are thousands of crosses and Stars of David marking the graves. It was cold and rainy. On the train from the cemetery back to Brussels, a gentleman sitting opposite me asked in excellent English if he could help me in any way. I was soaking wet and muddy, and he knew I had been to the cemetery. I asked him how far it was from Brussels to Mechelen and told him briefly the story of my husband's meeting the family in Mechelen. He immediately offered to drive me there, whereupon he produced all sorts of personal identification, photos of his family, and business credentials. He needed only to telephone his wife in Brussels. It seemed such folly, and an imposition on a stranger, but he said, "The American soldiers gave their lives for us. It is a privilege to meet you and assist you."

We had nothing to go on except a name and address from 1944, but luck was with us. We located the house, and my friend (by now) conversed in Flemish with a young man in his twenties who answered the door. At first he did not understand who we were, but then he shouted, "Of course, the soldier Lavine!" The young man was the husband of the girl Sandy had written me about in 1944. He told us that his in-laws were living about a mile away and he would take us there immediately—he was so excited he forgot to put on his shoes!

When we reached their home and explained who I was and how I came to them, there was disbelief on all sides that our meeting had come about after so many years. They welcomed us warmly and happily, and there was much talking at once, and many tears. My benefactor had to get home, but Sandy's friends (now mine) insisted that he leave me with them for the evening. They would drive me back to the hotel in Brussels in time for my departure. I gave my train companion heartfelt thanks, and we exchanged addresses. Some years later, his daughter visited me in the United States.

Feelings came pouring out between the family and me, in a mixture of languages and gestures. They showed me the sofa bed where Sandy had spent the night; they told me of his kindness to them; and when they said goodbye to him, it was for the last time. They learned much later, from one of his friends, that he had been killed in action. When the war was over and the military cemetery completed, they visited there and put flowers on his grave.

For the first time in my life, I realized what strong and lasting bonds could exist between strangers—and between *countries.* Somehow I grew a little, and my outlook was broadened: the pain was made more bearable, and the sacrifice of so many lives was placed more sharply in perspective. Inwardly I vowed to try, for the remainder of my life, to become worthy of the gift of freedom bestowed upon me.

And I am still in touch with my friends in Mechelen.

THE ROAD TAKEN

Nancy Houghtaling

War seems to accelerate the process of living. Normal events such as marriages, graduations, even funerals—occasions that call for a certain stateliness—are rushed, and looking back, you see those special days played in fast-forward.

The year was 1941. To young women in those early days of World War II, marriage seemed the most vital move, and I was no exception. I was working in the dean's office at college (for twenty-five cents an hour!) when a former graduate, now an Army Air Corps serviceman, came back to visit his alma mater. We met, we talked, we laughed. A week later we went out for dinner and dancing. Three months later we were engaged. He was sent to Italy, where he flew with the Fifteenth Air Force. He came home safely, and we were married. End of story.

Not quite. Three little girls (with another en route) and five years later, he was sent to the forgotten war, to Korea. He did not complain. He was a career officer and felt he should be involved in the war. The girls and I settled in Washington. My sister lived in the next apartment building, and she helped me maintain my strength and courage.

Soon the children were two months, two years, three, and four. They had a great time in our Chevrolet station wagon, which I learned to drive over ice in the winter and potholes in the summer. Once a week we went grocery shopping at Fort Myer, one of the oldest army posts in the country. It also stands guard over Arlington National Cemetery. As we left, we would pass the parade ground, a beautiful field of green used for the daily trooping of the colors. Young men in their dress uniforms would pour from the barracks and stand at ready. The review stand would fill, the flags would unfurl, the band would strike up a Sousa march, and the parade would begin.

The girls and I always got there at the best possible moment. Rushing, I would grab the baby, give the two-year-old's hand to the four-year-old, and clamp the three-year-old's hand to my skirt, and we would stand there in brilliant sunshine as the colors passed. Precision and grace personified the parade. We would wait until the last note faded and return to the car in high spirits. It was almost too good to be true.

In the world of reality, however, the wife of any air force man expects someday to receive the three-officer visit bringing grim news that strikes the heart hammer blows. So I waited. I held my breath. I hoped. I prayed. And he came back in two years—older, quieter, taking silent joy in the four girls.

Now it was time to get on with the happiness of life. We rented a small saltbox in a neighborhood of similar homes, we enrolled our oldest in the first grade, and we bought a gym set for the girls to enjoy in the fine backyard. I finally stopped worrying about the messengers of death.

Strangely, death came unannounced and struck the brave warrior without warning. A cold became polio, and four days later he whispered to me, "I'll love you forever," then, "The aircraft is coming down around me." Closing his soft brown eyes, he died. He was buried in Arlington National Cemetery with other heroes.

Months passed. I started traveling all over the United States looking for a friendly small town in which to rear the girls. At a friend's suggestion, I visited the Gulf Beaches and found a pretty little house just one block from the Gulf of Mexico. The girls and I spent many magic hours on the sandy shores and in the blue water. I enrolled the oldest girls in the Catholic school on the beach, and the principal offered me a job teaching. Would I like that? I tried to to look into the future. We were not comfortably fixed—in fact, we were limping along—so I said yes and began a career that lasted thirty years and took me to sunny Virginia, snowy Germany, sweet Georgia.

Eight years after the death of the young air force major, I remarried, but I never forgot the dear one with the deep brown eyes. Last summer I returned to Fort Myer to visit him in Arlington. I was leaving with my sister and brother-in-law when I noticed barracks doors suddenly opening and young soldiers falling into formation. "Wait!" I said. "There's going to be a parade."

We stood and watched as the review stand filled. As if by magic, each soldier took the appointed place promptly. The chords of "Under the Double Eagle" sounded, the bandmaster blew his whistle and stepped off, and the parade began.

Standing there, I could almost see a little girl with long brown curls holding the hand of a littler one with cornflower hair. I could feel a slight tug on my skirt as I adjusted a baby determined to slide through my arms.

I blinked my eyes quickly in the golden autumn sunshine and turned toward the car. Somehow I felt the circle had been closed. In my mind the band will ever be playing, the graceful young men and women will ever be marching, and the flags will be snapping crisply in the fall air.

Reaching deeper, deeper into the recesses of memory, I see a youthful man with brown eyes smiling at me as he says, "Is the dean in?"

A COMING OF AGE

Linda M. Hardin

I was a GI war bride, one of almost a million European women who married American soldiers who fought in World War II. I crossed the ocean on one of the many small troop carriers that were detailed to transport us from Europe to New York.

The U.S.S. *George Goethals* left Le Havre on March 5, 1946, with 452 brides. We should have been 454, but two brides got cold feet at boarding time and went home. By the time we reached New York, we were 454 again; two babies had been born at sea during a raging storm. One was named George. I cannot recall if the other was Georgette.

Why would two young women suddenly turn their backs on a chance to join the men they loved and had promised to follow? Perhaps it had something to do with the five days before we boarded, which we spent at Camp Philip Morris, one of many army bases that had been used to house thousands of Allied soldiers after they landed in France. In Le Havre these camps were named after American cigarette brands. Each prefab barracks inside these wire-walled compounds was furnished with twenty-four army cots and a wood stove. The Ritz it was not. Outside, the grounds were a mixture of runny mud and brown snow that did not have time to melt before the next flurry.

Throughout our stay, our lives were regulated by blaring loudspeakers ordering us to form lines outside various buildings. We waited, often under falling snow, for document checks, food, physicals, questionnaires. We took the food and the questionnaires back to our quarters and lined up again to bring the filled-out documents back. These lines were the longest because the people who read our answers had questions to ask and sometimes made us change an answer. I have a vivid memory of being told to change the word "*feminin*" next to my gender and replace it with the word "female." Female! In my country we only used "female" to describe animals. Human beings were either "*masculin*" or "*feminin.*" That was my first cultural shock.

We never saw the women who had babies. They were housed in the officers' quarters with the army nurses. We were happy for them, but we would have welcomed a chance to hear their bedtime stories instead of ours, which were not the type to prepare us for dreams of fairyland.

First there were the rumors that tend to circulate like wildfire when people are isolated from the outside world and cut off from the only security they have known. We also exchanged articles we had saved from our hometown newspapers, by columnists poking fun at us for having chosen American husbands instead of nice French boys. A couple of examples are still vivid in my memory. "So long, slaves! Remember that American men have three loves: their mothers, their dogs, and their wives—in that order. If you don't get along with the first two, you're out of luck." Then there was the story of the ship that had left Southampton two months before, carrying English war brides. "It never reached New York because the American women who had lost their men to their English sisters got together and paid the Mafia to sink that modern *Mayflower* in the Atlantic."

Five days of camp life, five evenings of such stories, five nights of taking turns to put wood in the stove and remembering the horror stories our parents had told us to try to stop our marriages all took their toll. When we lined up for a free three-minute phone call to say a last goodbye to our families before boarding, there were few dry eyes in the crowd. As each woman took the receiver, the whole range of complaints came forth. The frustrations, the fears, the loneliness, and the emotion at hearing the voices of loved ones at the other end of the wire brought on the sobs down the line of waiting women. Then the tears stopped and we were silent as we listened to the woman who now had the phone.

"Yes, Mama, everything is wonderful! Yes, we are served fabulous foods, and on white tablecloths. We spend our days in the recreation room playing fascinating games. Everyone treats us as if we were princesses. Please don't cry—as soon as I get to America,

I'll start planning my visit home. Yes, yes. I'll write every day. Don't worry about me, I am on my way to paradise. Au revoir!" When she hung up, she passed the phone to me and walked away, head high and shoulders straight. We had witnessed how to face the responsibilities of our new lives.

Looking back on the past forty-five years, I don't have a doubt as to when or where I became an adult human being. It was on March 5, 1946, at Camp Philip Morris, somewhere near Le Havre, a port city in northern France.

When we arrived in New York twelve days later, we were not pelted with overripe tomatoes or rotten eggs. While our little ship was being towed into the harbor, dozens of sailing and fishing vessels of all sizes and descriptions surrounded us and escorted us into port with their whistles on full blast in welcome salutes. As we pulled into the dock, a band in colorful uniforms played "La Marseillaise," then "The Star-spangled Banner." Down below, hundreds of white handkerchiefs were fluttering in the wind. As we walked down the plank, the crowd that was waving those handkerchiefs began to applaud and shout, "Bienvenue! Welcome!" The husbands, the new families, the new friends, and entire neighborhoods, it seemed, were there to greet us.

About a dozen buses were waiting for the brides who had to get to the railroad station. I was among them since I was going to Miami. As we crossed New York City, there were more bands in the streets. Thousands of people were marching, singing, dancing, shouting, laughing, and waving at us. It was a wild crowd giving us a rousing reception. We really felt like princesses being welcomed to their paradise. Even the sun greeted us!

When I arrived in Miami the next day, my husband set me straight. That wild celebration in New York had not been for us. It was the Saint Patrick's Day parade, March 17, 1946.

The Chaplain's Assistant

Sheldon Leibowitz

The flying boxcar touched down on the snowflaked runway. The nose of the C-119 opened, the soldiers walked down the metal staircase and into the cold winter of Korea. December 1952. The moonlit night was cold and damp. Green army fatigues clinging to my sweat-soaked body, I walked along with the disembarking troops. A duffel bag hung over my right shoulder; my M-1 rifle was balanced on the other. A steel helmet fit loosely on my head, exposing brown curly hair. It was a slow, cold walk toward the Quonset hut.

Suddenly, a loud explosion. Then, off in the distance, the sky lit up. Fourth of July fireworks.

"Welcome to Korea," shouted Sergeant Jackson. "It's only a fire fight. We won't see any action for a while."

I shivered, then stumbled, almost falling.

"Hey, Private, watch your step or you'll fall on your ass." Jackson laughed loudly.

The soldiers approached the entrance to the Quonset hut. Jackson bellowed, "Squad halt, face front, and stand at ease."

Four army trucks with green canvas covering waited silently near the hut.

"When your name is called, get into one of the trucks," grunted Jackson, starting down his list. My name wasn't on it.

"Sergeant, what about me?" I asked.

"Who the hell are you?"

"Leibowitz, Private Sheldon Leibowitz."

Jackson glanced at his list. "Sorry, kid, you're not here. Wait inside. Somebody will be along soon." Then he turned toward the trucks. "Move 'em out," he snapped, and hopped onto one of them. The trucks departed, leaving me alone, cold, and frightened.

I walked into the Quonset hut and immediately felt the warmth of the potbelly stove.

"Hey, close the door," came a voice from the corner. An officer was seated at a table at the far end of the room, a chessboard in front of him with the pieces arranged as though a game was already in progress.

"What's your name, Private? Where are you from? Do you play chess?" His heavily New York–accented speech was deep and melodious.

"Private Sheldon Leibowitz, Brooklyn, U.S.A., and yes, I certainly do play."

The officer emerged from his corner, a large teddy bear. Putting one of his paws on my shoulder, he firmly led me to the table and proceeded to rearrange the chess pieces.

"I'm James A. Mayo, Bronx, New York. Enough small talk. I'll play black." And he flashed a smile, exhibiting a perfect set of ivory teeth.

We played in silence, for what seemed like hours; finally the game ended in a draw.

"Private, you're good, and I need the practice. Can you type?" Before I had a chance to answer, he put on his cap. The cross of an army chaplain was shining into my eyes.

"Never mind about typing. Are you Protestant or Catholic, Leibowitz? I want you to be my new assistant."

"I think there might be a slight problem, sir. I'm Jewish," I replied.

"No problem, Leibowitz. As you can see, I'm black." Pointing to the colonel's eagle on his collar, he continued, "With my new position as commander of all chaplains in this area, you, Private Leibowitz, will be my new chaplain's assistant.

And for a period of time I was. But that's another story.

Heroes and
Friends

BEST FRIEND

Lola DeVaughn

I grew up in a small community in the rolling hills of Mississippi more than fifty years ago. My best friend was Laverne, a little girl my own age who lived near me. We spent as much time together as possible, sharing all our sorrows, joys, and secrets. Our parents made a meager living raising corn and cotton with a couple of mules and a few plows, and we each had chores to do to help them out.

Laverne and I grew up and married neighborhood boys. We lived about fifteen miles apart. With rugged dirt roads and no cars of our own, we didn't see each other often, but we kept in touch by letter and with an occasional long-distance telephone call.

When her mother died, Laverne phoned me and I went to her immediately. Her mother had to be laid out for burial, and she had asked me to do it. A dead person was not sent to an undertaker in those days, not in that part of the country. People couldn't afford it in the first place, and a woman just wasn't exposed.

Soon after arriving at Laverne's home, I was taken to a bedroom where the corpse was. A neighbor woman came in with hot water, towels, and soap. This task would be hard for me because I had known Laverne's mother all my life and loved her dearly.

We bathed and dressed her and laid her out on the bed. While we were waiting for the casket to arrive from the city, I saw her false teeth on the mantel in a cup of water. After washing them, I tried to put them in her mouth, but I simply couldn't get it open. I slipped off my shoes and got on the bed with the corpse. I pulled on her mouth as hard as I could, finally prying it open enough to get the top plate in. Now to push it into place. It just didn't go in right. I tried the bottom plate and it was the same. Her mouth looked too full and would not close. I opened it wider and pushed the teeth farther back. That helped. For more than an hour I labored to get the teeth in. I finally ended up tying a white cloth under her chin and pinning it on top of her head to keep her mouth closed. I was completely exhausted and so nervous I could hardly stand up.

Just as I finished and was about to leave the room, there was a light knock at the door. I opened it slightly, and Laverne looked up at me with a tear-stained face. She held out her hand and said, "Lola, here are Mother's teeth. I almost forgot. I've washed them." I thought I would faint, but I took the teeth and assured her that I would put them in.

I could not go through that again—I just could not. Later, when the corpse was laid in the casket, I wrapped up the teeth Laverne had given me, and when no one was around I slipped them into the casket under the body. I had kept my promise. I had put them in.

I went home after the funeral. A few days later I called Laverne to ask how they were getting along.

"Oh, we're making it fine, except for Papa. He lost his false teeth and hasn't eaten any solid food. I can't imagine where they are—we've looked all over the place. He hasn't seen them since Mama died."

Laverne was my best friend, and I had always told her all my secrets, but I could not tell her where the teeth were. To this day, she doesn't know. She's still my best friend.

Spring Burial

Sister Irene Houle

Seventy-five years ago, when I was six, we were quarantined. My father had to find another place to live while Mama stayed home to nurse the sick ones, me and my five brothers and sisters. We had the measles, I mean the killer measles.

It was a brutal winter. The fierce wind came tearing off Lake Superior and stormed into our little copper mining town, Houghton, Michigan. It screamed up the hills and swept down into the village. Its icy breath bored through the drafty walls, forcing us all closer and closer to the wood-burning stove, whose isinglass windows revealed orange and pink flames doing their best to keep us warm.

Every morning we kids stood at the window, looking across the snowdrift that almost covered the picket fence between our apple trees and Mrs. Coon's chicken yard. We strained our eyes and watched in silence.

"Here she comes, here she comes," we all shouted to our mother when Mrs. Coon's shadow loomed over the drift. Coat bundled about her, scarf flying, snowshoes flipping expertly through the driving snow, she was soon in our yard, and Mama was at the back door to let her in.

Mrs. Coon was an R.N., only she didn't work in a hospital; she just showed up where people were sick. There was never any money involved. She heard about sick people and came. She was a Seventh-Day Adventist, and we were Roman Catholics, but that didn't seem to make any difference. Mama loved Mrs. Coon. I don't know what she would have done without her. Her cheeks were pink, her eyes sparkled, and red-gold wisps of curls escaped from the firm bun she had formed at the back of her neck to make her hair mind.

Mrs. Coon would stand her snowshoes in the shed so the snow wouldn't bury them, and then she'd come in. Mama had water heating on the kitchen stove, and they would bathe us and get us into warm clothes, and Mrs. Coon would help Mama with Georgie, who was four, and very, very sick.

Mama said, "I think she is going to die, it's so hard for her to breathe," and Mrs. Coon would hold Mama's hand and say, "Yes."

One morning Georgie was still and white. Mama was crying. Everyone was very quiet. Mrs. Coon came with a beautiful white dress that was her little girl's. It went way down past Georgie's feet. Georgie just lay there and didn't seem to notice her beautiful dress. They tied a lovely blue satin ribbon on her flaxen hair and lifted her into a box all quilted with silk and lace, and there were tall candles whose flames danced.

"No one will come," Daddy said. "They can't make it in this blizzard." The wind whirled around the big old house, and the snow piled higher. The house sighed as it stood up to the mean, cold wind.

The next day Mr. Krall came with his black rig, his horses blowing great puffballs of frosty vapor into the freezing air. We watched at the window as he trundled in. Georgie lay there on her silken bed, her pale gold hair and blue ribbon gleaming in the candlelight. I had never known her to be so quiet for such a long time.

"Come and say goodbye to your little sister," Mama said. Each one of us went up and said very solemnly, "Goodbye, Georgie," and touched her brow or her hand—so cold. Georgie didn't say a thing.

Mama was crying. Daddy just stood there, his arm around Mama. Mrs. Coon was helping with the coats, blowing out the candles, putting the cover over Georgie. We watched from the window as Mama and Daddy went out and got into the rig. Then Mr. Krall handed in the little box that had Georgie in it, and Mama and Daddy held her on their laps. Mr. Krall got into the driver's seat and flicked the whip, and the little black horses started down the white road, their bells jingling. The brilliant sunlight blinded our eyes as the horses disappeared in its sparkling radiance.

"Georgie is with God," Mrs. Coon said.

BROTHER'S KEEPER

Celia Ashton

Before taking my worn kid gloves and purse from the hall table, I went to my husband's desk and picked up two long white business envelopes. I put them in my purse and left the house. Glancing at my watch, I noted that I had time to make the daily mass at Saint Agnes.

I smiled as I backed out of the driveway. My year of prayers had been answered. Given a chance, Joe was going to make a comeback. I was sure of that when I kissed him goodbye and put him on the seven o'clock plane for Chicago last night for his first job in over a year. My throat constricted when I thought of how willingly Joe, Jr., had given his father his week's pay from his after-school job at the local variety store. Kathy and Lorraine had contributed their baby-sitting money. The younger boys, not wanting to be outdone, managed to scrape up a lawn to mow yesterday afternoon and proudly gave him three dollars. Touched by their gesture, Joe tried to thank them. Jim blushed and said, "It's nothing. You're a good dad." "The best," Thomas added.

Noon saw me entering the Mid-State Savings and Loan. It took a lot to come here. Joe probably wouldn't have approved, but I felt that one last effort should be made. George Wheatly, the bank's president, was a personal friend of Joe's.

I approached the receptionist, Peggy Sheehan, and asked for Mr. Wheatly. My, wasn't I formal. Peggy was an old classmate of mine. She went to the inner office. Returning to her desk, she announced professionally, "He'll see you in a few minutes, Mrs. Ashton."

I waited.

A buzzer sounded.

"Ah, Celia, come in." Mr. Wheatly rose from behind his mahogany desk and indicated the chair across from him.

I sank into the soft leather cushions, well below his eye level. How uncomfortable, I thought, placing my gloves on the desk and opening my purse. I took out one of the white envelopes and moistened my lips.

"I'm here to ask a favor, Mr. Wheatly. We both know the situation." I waved the envelope. "Joe's been unemployed this past year, but he's employed now." I hesitated, then added, "Soon we'll be able to make up our back payments. All we need is a little time." There, I had done it. Humiliated myself before George Wheatly, an elder of the Northern Baptist Church.

Our eyes locked for a moment. Then he lowered his. During the lengthy pause the only sound in the president's office was the ticking of the grandfather clock against the wall.

Straightening himself in his high-backed chair, he said, "Can't be done, Mrs. Ashton." His voice was businesslike. "Public notices are already out. The auction will take place tomorrow—unless you can come up with the face value of the mortgage by then."

Defeated, I rose and prepared to leave.

"I wish Joe the best with his new job," he said, smiling as he held the walnut-paneled door open for me.

I made no reply. There were hot tears behind my eyes as I walked through the bank, head high. Peggy Sheehan busied herself with her files as I passed.

Outside I paused and extracted the other white envelope, checking the address in the upper left-hand corner: 835 Main, Room 304. As I climbed the dark staircase to the third floor, I felt anger mount with every step. I had been brought to the point of asking a favor of Jacob Miller, a Jewish attorney. Jews. Money changers demanding their pound of flesh. But for Joe I would face any humiliation. After George Wheatly, this should be easy.

I entered quietly. There was no receptionist, and the door to the inner office was ajar. Miller was at his desk, phone in hand. He waved, indicating he'd be with me shortly. I surveyed the sparsely furnished office. Bookcases filled with law books lined the walls. A recent diploma from Harvard Law School hung conspicuously over an end table.

Miller came out, his hand extended in greeting. "Good afternoon. I don't believe I know you."

I rose. "I'm Celia Ashton, Joe Ashton's wife."

"Mrs. Ashton, I'm glad to meet you." His hand felt warm, young and strong. "Come in. What can I do for you?" He moved a chair closer to his desk.

"I'm here because of your recent letter to us." Attorney Miller represented Morris Brothers, a business supplier to whom Joe owed forty-five hundred dollars. I put my gloves on his desk and took the letter from my purse. "We'd rather not take bankruptcy, Mr. Miller, if we can avoid it. If we can make arrangements for monthly payments on the Morris account, in time we would get the balance paid off. I know it's a lot to ask, but that's the best we can do." I fumbled nervously with the strap on my purse. I hardly heard his next question.

"Your husband is working now?"

"Yes. He started this week. He's out of town, otherwise he'd be here." Why did I say that? Joe would never have come *here* asking for favors.

"I understand your home is being foreclosed."

"Yes. It's too late to do anything about that. And I fail to see how it has anything to do with this." Annoyed, I tapped the white envelope in my hand.

Attorney Miller sat silent, observing. Then, taking the phone from its cradle, he dialed a number. I shifted nervously in my chair. I wanted to run out of the room.

"Sam, Jacob here. I'm sending a Mrs. Ashton down to you. See what you can do for her. Right away." He hung up. "Now, Mrs. Ashton, bankruptcy isn't what you want, I can see that. My client and I will work out a payment plan, something you and your husband can handle."

"Thank you." My voice caught.

"I want you to go downstairs to Room 201 and see my uncle, Sam Levi." I rose and reached for my gloves, but Attorney Miller picked them up. Examining their worn fingertips, he said, "Mrs. Ashton, you should never wear gloves like these, no matter what your circumstances may be. Look prosperous even if you're not. Then no one takes advantage of you." He threw the gloves into the wastebasket, smiling to ease my shock. "Buy yourself a new pair. Now you'll see Sam, and I'll take care of the Morris matter."

See Sam. I might as well. Every other avenue had been explored. Even Joe's brother had refused to help. I squared my shoulders and entered Room 201.

Before leaving for my secretarial job the next morning, I securely locked the house. As long as it was ours, privacy would be maintained. The auction could take place in the yard. Attorney Miller had a point, I thought as I drew on my new imitation kid gloves. I did feel better.

The morning dragged. At noon Sam Levi, a short man in his mid-fifties with bushy hair and eyebrows, came in to take me to lunch. He seated himself opposite me at a secluded table in the rear of the restaurant and took a packet of legal papers from the inner pocket of his loosely fitting jacket.

"I had a little difficulty with Mr. Wheatly, and also with an obstinate bidder against me. A woman, a Mrs. Sheehan. But I took her aside and told her I was buying your property so she'd damn well better go home."

I shivered. Peggy Sheehan, Wheatly's secretary. The straw buyer for the Mid-State Savings and Loan.

"Mrs. Ashton, when you and your husband are in a position to refinance your home, I'll sell it back to you."

I started to speak. Sam Levi waved me silent.

"Whenever you're ready. Take your time. Interest rate the same as before, five percent."

How could this be? My image of Shylock shattered. Through my tears, I saw Sam Levi smiling.

"This has nothing to do with business, Mrs. Ashton. A Jew is called upon sometimes to be his brother's keeper."

Brother's keeper. The tears flowed. Sam Levi reached over and patted my hand.

"Thank you," I whispered.

Sam Levi's shoulders shrugged under his baggy jacket. Picking up the menu, he said, "Now, how about some lunch?"

DON'T STOP—PLEASE
DON'T STOP

Lee Hames

On the hot, bright sands of a Lake Michigan public beach in Milwaukee, a lifeguard was straddling the unconscious body of a man he had just pulled out of the rough water. The lifeguard was Jerry Hanson, a friend who worked at the same office I did. Now he was strenuously thumping on the man's chest while Joe, another guard, gave mouth-to-mouth resuscitation. The man wasn't responding.

"It's no use," said Joe. "The poor guy is gone. There's no pulse or breath."

Jerry had to admit that things looked hopeless, but for some reason he couldn't explain even to himself, he insisted they continue. But he did suggest that exchanging places might seem like a rest for both of them. Now, although they were exhausted, when one suggested stopping, the other urged they continue.

After what seemed like hours, they were at the point of passing out in the burning sunshine when Joe suddenly whispered excitedly, "I've got a faint pulse." As Jerry reached for the man's wrist to check, he heard an ambulance screech to a stop on the beach road near them, and two attendants rushed over to relieve them. The man was soon out of danger and on his way to the hospital. Jerry and Joe calmly shook hands.

Two weeks later, the man they had saved came into our office to thank Jerry. He said his name was Kramer and offered Jerry a large reward. Jerry said he couldn't accept it because he was only doing his job.

"No, you went far beyond it," said Kramer. "The first time you exchanged places, you would have been justified in stopping."

"Who told you that?" Jerry asked.

"I heard what you were saying."

"You what?" Both Jerry and I were stunned by Kramer's words.

"Yes," Kramer continued, "I could hear everything, but I was powerless to communicate in any way. I just prayed you wouldn't stop."

After Kramer left, I wondered whether what he had told us was possible. A doctor friend doubted it. He thought Kramer had heard the details of the rescue after the event and merely thought he heard Jerry and Joe at the time. Whatever happened, nothing lessens what the lifeguards did.

Stories of struggles against seemingly hopeless odds are not uncommon. What child has not learned about Columbus, who urged his almost mutinous crew to "sail on, and on, and on." And I always loved the story of Bruce, an ancient king of Scotland, who was imprisoned in a dungeon and was inspired to escape, and eventually defeat his enemies, as he watched the tremendous efforts of a spider that finally attached its web to a distant beam after failing for days.

But none of these stories moved me as much as the effort of Jerry and Joe, who *just refused to give up*. Ask Kramer.

A Triumph of the Heart

Bessie Aspan

His name was William Thomas Shropshire. When he grew up, he would be known to his friends and acquaintances as Willie. To his family, and only his family, he was Bud.

Bud was my uncle, my mother's younger brother. Their father had died when Bud was quite young, and he and my mother grew up in the home of their maternal grandfather, along with two young cousins whose mother had died. They were all in the same age range, and they loved, laughed, and played together throughout their childhood years. My grandmother helped in the fields to pay their way. She also served as the lady of the house for her father and the four young orphans.

Bud must have been around six years old the day he fell from the high porch where he was playing happily with his sister and cousins. He didn't appear to be badly hurt, but by the next day he had developed a very high fever, and the doctor was called immediately. There were no hospitals to rush him to, since they lived miles out in the country. The doctor came every day for the many days it took to bring his temperature down to normal. But then Bud couldn't walk! The infantile paralysis, or polio, as it is known today, had taken its devastating toll, rendering his legs practically useless. They never developed to normal size.

Bud was never able to do any heavy work on the farm, but that didn't deter him from developing a ready smile and a sunny disposition. And the things he could do, he did well. He would cut a long pole, put a line and hook with a worm on one end, and crawl down to the creek, never failing to catch a mess of fish for dinner. He whittled, and made the best slingshot in the entire county. He cut saplings in the woods and wove beautiful baskets of willow and oak strips. I especially remember seeing my grandmother use the sewing basket he made her.

I must have been around four when Bud left home to enter a hospital in Memphis, Tennessee. There he was given extensive therapy on his legs, put in braces, and trained in the art of shoe repairing. He was gone for at least ten months, perhaps longer. Once when Grandma and Mamma were writing him, I added a note, with a much larger hand on top of mine guiding it, I'm sure. It was probably the first letter I ever wrote. When he wrote Grandma again, he turned her letter over and wrote to me on the back. I was thrilled half to death.

One day Grandma and I had been over across the creek in the pasture. When we came home, she stopped by the mailbox and wondered aloud whose buggy had left the road and gone all the way through our front yard up to the porch. Mamma was standing in the doorway, and when Grandma asked who made the tracks, she only smiled. All of a sudden it hit Grandma! She went tearing down the long, wide hall crying, "Oh, my boy's home! My boy's home!" The mail she was carrying went flying all down the hall.

Bud was sitting at the kitchen table with a smile on his face and a cup of coffee in his hand when Grandma grabbed him in her arms. It was a joyous day for everyone, and for Grandma, I expect, most of all. Our mail carrier, Mr. Audrey Stuart, had picked Bud up at the depot in Gloster and brought him the fifteen miles to our home.

Bud had been fitted with heavy metal braces reaching just below his knees, and the crutches the hospital had provided enabled him to walk slowly, one single small step, then another. However, as summer and very hot weather arrived, Bud could barely endure the braces with their heavy padding, so he took them off. There was no air conditioning in those days, and since we didn't have electricity, he couldn't even have a floor fan. Grandma always felt that if he had worn them, he might have been able to walk some. Outside, Bud used his crutches and threw both feet ahead of him to get along; in the house he sat upright on the floor and crawled. He never let his handicap stop him.

Soon after Bud came home, he and Grandma moved to Gloster and rented a tiny house. I believe it was the state that set Bud up in his shoe repair business. Grandma's first cousins, Tiny and Douglas McNeely, owned a small café and meat market with a room in back where Bud had his first shop, a very meager beginning, though he soon had enough business to meet his and Grandma's expenses. He hobbled clear across town to and from work, and Grandma carried him a hot lunch at noon each day when the sawmill whistle blew. Whenever I stayed with them, it was a treat for me to go along.

After a while Bud was able to move his shop to a much better location. His business grew and prospered, and Grandma managed his money well. He paid the state back for its investment in his shop and bought a large two-story house for Grandma and himself, across the railroad tracks from downtown. They loved it, and Grandma had beautiful flowers and a large vegetable garden. After he paid off his home, he bought his first car, which had special hand brakes. Bud became a proficient driver, going wherever he wished.

When my older sister finished high school, Bud sent her through business college in Chillicothe, Missouri. A couple of years later, he paid for a secretarial correspondence course for me and bought me a typewriter. I stayed with Bud during my last year of high school and on until Grandma died, a year after my father died. Then Bud and I moved out to the country with Mamma and my two younger sisters.

After I got married and moved away, Mamma and Bud had a large home built in town. By then his shop had been located on a good corner spot for many years, right in the heart of Main Street. His friendly face was a familiar sight to one and all.

I cannot begin to imagine what my life would have been without Bud. I went home to be with him just before he died of heart failure at age sixty, and for years afterward, whenever I went back, I halfway expected to see Bud sitting there in his shop, smiling. He was kind, gentle, unpretentious, understanding, generous to a fault, and always a strong anchor of support. He loved life, and lived it to the fullest. And how good it was that Grandma was able to see and share in his success.

Certainly God poured out His blessings on him, and Bud shared those blessings with his loved ones, his friends and acquaintances, as well as the town of Gloster. Truly his life was a triumph of the heart.

DUKE

Rosina Hemshorn

When we bought our farm, my husband knew we needed a good cattle dog. We had over a hundred acres, half of them woods and brush, and sometimes it took hours to get the herd home so the milk cows could be milked.

A friend of ours had a good female dog that was expecting pups, and he promised us one. Three months later he brought us Duke. When the puppy was about six months old, my husband started to train him.

One day my husband had a job that would keep him out after dark. It looked like rain, and I thought how nice if I could get the cows home so he wouldn't have to go looking for them with a lantern. There was one cow that just had a calf, and I knew she might head for the woods, as cows will do. My husband would have a hard job finding them later, because a cow can sure hide herself and her calf. And since a calf usually sucks from only one or two teats, the cow might have her udder ruined if I didn't get her home and milked out.

I took my two-year-old girl along, plus an umbrella and Duke, who still didn't seem too savvy about what to do. We found the herd, including the cow and calf, and headed home.

I was doing fine until it started to rain. Going around a bend, the calf slipped on the wet path and let out a screaming beller. The mother cow of course thought I was hurting her calf, so she turned on me with her horns lowered. I threw my little girl over the fence and started to jump after her, but there was the cow, only inches away. Duke ran up and nipped her on the heels, and she turned to see what was happening, which gave me my chance to clear the fence. I was so shook up that I snatched my daughter and made for home, not caring if I ever saw a cow again.

When I looked for Duke, I saw him rounding up the cows. He had them home before I reached the gate to close it behind them. From that day on Duke was king. He was so proud of himself when he realized that those cows were afraid of him and he was the boss. In a few weeks he was on his own. He would be lying down watching the sun, and at five o'clock he would run and get the herd home.

About a year after we lost Duke, my husband sold a steer to a neighbor. I could hear them trying to load the steer for over an hour, but he wouldn't go up the chute into the trailer. I went to see if I could help. They said they had tried everything, like twisting his tail with a stick and prodding him. I hollered, "Here, Duke," and you should have seen that steer move. In one second he was in the trailer.

What a dog! Duke was the only good cattle dog we ever had, and I still think of him as my lifesaver.

SEÑOR SANTA CLAUS

Red Stevenson

Many years ago, I owned a large diesel truck and trailer and made weekly trips between Oklahoma and California. Fatigue and loneliness were my constant companions.

Sometimes I had to pull over on the shoulder because tears blurred my vision as I thought about my wife and three small children waiting at home. The two nights and one day a week I got to spend with them were my reward for a hundred-and-thirty-hour work week. More than once, I came out of a truck stop so tired I couldn't remember whether I was on my way to California or on my way back to Oklahoma. I'd open the doors of my trailer, and if I had a load of produce, I knew I had already been to California. If I had chickens, I knew I was still headed west.

One Christmas Eve, I was running late getting home. Because I was paid by the number of cases I hauled, I'd loaded an extra hundred cases of oranges. They made me overweight, but I was sure all the weight stations would be closed on this special night.

I was almost right. All but one on the Arizona–New Mexico border. I parked to one side, shut my truck off, and walked over to the small building that housed the attendant.

It was a night like it might have been in Bethlehem when Joseph asked the innkeeper for a room. There was not a breath of wind, and large snowflakes filled the darkness, falling so slowly they seemed suspended in midair, gently caressing me as I approached the building.

There was a lone Mexican-American on duty. "Señor," he said, "why didn't you park on my scales?"

"There's no use in me lying to you, amigo. I'm overloaded."

Something about the way he asked the next question told me that it did not please him to think about giving me a ticket this particular night. I felt we were kindred spirits, both having to work on the holiest night of the year.

He pursed his lips. "How much you think you're overloaded, señor?"

There was a radio turned low. A high female soprano voice was singing in Spanish, and though I spoke no Spanish, I recognized the words. "Peace on earth, goodwill to men."

I thought for a minute and replied, "One case of oranges, amigo."

The corners of his mouth crept upward, and suppressed laughter showed in his eyes. Finally he said, "Just set the case of oranges you overloaded off, señor, and we'll both make our families very happy."

I went back to my rig and managed to pry one case loose from the tightly packed load. I wrestled it to the ground, carried it over to the scale house, and set it down just outside the door.

As I climbed into my truck, I looked back and was surprised to see three little Mexican kids eagerly breaking open the crate. Evidently they had been keeping their daddy company on this Christmas Eve and had been hiding so I wouldn't see them.

No artist could have painted a prettier scene for a Christmas card than this tableau of a father and his children standing in the softly falling snow beside an unexpected Christmas gift, waving goodbye to me. The perfect whiteness of the snow accentuated the bronze of their smiling faces. The sight eased the heartache I was feeling at not being with my wife and children on the one night of the year every family should be together.

As I slowly let the clutch out and my truck began to move, the three children all shouted in unison, "Merry Christmas, Señor Santa Claus!"

THE ARGYLE SOCKS

Patty Kayser

For eight years I lived in a small village on the Sea of Marmara, about thirty miles from Istanbul. It was a summer resort for the wealthy of Istanbul, but in winter the only inhabitants were the villagers and the foreigners who worked at the nearby airport. There was a small mosque at one end of town, a Greek Orthodox church and a Catholic church at the other end. I was from Brooklyn, the "city of churches," and I felt very fortunate to have a Catholic church so near.

During the winter, attendance at Sunday mass dwindled to three elderly village ladies, myself, and another airline wife, Eileen. The winter of 1949 was very cold, and with coal rationed the church was like an icebox. Christmas was fast approaching, and we noted that the old Italian priest and the brother were still wearing the open sandals of their order! Since we couldn't get to Istanbul before Christmas to buy them some warm socks, Eileen decided to knit them each a pair and put them in the collection basket along with our monetary offerings.

The next Sunday we met at church, and she proudly showed me the socks. They were brightly colored argyles, very popular in those days but hardly suitable with the monklike brown robes of the order. When she saw the expression on my face, Eileen explained that it was the only wool she had at home.

The following Sunday when the priest and the brother lifted their robes to ascend the altar steps, there were the argyle socks in all their glory. The brother came by with the collection basket and smiled a bashful smile. Eileen poked me, and I had to admit that the socks were certainly brilliant Christmas gifts.

A Christmas Past

Myrtle Cooper

It was nearing Christmas in the small town north of Spokane, Washington, when my mother announced to us three small girls that Santa Claus would not visit our home that year. In fact, we would not even have a Christmas tree because there was no money for a horse and sleigh to go out and cut our own. The church had not paid my father's salary for several months. The lumber mill, the livelihood of many of the church families, was closed down.

But we still enjoyed the Christmas Eve program at the church, where we admired the gaily decorated tree and received gifts of candy and apples donated by the merchants. Afterward, as we were wandering sleepily home through unlighted streets, guided only by my father's kerosene lantern, we heard sleigh bells and carols in the distance. Our hearts were happy for the candy and fruit we clutched in our small hands.

The parsonage had a long front porch the width of the house. As Father fitted the key into the lock, he stumbled over something that in the light of the lantern appeared to stretch an interminable distance into the darkness along the porch. We dragged it into the house and found ourselves gaping at a big net stocking filled with colorful packages.

It was time for bed. We children were told we could unwrap the gifts in the morning as Mother shooed us upstairs. The stocking must surely have come from Santa, who had appeared briefly at the church.

Just as we were dropping off to sleep, we heard the doorbell and a terrific commotion in the front hallway. By the time we got to the top of the stairs, Santa was disappearing into the parlor.

The next morning we bounded down the stairs half-dressed. Standing by the fireplace was the most beautiful tree we had ever seen, but instead of tinsel and glittering ornaments, it was festooned with colored paper, cranberries, and popcorn. Underneath were gifts from the huge stocking we'd found at our door the night before. The tree was vaguely familiar. The school Christmas tree, perhaps?

Mother let us pinch the candle holders tight under the branches, and as she drew the shades, we gazed in wonder at the gloriously lighted tree. There were dolls for us girls, and mittens and caps; pots and pans for Mother, a bright shawl, and a tortoise-shell comb for her long brown hair; shirts, ties, and socks for Dad.

It was a memorable Christmas for us all when grateful parishioners sacrificed so that Santa Claus, the eternal spirit of Christmas, could gladden the hearts of their young pastor, his wife, and their three small daughters.

FRIENDS IN DEED

Gilda vanSand

The neighborhood where I grew up wasn't called *el barrio* then, or Harlem or Spanish Harlem either. The families who lived on the blocks bounded by Central Park on the south, Fifth Avenue on the east, 116th Street on the north, and Lenox Avenue on the west would say they lived "uptown." It was a neighborhood with a diversity of cultures, where Spanish, Italian, Greek, Yiddish, and sometimes English were spoken in the homes and in the streets. In our house we spoke Spanish.

Thanks to the slow recovery that the Roosevelt administration was bringing about, our neighborhood was reclaiming its working-class status. Men went off early in the morning, not to stand for hours on breadlines, but to jobs, or at least to answer the Help Wanted ads that were appearing in the paper. The WPA, CCC, NYA, and other three-letter agencies spelled J-O-B to artists, actors, construction workers, high school dropouts, and college students who considered the twenty or so monthly dollars a windfall.

The end of Prohibition had brought a beer garden to our neighborhood. That was what it was called, not a saloon or a bar. On the first warm days of spring, a cluster of little tables draped with red-and-white-checked cloths sprouted on the sidewalk. Overhead a green trellis entwined with fake grapevines and tiny lights gave the entire street a festive look. My brother and I were never allowed to go in there, but sometimes my father let us sit outside and have a root beer. I didn't learn until much later that his beer was different.

One Saturday morning my mother sent me around the corner to my father's barbershop with a note and a little brown bag. I knew what the note said and what the bag was for. She needed a few extra dollars to finish her marketing, because my godmother and her family were coming for dinner that night.

I wasn't often allowed out alone, so this errand was a godsend. All morning I had been plotting a way to telephone my friend Amelia so that her mother would invite me over to play after Sunday mass. I hoped that her father would take us to Central Park for rides on the carousel and boxes of Cracker Jacks. This call had to be made from the privacy of a booth, because even if my mother was too busy to listen in, my brother certainly would, and then he'd hear about the nickel I'd found in my Sunday coat pocket and tell on me. Sometimes the money I was given for the collection basket would get stuck in the lining of my coat.

My father, the barbers, the manicurist, and the bootblack were all too busy to pay much attention to me. Papa read the note, hit the No Sale key on the cash register, pulled out a few bills, and put them in the bag, giving me a quick peck on the cheek. I ran to the candy store next door, dialed the number, and got a busy signal. I dialed again, with no success. A lady was waiting impatiently to use the phone. I was afraid she'd ask Mr. Krasnoff to intervene and he would want to know why I was making calls from his booth, so I left quickly.

The beer garden a few doors down was crowded, but the phone booths were empty. Did I dare? I walked quickly down the long aisle past the bar, looking neither to the left nor to the right. I made my call and was promised an invitation. My Sunday treat was assured. Tucking my hands in my pockets, I hurried to the door—and then my heart stopped. No paper bag! I rushed back to the booth and ran my hand under the seat. Only cigarette butts and gum wrappers. I must have left it in the other booth, and by now it surely was gone. I tried not to cry, but the tears just flowed. I had never done anything so terrible.

One of the men standing at the bar noticed me and asked, "What's the matter, little girl?" I couldn't speak. Others began to crowd around me. "Who is she?" "What happened?" One man pushed forward and looked at me. "She's the daughter of the barber next door. Go get him." I certainly didn't want that, so I blurted out my story. "My father gave me some money for my mother for the marketing, and I ... I lost it."

After a great deal of clucking and tsk-tsking, I heard one man say, "Her father has been a good friend to many here." "That's true," said a tall, skinny man they called El Flaco. "He has given money for funerals and for families left homeless by fire." Another added, "And if you're out of a job, you know he'll let you put the haircut on the bill." El Flaco took off his hat and passed it around. In a flash I was holding a brown paper bag not unlike the one I had started out with. "Now hurry home with this, and not a word to anyone," said El Flaco.

I ran all the way home, up three flights of stairs, and thrust the bag into my mother's hands.

"What can your father be thinking?" she cried when she opened it. "I ask for three dollars and he sends eleven—and four of them in change! I have a good mind to send you back, but it's too late. I must go out to shop now, but we'll talk about it tonight."

My lucky day was not over. When Papa got home, Mama was occupied with her guests, who stayed too late. The subject of the dirty bills and all that change never came up. Still, I had a problem. Whenever I walked past the beer garden with my mother, the men at the bar winked and smiled and waved. I couldn't tell Mama about my new friends, but I couldn't ignore them either, so I would bend down and pretend to lace my shoe and wave at them behind my mother's back. I think they understood, because after a while they stopped waving.

SIMPATICO

Marty Silverman

I was born and raised in Troy, New York. When I was bar-mitzvahed I made a good speech, and my mother immediately concluded that I would become a lawyer. There was no way I would disappoint her. When my friends were asked what they were going to do when they finished high school, no one ever seemed to know. I knew. When asked why I was going to be a lawyer, I simply responded, "My mother says so."

By 1933 we'd been living in New York City for many years, and my dad found that the harder he worked at his tailoring and dry-cleaning store, the more he fell behind. We decided to move back to Troy, where we had relatives and friends and he might do better. There was one problem. I had just completed my first year at Brooklyn Law School. How could I continue?

There was a law school in Albany, about six miles from Troy. It prided itself on being extremely selective and generally did not accept transfer students. Every friend and relative assured me that with barely a B average I would never get in. I suspected that if I sent my application along to the registrar it would be summarily rejected, so I called the dean's office and requested an interview.

On the appointed day and time I entered the dean's office, full of trepidation. Dean Alexander greeted me warmly and offered me a chair. He was a man of about fifty, with an easy way that soon put me at ease. After glancing at my transcript, he asked, "Why do you want to come to Albany Law School?"

I started with my family history, how I'd worked my way through high school and college, how my mother had this dream of seeing her son become a lawyer and I had to make it come true for her. He leaned back in his chair and lit a cigarette, and nothing more was said for what seemed like ages. I said a little prayer.

Finally, speaking very softly, Dean Alexander asked me if I had any idea what I was about to undertake. He explained that there would be four hours of classes every day, followed by at least four hours of homework, all casework that would have to be done in the school library. Times being what they were, I probably wouldn't find a night job in Albany, and even if I did, I probably wouldn't be alert the next morning. Then he looked at me with a twinkle in his eyes and asked, "How would you be able to handle that?" I could only think of one reply. "Sir, the good Lord will provide me with the answer." The dean looked at me intently, extended his hand, and said, "Let's give it a try."

It was not until after I left his office that the realization hit me: despite all the doomsayers, I was going to Albany Law School! I got into my car and sat stunned, trying to review in my mind the events of the last hour. But after the euphoria of the moment wore off, I began thinking, Where do I get a job? How do I get a job?

I drove toward the new bridge that had just been built across the Hudson to link Albany and Troy. As I started over the approach to the bridge I passed some farmland, and a voice seemed to call out, "Build a gas station here." I drove back and forth across that bridge three times, and each time the voice repeated its message.

The next morning I telephoned the Standard Oil Company office in Albany. I explained that I had found an excellent site for a gas station and wanted their help. Within a week I had their approval. They would furnish the tanks and pumps and would loan me $6,500 to build the station, the loan to be repaid by adding two cents a gallon to my cost of their product. I arranged to purchase the land from the farmer who owned it. The price was right, I borrowed the modest down payment from a relative, and we were off.

Shortly after school started, the station was up and running. It was an instant success. Word seemed to have gone out that the kid running the station was trying to work his way through law school. On Saturdays and Sundays, friends, relatives, and total strangers would drive from Troy, Albany, Schenectady, and towns in between to fill up. Sometimes a child would ask from the back seat, "Why do we have to drive so far for gas?" The parents would turn and proudly proclaim, "We are helping this young man go to college." I should add that my most dedicated customers were Jewish. They were the ones who drove the farthest, felt the greater need to help, and always seemed to drive away happier for it.

One Saturday night a car drove in about 11:00 p.m. I recognized the driver as a customer and the father of a classmate of mine. After I filled his tank and washed his windshield, he paid me and said, "Marty, if I were you I'd get tomorrow's *New York Times*." I thanked him and froze in my steps as he drove off. It was customary to print the names of those who passed the bar in the *Times*, but no one ever knew when. Would this man go out of his way to drive to my gas station so late at night and tell me to buy the *Times* if my name was not in it?

There was only one place to go for the next day's *Times*: the Albany railroad station. The train from New York would arrive at about 3:00 a.m. I called home and said I would be going out with a couple of friends and would be back late. Then I closed up and went down to the railroad station to wait. When the train arrived, I grabbed the first paper I could get my hands on, found the section with trembling fingers, read the list—and there was my name. I passed. I passed! And in the top group, too! Overcome with emotion, I put my hands over my eyes, bowed my head, and thanked God. I was so drained that I sat and cried like a baby. Twenty years of work and schooling had all culminated in the paper I held in my hands—but it was more, much more, my mother's dream come true. Her son was a lawyer.

Not long before, when my mother was visiting my older sister, they had gone to a tea leaf reader as a lark. Reading my mom's leaves, the woman had said, "You will be receiving some very good news, but you will not believe it until you see it in black and white." Armed with the *New York Times* and knowing that little story, I went home.

The next day, Sunday, was a very important day in our house. It was the one day of the week my dad could sleep, the one day of the week no one made any noise until he awoke, the one day of the week we could relax as a family and my sisters and I could show our love and respect for our parents. My dad arose, and we sat down to breakfast together. When all was quiet I announced, "I believe I have passed the bar exam." My mom promptly responded, "I won't believe it until I see it in black and white." Slowly I got up and reached for the *New York Times.* Bedlam broke out. It was a moment of great joy, excitement, and of course congratulations. At the time, Max Steuer was known as a great litigator; my dad broke out a bottle of wine and toasted the *next* Max Steuer.

A Dollar Down

Norbert Seif

When I arrived in New York City in the spring of 1939, I lived with my cousin Helen in an apartment on Spring Avenue in the Bronx. I was seventeen, a refugee from Vienna, Austria.

Four days after my arrival, Helen found a job for me. On Spring Avenue, dwarfed between apartment buildings, were three single-family dwellings. The largest, the entrance flanked by two lilac bushes, belonged to Mr. Sam Rabinowitz, my boss-to-be.

Mr. Rabinowitz was in the "customer peddler" business. "A dollar down, a dollar a week, I trust everybody" opened doors for him. His customers were located in a development of small homes about ten miles north. He sold them linens and miscellaneous housewares.

Mr. Rabinowitz had decided to expand, and that was where I came in. I was invited to his house for a Sunday brunch. Mr. Rabinowitz was waiting for me outside.

"You speak a little English, boy?"

"I took it in school over there. I'm okay."

"Good. Come in now."

In all my seventeen years, I had never set foot in a private home. I was awed by the marble tiles in the foyer, and the kitchen seemed as large as Helen's entire two-bedroom apartment. A huge, round oak table with claw-footed legs was covered with dishes and platters filled with fish, cheeses, and fruit. Some of the dishes were foreign to me: smoked salmon, rolled, pickled, and schmaltz herring, and cheeses I had never seen before.

"Have you never eaten herring and lox before?" Mrs. Rabinowitz asked me, her eyes smiling behind thick lenses. "You know, you eat more than my son Julius, the doctor. He is married to a lovely girl from a very wealthy family, and has a big practice on Fifth Avenue, and lives in a mansion. A heart specialist, my Julius," she added with pride.

"All the children of Israel should have a son like my Julius!" The host, who had been slouching with both hands on the table, sat tall and straight in his chair.

Sam Rabinowitz was in his late sixties, a little over five feet tall, compact and chunky. The quickness of his movements belied his age. I thought he looked like a peasant. The hair was white, thick and shiny, fitting like a cap over a creased round forehead, high cheekbones, a wide nose, and a square chin. He was cross-eyed, and when I spoke to him, I took care to focus on his bushy eyebrows, not sure which eye to look at.

After we ate, Mr. Rabinowitz sipped hot tea out of a glass, and while his wife washed the dishes, he described the job. I was first to accompany him on his route to learn the business. Later, I was to canvass for new customers. The work was seven days a week from nine to four, except Sunday, when in deference to his Catholic customers the hours were one to five. The pay was seven dollars a week, a dollar a day.

The next few days I accompanied my boss on his route. I watched him carefully as he called on his customers, and I helped with deliveries. And then I was on my own.

Mr. Rabinowitz coached me carefully. "Now, you'll have a dozen Cannon towels under your left arm, and a dozen Pepperell sheets under your right arm. You'll ring the bell. People will not open the door. They'll yell, 'Who's there?' You'll yell back, 'I sell sheets and towels!' If they let you in, you'll say good morning or good afternoon. Say that you don't want to bother them.

"Say that you're new in this country and have no relatives. Say that you're selling first-quality towels and sheets, as cheap as anybody. Say that you give credit. 'One dollar down, and one dollar a week.' Say your feet hurt, but smile while you say it. I'll pick you up at four at the same spot I drop you off in the morning. You do what I tell you, you'll make out okay."

As Mr. Rabinowitz chanted his instructions, I looked first at his right eye, then at his left. To my amazement the left pupil was significantly larger than the right. He stopped, turned his face away from me, and spoke in a different voice. "Boy. What are you looking at?" I opened my mouth and my tongue froze. The old man turned back to me, chuckled, and continued his sermon.

I did what Mr. Rabinowitz told me to do, and I made out surprisingly okay. Some doors never opened, and at times people screamed curses I didn't understand. Dogs followed me, sniffed my sheets and towels, and trotted off in peace. And I met warmth and kindness. Often I didn't comprehend the words people spoke, but I read their eyes and it was enough. Women kept buying my sheets and towels. They referred me to endless nieces, aunts, sisters-in-law, and new brides, and my pay increased from seven to eight dollars a week.

In July 1939 my parents arrived in New York City. We rented an apartment on East Ninth Street in Manhattan, and Mr. Rabinowitz patted my cheek when I said goodbye to him.

From South Carolina to Heaven

Eva Bell Williams

When I was a little barefoot girl in the South my days were frightening. Every morning my father would leave his chores on the farm and walk my younger sister and me to school through the town. In the afternoon he would come back and call for us. He had to, because if we were alone the white boys threw rocks at us.

In the next few years everything changed. Papa died, and Mama and my older sister Rosa had to go out to work. Then Rosa was seduced by an older boy and got pregnant. I had to drop out of school and stay home with the baby.

When I was fifteen I got a letter from one of my girlfriends who had gone up to New York to work: "Eva Bell, you must come here. It's heaven!"

"The only time you go to heaven is when you die," said Mama. But my stepfather said, "Let her go. She deserves a chance to better herself."

My girlfriend sent me the train fare ($11.34) and met me at the huge railroad station. I had never seen so many people in one place before, and I could not understand what they were saying. She took me over to Brooklyn and left me with the family I was to work for, an Orthodox Jewish rabbi and his wife and their three children. The parents spoke no English, but the oldest child, about five, acted as interpreter. They were kind and patient but firm. Within three weeks I was speaking fluent Jewish, and in a matter of months I knew all the rules of keeping a strictly kosher house. Not only were all the fleishigs and milchigs kept separate but the house was scrubbed from top to bottom.

I had Thursday afternoons and every other Sunday off. The rabbi wanted me home by ten o'clock, but I complained, "The fun is just getting started at the Apollo at ten." I loved to dance, and my friends and I had good times. I said I would leave if I had to be in by ten o'clock.

The rebbetzin said, "I'll tell you what. When you come in don't make any noise. Above all, don't run any water—don't wash your face or flush the toilet. Then the rabbi won't know what time you get in. It will be our secret."

One day the rebbetzin's sister was visiting from Chicago, and the two ladies went out shopping. While I was washing the kitchen floor the doorbell rang. It was a messenger with a parcel for Mrs. Epstein, the sister. I signed for it and went back to my pail and scrub brush (no mops in those days—mopping was the lazy way, and you couldn't get into the corners). A few minutes later the ladies came in, and I said, "There's a package for you, Mrs. E."

"How did you get it?" she asked. "Didn't you have to sign for it?" She could not believe I could write, and I signed my name again in her presence.

"Get up off that floor at once," she ordered. I quaked. What had I done wrong?

"You will not scrub another floor or wash another window again unless it is your *own!* I am taking you back with me to Chicago, and you are going to nursing school."

She did, and I did, and two years later I received my diploma as a full-fledged licensed practical nurse. I elected to work with the newborn and did that for twenty-five years, until they made me retire on my sixty-fifth birthday. I wasn't ready to stop working.

The rabbi and rebbetzin are still my family. They come to visit me and invite me to their house on holidays. Their children (there were nine in all) are grown and married and doing well. They never forget my birthday and always keep me up on the news about their doings and their own children.

SOL

Ed Denzler

Everyone called him Sol—that is, everyone except Mrs. Buxbaum. She called him Sweetie. I don't remember Sol's family name, but I will never forget Mrs. Buxbaum. To a fifteen-year-old in 1938, a person like Mrs. Buxbaum was like Madonna today.

Sol owned a pharmacy in the neighborhood. Unlike modern drugstores, Sol's store concentrated on drugs, prescription and patent medicines. Of cosmetics he had none, and the only cigarettes or cigars in the place were the ones between his lips or in his pockets. He did sell personal hygiene items, though, and that made me the envy of every teenage boy in my high school. Although I didn't realize it at the time, it also made me someone to be feared by all the parents of the girls I so badly wanted to date. Well, almost all. Mrs. Bricault, the French lady, Michelle's mother, she … but that's another story.

The families that traded at Sol's, particularly the mothers, considered me fast. After all, I knew about menstruation and contraception and God knows what else, things they would never talk about among themselves or with their children until the children were married and could handle adult topics. Sol himself shared some of these same Victorian notions. He had hired me to work after school dishing out ice cream, making two-cents plains, and generally assisting customers when he was busy. But let him see me approaching a lady customer near the few feminine items he carried and he was out of the drug section like a shot. "Boychick, let me help this lady, this lovely lady," that was Sol's way. Ugly as sin she could be, but to Sol she was a doll, a lovely lady.

Sol also reserved a few of the men customers for himself, and for a while I thought he was running a bookie business like Mr. Castrato, the barber. After I'd worked there a month, I realized that the mumbled whispering words and the stealthy under-the-counter fumblings and the swift exchange of money all had to do with the purchase of condoms. Sol was protecting me from the nasty world of growing up. Little did he know that I had one in my wallet, purloined from my father's dresser drawer without the faintest notion of how or why it was to be used. I was very embarrassed when Sol told me.

I only saw Sol in trouble once. Yes, you guessed it. Mrs. Buxbaum. She came into the store late one Friday afternoon, as she usually did, and took Sweetie, as she usually did, back to the storeroom and closed the door. Sol told me once that they had to talk about "temple matters," a subject a Gentile boy wouldn't understand. Anyway, this time Mrs. Sol, who should have been home preparing the Friday evening meal, showed up. When I told her Sol was having a temple discussion with Mrs. Buxbaum, she wanted to join them in a hurry. She opened the storeroom door and started shouting in a language I did not understand but which left no doubt in my mind that my boss was in trouble.

Sol wasn't angry at me for telling, though our relationship was slightly strained after that. He would look at me, shake his head, and say things like, "Boychick, when are you going to grow up?"

I went looking for Sol after World War II, wanting to show him I had grown up and thank him for helping me along the way. But his building was gone, replaced by a strip mall—no drugstore, just a beauty shop, a Chinese restaurant, and an Arthur Murray Dance Studio.

Sol, too, was gone from the neighborhood. According to Mr. Castrato, Jr., the barber's son, Mrs. Buxbaum and Sol had been partners in a land development scheme near Fort Lauderdale until she caught him having one of those temple talks of his with the developer's secretary. Mrs. Sol became famous as the chicken soup queen of a commune near Haifa, where she cured more people (victims of the Holocaust) in one week than old Sol had cured in all his years as a druggist.

Me, I'm an old man now, but I can still remember Sol's last words of advice when I left his employ: "Ven du gehst zu shul, geht zu davenen." I think he was telling me, "When you go to temple, go to pray."

SOCCA SOBER

Irma Moss

I was sixteen, and as his only child, I accompanied my father on what was now my third or fourth trip to Havana. It was half business and half vacation for him, but since I was taken out of school, it was all fun for me.

We traveled by ship in those days, with large steamer trunks. It was before jeans and sneakers. My blouses, suits, shoes, hats, and gloves all had to match—hot under the tropical sun, but very lady-like. Each night I wore a long gown, ate dinner to the strains of Latin music, and was graciously served by waiters wearing white gloves.

There was no shortage of deckhands, often more numerous than passengers. Working aboard a ship was the window to the world for poor foreigners. They were trained in the European tradition that our wish was their command. I didn't mind having my shoes polished or my bath drawn, but at sixteen I was very embarrassed to have a matron waiting for me with outstretched arms, holding a huge towel. Instead of stepping out of the bathtub gingerly, I jumped out to get covered as quickly as possible. I could feel her large arms envelop me and her breasts heave up and down as she vigorously dried me. Thereafter, I preferred to swim in the pool on deck.

As soon as our ship docked in Havana and we cleared Customs, we'd rush to the taxi station to find our driver. He was young, and quite handsome, I thought. He was always there and greeted us warmly. How he managed to transport us and our trunks smoothly over cobblestone streets remained a source of wonderment to me. He was not only our chauffeur but also our guide. He seemed to be omnipresent, always waiting patiently for us in front of our hotel, the Nacional. His English was sparse, and our knowledge of Spanish was even more limited. He often repeated something that sounded like "Socca Sober," so that was what we called him, assuming it was his name. He responded with a grin.

Socca Sober saw to it that I danced at Sans Souci under the stars. When one orchestra stopped, another would begin. I would dance all night, and then faithful Socca Sober would take me to Sloppy Joe's, where all the young people congregated in the wee hours of the morning. I was the image of the rich American debutante, seeking only fun. Socca Sober knew better.

When my father was busy, Socca Sober took me to the tobacco factories. There I saw other sixteen-year-olds making cigars and cigarettes. I can still smell the tobacco fumes that shortened their lives, and I can still hear their hacking coughs, but I knew poverty forced them to remain.

One day I asked Socca Sober to drive me into the countryside. "No tell Papa?" he asked. "No tell Papa," I promised.

The adults sat in front of their hovels, staring into space. The children ran bare, stomachs preceding them, through the squalor that was their playground. Socca Sober watched me walk through this children's cemetery, then saw me totter, and quickly caught up with me, slipping his hand in mine. I could feel the callouses from his constant driving, but more than that, I could feel his reassurance and caring. He guided me gently.

Another day the peasants marched through the streets of the city with the head of the chief of police on the point of a sword. It was a release to them, a celebration of sorts. Americans were ordered to remain indoors, but I was sixteen and hadn't learned fear yet, and so I stood there, fascinated. With no regard for his own safety, Socca Sober pushed me into the taxi, and as it was an open car, he recruited six policemen, three on either side, to form a human shield against the flying bullets. I didn't tell my father I was in the midst of an anti-American demonstration staged by the Communists until we were safely back home.

On our last day, my father returned to our ship with a Cuban businessman who was seeing us off. In his perfect English he wished us farewell, then asked for the name of our driver so he could give him instructions for his own trip home.

"Socca Sober," I replied.

The businessman spoke to Socca Sober in Spanish and then informed us his name was really Jorge, George in English. We learned that Jorge was always bragging about his car, which could transport us and our trunks because it had such good "socca sobers"—shock absorbers.

These many years later, when my mechanic told me I needed shock absorbers, I recalled Havana and Socca Sober.

I will remember the girl who reached for the stars lighting up the dance floor as she twirled to the beat of Latin rhythms. I will remember the warmth of the tropical sun and the blue-green waters enveloping me like the arms of the matron after my bath. And my heart will always remember the pain of a people long too poor and oppressed to rise up against Batista, a people whose dream died hard under Castro and Communism.

Now, when darkness engulfs me and uncertainty makes me totter, I feel a warm, reassuring hand slip into mine. It guides me gently and firmly. Somehow I make it through another storm. My fingers lovingly caress the hand in mine. The skin is rough. I can almost count the callouses.

LOUIE

Ben Levine

In 1925, Bloom's was not the worst dairy restaurant in New York City. There were many people to dispute this, with passion. Situated on the Lower East Side, it flourished against all odds.

People sought out Bloom's for different reasons. Some came to socialize, to seek new friends or mates. Some came to spar with the waiters. There were even customers who came to eat the food.

Of the three waiters, Louie was there the longest. His gaunt face and bushy eyebrows were a familiar sight in Bloom's.

Whatever good humor existed in the waiters reached its peak at two in the afternoon. It declined rapidly after that. Cynicism and fallen arches were prerequisites for the job. The waiters couldn't stand indecision, as it caused their feet to swell. Certain common words lowered their tolerance and raised their blood pressure. "Fresh" set off an emotional cycle: anger, its repression, psychosomatic pain, guilt, and finally despair. "What you got for dessert today?" was an unnerving question because the menu never changed.

It was an hour before closing when a burly middle-aged man with no neck came into the restaurant. Louie took an instant dislike to him. He was not from the neighborhood, he read the wrong newspaper, and he sat at a table for four.

"You'll be so good as to sit at this table for two," said Louie, "Mr. Bloom asks."

The stranger bit into a roll, shook his head, and glared at Louie. "So sue me."

Something came alive in Louie. This man I could hate, he thought.

"I could buy and sell Bloom ten times over," said the customer, blinking rapidly. "And throw you in with the bargain."

God sent him to me in my great boredom, thought Louie, smiling down at him.

"You could call me Louie, Mr. ... Mr. ..."

"Mr. Goldstein," said the little man, tapping nervously on the table with a hard roll. "You got a toilet in the back?"

Louie nodded, brushed some crumbs off the table onto Goldstein's lap, and asked, "You want a menu?"

"No, I want a stuffed gorilla."

Louie went for a menu, put an Out of Order sign on the bathroom door, and returned to Goldstein.

"Tell me, Louie, this is a good restaurant?"

Louie flicked some flies toward him with his towel and replied, "I eat here all the time."

Goldstein looked at Louie's thin figure and sunken eyes. "You don't look too good."

"What I got, I got from the customers."

"You don't like it here? Quit. Do like I did—go into business."

"I did."

"So what happened?"

"The horse died."

Louie left to serve some customers, then retired to the back to smoke and relax. After fifteen minutes he returned to Goldstein.

"Hello, stranger." Goldstein looked down at the menu, then up at Louie. "Why didn't you tell me the toilet was out of order?"

"You didn't ask."

"I'll wait till I get home. You'll give it to me fast?"

"Oh, I'll give it to you."

"So, what's good today?"

"'So, what's good today?' he asks," said Louie to an imaginary person in back of him.

After a long pause, Goldstein said, "Well?"

"Mr. Goldfarb—"

"Goldstein."

"If I said pirogen and you got terrible cramps, you wouldn't like me no more."

"What's your advice?"

"Don't eat the chopped herring."

"So what should I order?"

"The fried herring. It goes good with all the rolls you already ate."

"First I'll have borscht and a potato. Then you'll bring me the halibut with rice. And tea. And hurry."

Louie picked up the menu, deliberately removed the soup spoon, and sauntered to the back. Then he took the Out of Order sign off the toilet and served three tables. For a customer at the first, he prescribed medication for a rash. At the second, he dispensed legal advice. At the third, he settled a marital dispute.

Louie returned to Goldstein, who watched as the waiter slowly withdrew his thumb from the borscht and wiped it on his towel. "This soup is hot!" said Louie, smiling.

"Who ever heard of hot borscht?" shouted the little man.

"The potato is cold," Louie triumphantly declared, and left.

Ignoring Goldstein's plea for a spoon, Louie catered to his other customers.

"Louie, I got here a dirty glass."

"Hurray for you."

"The bean soup is delicious. You got a new cook?"

"New beans."

"Why is always missing a knife, a fork?"

"I got my own troubles."

Finally Louie brought Goldstein's halibut. "You didn't eat the borscht."

"There's a fly in it."

"It came in with you."

"It's dead."

"Nothing lives in Bloom's borscht."

"Take it away. Take it away."

As Louie turned to leave with the borscht, he was called back. Drumming rapidly on the table with his fork, Goldstein asked, "Since when I ordered fried potatoes?"

Louie raised his order pad high and pointed. "So what I got here?"

"Take it away and bring me rice."

Louie crossed to the kitchen and continued bantering with his customers.

"I don't need a glass of water. It's in the soup."

"So put a bullet in my brain."

Louie put the rice on Goldstein's table, saying, "Enjoy, Mr. Goldback."

"Goldstein," said the customer. "You're leaning on me. This fish is fresh?"

"The eyes are still moving."

"It don't look that good. You sure this is a healthy halibut?"

"Not now."

"I mean before he was cooked."

"He looked better than you do."

Louie watched him as he ate. "You asked me why didn't I go into business. I could tell you a story, it would make you cry, Silverstein."

"Goldstein. You could keep it a secret. This fish tastes funny."

"Maybe if you went to the bathroom across the street?"

"You had to remind me?"

"Anyway, what do I know about horses? The day he died he looked like the day I bought him and the wagon."

"I don't feel so good."

"So soon?"

"What do you mean, so soon?"

"You're lucky you didn't eat the tzimmes. But I didn't tell you about my swollen horse, lying there in the gutter..."

"Right away I said, 'What's with this fish?'"

"And you ate it, God forbid?"

"Just give me the bill. Now."

"Listen, nobody ever died from it." Louie again addressed the imaginary person over his shoulder. "No, nobody ever died!" He placed the bill on the table.

Goldstein grabbed it, threw some coins on the table, and rushed to Bloom at the register. Louie trotted alongside, shouting, "Come again, hear? Anytime."

As Goldstein left, Louie said to Bloom, "A little of this and a little of that fell in his fish."

"It could happen to anybody," replied Bloom.

They smiled warmly at each other, and Louie walked back to his customers. He was unaware of pain in three parts of his body. Louie was as close to happiness as he could get.

BENNY BINION

Emerson Emory

All the local papers carried the story when Benny Binion of Las Vegas died. The wire-service article centered primarily on Mr. Binion's encounters with the law more than fifty years ago. Perhaps little attention was paid to the account by present-day black citizens of Dallas, but a few remain who recall the good Benny Binion did during his stay here.

The 1929 crash, although its effect on black families is seldom considered, deprived many black men of jobs as janitors in local corporations. Black women were forced to support their families by working as domestics in the Park Cities. Things didn't improve until the Japanese attack on Pearl Harbor in 1941 and the increased government spending that followed.

It was during this in-between period that Mr. Binion introduced the game of policy to the black community. The media described policy as a rigged quarter and fifty-cent game, but you could actually play for a nickel or a dime. Ten cents would get the winner ten dollars. Even better, the game provided work for black men who had no other means of employment. The media seemed to take great joy in pointing out that policy was illegal, but as one who reaped some of the benefits, I shall always remember Benny Binion for other reasons.

I remember Benny as the man who gave my father a job so that my mother and I could eat. I remember my father's pride when he collected his small earnings, the result of miles of walking through the community.

I remember the expression of joy on my mother's face when ten cents of her hard-earned money netted her ten dollars. Yes, there was a look of dismay when she lost, but play again she did, as soon as possible. You see, ten dollars was far more than the sum she earned in the kitchens of University and Highland Park from sunup to dark, six and sometimes seven days a week.

I remember the opportunity given me as a boy to earn money by delivering policy slips to the customers. Illegal, maybe, but no more so than today's football pots. I wonder whether I'd be a doctor now if it hadn't been for policy.

I remember the trucks parked next to the policy shack behind the old State Theater during the Christmas season, laden with apples and oranges—sometimes the only gifts the neighborhood kids would receive from Santa, a.k.a. Benny Binion.

As far as I'm concerned, Benny Binion did no wrong. Until our society realizes that brushes with the law do not always destroy the compassion of the men who are unfortunate enough to encounter its wrath, we will continue to be reminded of their "crimes," under the guise of justice, and forget their good deeds. As it was said of Caesar,

> The evil that men do lives after them,
> The good is oft interred with their bones.

If my parents were alive today, I'm sure that they would join me in saying, "Thanks to you, Benny, for having been a part of our lives. Thanks for giving hope when all was despair, for bringing happiness when all was lost. May you forever rest in peace, knowing that there are still those who remember."

A GOOD LITTLE GIRL

Marcia Cohn Spiegel

My aunt Lottie died the other day. As we gathered to close the house and divide the memories, we found the treasures, the souvenirs and reminders of other lives and times. The pictures of the shtetl from which my grandparents came, the ghetto to which they moved, the American children growing up, dressed in their finest, the certificates, the honors, the awards, the diplomas. And as we sifted through remembrances of another life, I imagined the cost of each of the pictures, each of the honors: the struggle and sacrifice of my grandparents, my mother, my aunts and uncles.

At the funeral they read "The Woman of Valor" (Proverbs 31:10–31). They always read "The Woman of Valor" when a Jewish woman dies. It speaks of her sacrifice and the selflessness, but it doesn't describe how tired she must have been from her hard work and lack of sleep. It tells us that she was praised, but it doesn't tell us how she felt about herself. Were her sacrifices their own reward, the knowledge that she made the lives of her husband and children better? Did she have any pleasure in her life? Did anyone do anything for her?

I was projected back into the world of immigrants. Jewish, Irish, Greek, Armenian, Mexican, Asian—I don't think it matters where they came from. I could picture the families—too large, too many children to feed, never enough money. Life was a constant struggle for survival. While the parents worked, the older daughters stayed home to care for children or were sent to work themselves. The younger ones got the diplomas, the certificates, the awards. The older sisters anticipated their parents' wishes: cooked, cleaned, shopped, set the table, and waited for their reward, for hugs of thanks and recognition. But the parents were too tired to notice. They expected their daughters to behave this way; what need was there for special attention?

Some of the sisters never married but stayed home to care for the children as they grew, and later for the parents as they aged. They gave up their lives without a thought, waiting for their reward. Or if they married, they continued to focus their lives on their parents, helping with family celebrations and holidays, helping with bills, helping with living, helping with dying, still anticipating desires and gratifying them before they were even expressed. Still there was no reward. And when the parents died, the tears were copious and unrestrained, for now the reward could never be given.

I guess that's how it was for Lottie and my mother. My mother remembers how she would make the beds, start the dinner cooking, get everything ready for her parents' return. She mothered her brothers, watched over them, and did all she could to care for them. It's hard for me to realize how small the difference in ages was between the two sisters and their five little brothers.

My mother doesn't remember her father or mother being physically affectionate with her. I find that so strange, because my memory of my grandparents is one of loving, touching, hugging. I remember the good smells of Passover seders or Shabbat dinners and the joy of togetherness at those special meals; my mother's memory of the seders and dinners of her childhood is so different. She remembers tired parents, bickering brothers, the rush and struggle to get ready. She remembers anger and fatigue.

She also remembers shame.

"What's the worst memory of your childhood?"

"That's easy. When we were learning to read, the teacher told us to bring in a daily paper, the *Trib* or *Examiner*. But we didn't get those papers. Only the *Jewish Daily Forward*. How could I ask my mother for money for a paper? There was no money. Didn't the teachers know? My brothers had it easy. Lottie and I helped them to be Americans. No one helped us. We had to do it all alone. I was so ashamed that my folks didn't speak English good. So ashamed that they didn't read an English paper."

Lottie and my mother went to Marshall High for two years and got certificates. We found Lottie's in the box of treasures, yellowed and dry after all these years. They both went to work as soon as the law would allow—secretaries, salesgirls. They loved pretty clothes. There is a faded snapshot from around 1920 of the two of them in beaded dresses.

"That one cost me two hundred dollars," my mother told me with pride.

"How much did you make?"

"When I worked at Sears I think I took home eighteen dollars a week. That was good money for a girl, you know." How long had it taken to earn that dress, I wondered, when most of the money went to the family?

Yes, the boys were lucky. They had the same struggle, but there was hope that they would become professionals, real Americans. They got the education. They went to college. They worked too, but if the sisters hadn't been bringing in something every week it would have been impossible for the boys to make it.

As we looked through the pictures on the last day of shiva,

before closing up the house for good, my mother asked, "What are you doing with the refrigerator?"

"Selling it to the new tenant, I guess."

"That's my refrigerator. I gave it to the folks. It cost me two hundred dollars."

"But that was over twenty years ago. It's probably not worth much now."

A pained expression crossed my mother's face. "No one seems to respect what belongs to me. That's my refrigerator—and stove," she said with pinched mouth and flashing eyes.

"What's the matter, Mom? I'm sure you don't really want that old stove and refrigerator. It's about something else, isn't it? Tell me what's bothering you."

"You wouldn't understand. You always had a mother and father who loved you and took care of you. You wouldn't know how it is to feel that everyone else was loved but you. No one ever noticed anything I did. No one cared. No one ever said thank you. *I* should have been the one to go to college. *I* was the smart one. But girls didn't go. Girls only worked and got married and had children. No one ever thanked *me*.

"They all loved Lottie. She was the pretty one. She was the one they did for. People always did for her. Look at this, Lottie got all of Ma's things, even the stove and refrigerator I bought when Ma and Pa moved in here. No one ever told *her* no.

"I did everything I could. I was good, I never caused trouble. I didn't fight or stay out late. No one ever had to tell me what to do, I always knew. I did it before I was asked. I did it before it needed to be done.

"But *she* got kissed, *she* got thanked. Back then the boys were always so cute. Everyone loved them. Each one was the sweetest baby, no wonder Ma adored them. But none of it was for me. I did everything I could, and after she died I never even knew if she loved me."

And so on that sad day my mother sat with a bag, collecting mementos of a past that lived inside her. We made stacks of pictures for each of the boys, their bar mitzvahs, graduations, weddings, and babies. We wondered about faded pictures from Russia and Poland, lost relatives no one would ever identify. We divided up the crocheted doilies, tablecloths, and embroidered tea towels. We filled our boxes with special pots for Passover matzo balls and chicken soup, and mismatched silver from the days when Zayde collected scrap metal.

And my mother cried for a little girl who was never naughty and never knew if she was loved.

FIRST LADY

Douglas C. Rigg

One of World War II's many ironies was its impact on our prisons. Felons, society's pariahs, became wanted men in a new way. Labor shortages engendered by the unprecedented mobilization meant that convicts were a valuable manpower pool.

San Quentin, perhaps because of its size and location, changed more than other penitentiaries. After Pearl Harbor the new warden, Clinton Duffy, volunteered the institution's resources for the war effort. He recognized an opportunity to improve his old prison, plagued by overcrowding and idleness.

Soon prisoners were processing ration cards for the Office of Price Administration. Others recovered scarce copper by diligently stripping insulation from miles of electric wiring salvaged from the ravaged Pacific Fleet. The prison laundry expanded, working extra hours to sort, clean, and repair navy issue, some of it bloodstained. One prisoner turned in a loaded pistol he found among newly opened laundry.

The prison contracted to make cargo nets, antisubmarine nets from steel cable, and small boats. Inmates were housed in rural camps, available as farm labor to plant, prune, and pick California's produce. Work in the prison's notorious jute mill, previously unpopular for its noise, dust, and monotony, found willing hands once grain bags became sandbags for the military.

As the institutional parole officer, I released men to shipyards to work as welders, electricians, and machinists. Others went to the merchant marine as cooks or bakers. These were skills learned in the newly reorganized prison vocational training classes. I also served on the prison draft board to screen for 1-A men who could be paroled to the army under new legislation.

Convicts used their small earnings to buy War Bonds and gave generously to the Red Cross blood bank. The prison population declined with all the outside employment, and prison morale rose. Warden Duffy was later to say, "The war marked the coming-of-age of San Quentin." Beyond the high walls there were approving news stories and editorials, and the prison received a National Service Flag. But the ultimate recognition was an unexpected visit from Eleanor Roosevelt.

She arrived on a clear day with a small party. Her manner was easy and gracious, her stride purposeful during a long tour through the sprawling prison compound. She observed with attentive eyes, asking intelligent and direct questions as she conversed with staff and prisoners. Her tour ended in the huge dining hall, its high sides and ceiling dotted with gun walks. I estimated two thousand or more convicts crowded into a space with half that capacity.

There was polite applause for the blessedly brief commentary of military and civilian brass, and good-natured groans for a retired jurist who ascribed the prisoners' high output to their faith in criminal justice. But all attention was on Mrs. Roosevelt, America's best-known woman, a citizen of the world, a busy celebrity who had chosen to join us. Audible whispers pronounced her far more attractive than her photographs. A loud welcome dropped to a deep silence as she rose, tall and dignified, emanating an immeasurable warmth.

In an uneven yet pleasing voice, she spoke of her pride, pleasure, and gratitude at what she had seen and heard this day. She compared the prison's war effort favorably with that of factories she had visited "outside." She looked forward to reporting on her day at San Quentin to the President, and she could assure us that he would be pleased. We knew then, firsthand, why she was called his "eyes and ears to the country."

Recently, she said, she had visited a prison in Maryland, leaving the White House very early. "Where is my missus?" the President asked. "In prison," he was told. "I'm not surprised," he said, "but what's she in for?" She shared our appreciative laughter, and then her voice dropped as though in private conversation with each of us. Tactfully, she acknowledged the prisoners' status, unfree, away from home and family, in a life sure at times to lead to discouragement and despair.

But we had given her reason for new hope and resolve, and she wished the men and their families a better future. Surely this terrible war of pain, loss, and sacrifice could not be in vain. Men who had experienced pain and loss would be needed to understand and to help heal those scarred by war. Our country, though imperfect, was still a land of great promise. Unless we could help make our nation a better place for all its citizens, we would find no cause to rejoice.

She ended surrounded by a deep silence strange to that large hall and its gathering. No man there felt any shame for his tears. Mine return this half-century later as I reach to recapture the day one brave woman touched the lives of her captive audience and its keepers.

Then our cheers and chanting of her name threatened the sound barrier. She smiled and waved her farewell. Through her eyes we had seen our better selves. And we truly understood the words "First Lady."

SPEECH

Bush Satterfield

When I started eighth grade, I sensed that the carefree days of my youth were over and that school was going to be a serious matter from now until graduation. I was fourteen and was paying more attention to what Mama and Dad said about studying hard so I could "amount to something."

My knee britches had been replaced by overalls, the everyday costume of most of the males in town. I felt I had at last reached that mysterious plateau that separated the men from the boys, and the feeling was bolstered by my move to the second floor of the school, where I mixed with the high school students. I had become increasingly aware that the girls on the second floor looked more interesting than those on the first floor; they wore makeup, and their dresses fit in all the right places, just like in the pictures in the Sears catalogue.

Much to my surprise, my favorite subject turned out to be English, thanks to the efforts of our teacher, Miss Violet Hendershot, who heard enough "I seen's" the first few days of school to last her a lifetime. We finally got into Shakespeare, *Julius Caesar* to be exact. Nearly everybody in class liked that story! We would read aloud and have discussions, Miss Hendershot leading us in such a way that even the dullest boys were interested. Then she played a mean trick on us. She announced that we were to memorize Marc Antony's funeral oration over Caesar's body and recite it to the class! It took several weeks, but everyone managed to struggle through the ordeal.

Most of the girls, anxious to show off anyway, made it look easy, but it was a little weird to watch an awkward, overall-clad, barefoot bunch of boys stand in front of the class saying, "Friends, Romans, countrymen...," all the while nervously rubbing the back of one leg with the opposite foot, constantly putting their hands in their pockets, avoiding eye contact with their buddies. Muffled snickering would erupt, and Miss Hendershot would tap the desk with a ruler and frown at us.

One of the boys in class was Dick Cole, a member of our gang. He had what is now called a speech impediment; we called it "stuttering" or being "tongue-tied." Sometimes we would make fun of Dick until he was almost in tears and tried to fight us. Sometimes he wouldn't talk at all, just listen and smile, especially if there were any girls around. Mr. Will Pitts, one of the clerks at the company store, told us the story about the day Dick came in and said, "My mama w-w-w-ants t-t-two bits' worth of s-s-sow belly, and she says if it's got any t-t-t-its on it she'll send it right b-b-b-ack!" We thought this was the funniest thing we had ever heard, not because of Dick's stuttering, but because of that word for the part of the female hog's anatomy, which was never supposed to be mentioned.

Well, Dick was the last to come forward to recite Marc Antony's oration. An expectant hush came over the room as Dick took his position and looked at Miss Hendershot for the signal to begin. It seemed that the whole class was suddenly paralyzed. No one fidgeted in their seat; no pencils or books were dropped. Buckshot looked at me and grinned and winked, as though to say, "Boy, this is gonna be somethin'."

Dick got through the first few sentences with hardly any stammering. As he continued, his voice grew stronger, and he used gestures and facial expressions to make the speech come alive. His gray eyes bored into ours with such intensity that we could almost see sparks. His overalls turned into a Roman senator's toga, and his bare feet were bound in Roman sandals. I even thought I could see a dagger at his waist. It was a magical moment.

When he finished, Dick gave the class a little half-bow like he'd seen actors do in front of an adoring audience. Miss Hendershot sat silently at her desk with a thoughtful expression on her face. As he started to his seat in the back row, someone up front began to clap softly. Suddenly everyone in the room, including Miss Hendershot, was applauding like crazy.

Dick sat down at his desk, just across from me and Buckshot. He sat a moment with his head bowed and then looked over at us with a little smile. As he hurriedly wiped his eyes with his shirt sleeve, his smile became a wide grin.

Passages

ROOTS

Bertha Russ

As I grow old
My ancestors crowd me
Looking over my shoulder
Into my mirror
A small, tight, warm encircling group.

PAUM-MAN-AKE

Elaine Johnson

In the year of the great snow, around 1609, Henry Hudson, an Englishman, dropped anchor off the shores of Paum-man-ake. That is the Delaware Indian name for "land that is long"; we know it today as Long Island. Along these eastern shores the Algonquian language was spoken, as far north as the cold land of the Onondaga, the Mohawk, and the Seneca. I know, for we greet each other as cousins. The crew of the ship, *Half Moon,* was met by either the Rockaway or Canarsie Indians, in canoes called mushee. The Indians were friendly, staring in awe at the sight of men with blue eyes (like a clear summer day), blond hair (with the sun caught in it), and white skin. You see, in their custom of painting themselves for war, white meant peace, so they did not fear these strange-looking men. The whites landed at a place known today as Coney Island, in the village of Broken Land, now called Brooklyn, my birthplace.

I was a shy, lonely, only child who loved to read books. The stories my mother told me became a reality as I grew older, but the kids at school made fun of me whenever I repeated the Indian myths, legends, and ghost stories. They called me "Shittycock" instead of Shinnecock; they said, "Gee, you don't look like Tonto," or "Hey, Elaine, where are your feathers and your bow and arrows?" I was the butt of so many jokes, tricks, and nasty remarks that I shut up and stayed to myself. But one nut kept it up. He had a good time putting my braids in the inkwell, or throwing my dress up over my head, or stealing my pennies.

As a child I couldn't understand why I got beat up at school and beat up again when I got home. One time I ran away, but when it got dark I had cried myself out, and I was hungry and cold. I went home, and to my surprise I was greeted with open arms. "Oh, baby, Lainee-bunch, where were you?" I thought all kinds of things. We both cried, but we talked to each other, and thus began my first fighting lesson. "I'm going to teach you to hit first and ask questions later," my mother said. "I'm not going to be with you always, and you have no sisters or brothers."

The next day I waited for the nut to swagger into the classroom and hit him with all my might. His big mouth was swollen, his lips and eyes were black-and-blue. I jumped on his back and was pounding his head on the floor when the teachers finally got me off him. He went home crying, with a sore head along with his bruises. What could the principal do? They all knew how he had been tormenting me. I know one thing: after that he walked around me, no more did he call me names.

As time went on, I kept wondering about the truth of the oral history repeated to me by my mother. My husband died young, and in my fifties I was granted a scholarship to college. I was scared about going to school with kids young enough to be my grandchildren, but something said, "Go ahead and try it. You can always back out if it gets too hard." A whole new world opened up to me, and I was able to research and validate my ancestry.

I know there were thirteen tribes on Long Island. The Shinnecock descendants still live there, along the shores of Peconic and Shinnecock bays, and in the hills that still bear their name. The great chief Nowendonah took his braves to help the Americans transport a ship from one shore to another, since the British were coming. They carried the ship on their strong shoulders and backs, as was their custom, walking and swimming the bright waters. All were lost, leaving a village full of grieving women. When winter came the other tribes stole the fat, plump squaws to their lodges, as their bodies produced heat and shelter from the bitter-cold nights, but in the summer months they enticed the maidens away from their mothers. At the Battle of Long Island, on August 27, 1776, the warriors served as scouts and guides under the American general George Washington, marching to the northern parts of the state, using old Indian trails as shortcuts. Again the women were left alone, so they worked on the farms of the wannux (white men) and taught their children. The last known full-breed on record was Rebecca Kellis, "Aunt Becky," who lived and taught on the reservation for a hundred years. If you've seen the motion picture *The Amityville Horror,* it's the Shinnecocks who haunt that house; there are forgotten graves all over these sacred lands.

On dark nights, before the campfires, many ghost stories, deeds of bravery, and legends are told by the senior citizens. At their center traditional beadwork, needlepoint, sewing, music, and the ancient dances are performed. At sixty-three I join them to reminisce over tales told over and over again, then add my own to theirs. The English did not visit our village until 1640. We went to their churches, and until this day they come to our annual powwow, where we give thanks to God for a good harvest. We are the largest remaining confederacy of Long Island. We live in harmony and peace, as the caretakers of this land, its animals, and all who walk upright, on two legs. Wanitonka, the creator, planned it so. I am now a weena (old lady) and I grow tired, but I must repeat these words spoken by the ancestors and the great war chiefs Wyandanch, Poggattecut, Culluloo, Telewana, and Occom:

> For as long as the grass grows green
> and the rivers flow.
> This the land of the indian!
> Forever this will be so.

I know nothing of my other ancestor, the African. I'm just glad he found the Indians in the woods of Paum-man-ake and that those caretakers fed him, clothed him, and taught him the Indian way of surviving in this sometimes harsh land. They intermarried and stayed with the tribe, and became peaceful warriors and chiefs.

TEL AVIV TRAIN STATION

Sari Blacharski

In the back of my mind I recall a tall soldier racing into the station, searching for someone, pacing back and forth. All eyes were on this handsome figure attired in khaki shorts and a shirt open on a tanned neck. He wore the insignia of the Palestine Settlement Police on his rolled-up sleeve. His beret was tilted jauntily over his thick black hair, but his brown eyes were worried. The moment she breathlessly appeared, they ran toward each other and became one in their joy. Her braided blond hair came down over her blue cotton dress. They might have stepped out of a painting, its background the Tel Aviv train station.

Many years later, as I sat waiting for a train in the same station, I saw a couple shuffling toward me. I could not take my eyes off them. The figures nearby became stationary and unimportant, but these two were alive and impressive. He was bent with the years yet towered over the woman alongside him. His skin was taut across high cheekbones, and his brown eyes sparkled. The faded brown suit was neatly patched at the elbows, and the creases in his pants shone from being pressed repeatedly. The awkwardly knotted tie and the stiff white collar seemed to belong anywhere but on this tanned neck. His thinning hair appeared to have been cut by loving but very unprofessional hands.

One foot followed the other hesitantly, sure and yet unsure; it was the pace set by time's clock, and it could be no other way. One hand carried a suitcase bound endlessly with string, as well as a smaller parcel; the other hand supported the arm of the woman by his side. The grip was firm and protective. They walked in unison, guiding themselves toward the space near me.

As they came closer I noticed how stooped her shoulders were, surely from stubborn efforts to move her body faster. He spoke to her in Yiddish, with now and then a word of Hebrew. "B'vakashah, mein teiereh, zitsen doh." She smiled and looked up at him with eyes as blue as the sky. "Yah, it is time to rest." I almost gasped at a beauty that revealed itself despite the years. Her face was like a delicate cameo, complete with hues of peach and a clear white. The quiet gentleness that was hers softened all the lines etched by a hard life in a new country.

As she slowly sat down I noticed earrings of definite antiquity, and over a white lace collar a gold necklace from which a small gold watch dangled. I applauded her stubborn femininity. Though she wore a blue-flowered kerchief snugly about her head, wisps of white curls with an occasional blond strand framed her face. A matching blue dress modestly came down to her ankles to meet shoes split at the toes for added comfort.

They rearranged their packages, and she whispered, "You must make yourself comfortable." With gnarled fingers he slowly unbuttoned his coat. I smiled to myself when he stooped to untie his shoelaces and finally removed his tie. She opened the small parcel, neatly spread a white napkin across his lap and her own, then proceeded to peel the hard-boiled eggs, alternately slicing tomatoes and cucumbers. When they finished he took a small penknife from his pocket and cut an apple into quarters; peeling the skin, he offered her the first slice. They moved as of one thought and conscience, sharing and serving one another.

Suddenly there was the shrill whistle of an oncoming train and the final sigh as it pulled into the station. Once again, as long ago, figures came alive out of a painting. They dashed in all directions— young soldiers going to their destinations, sabras in starched uniforms, serious civilians with black briefcases, and curly-haired children nibbling on bread in the arms of their mothers.

THE GOLDEN YEARS

Oscar Ogman

It's been ten years my husband is dead. Now I will retire and live on Social Security, do all the things I never had time for.

The first few weeks I stayed busy, then boredom set in. It was no life for a young sixty-five-year-old widow. I was introduced to the Senior Citizen Center, the in thing. My first visit I had a meal and a container of milk all for the price of fifty cents—can't beat the bargain. After lunch there was dancing in a crowded room where the women outnumbered the men. Competition was keen, and it required skill and the proper bait to land one of these fish. I was determined.

It was on my third visit to the center that I met Jack. He danced well and held me oh-so-close. The next few weeks flew by. I saw him every day at the center, and in the evening we ate dinner together. It was quite a courtship. One day he suggested that we live together. He moved in with me, and we pooled our Social Security checks. It was all right with me; I cared for him, and this was one way to keep him. Now I had a man around the house, no more living by myself, no more being frightened of noises during the night. Now I had someone to go out with and would never have to touch the money put aside for my children. Life was great. Everything was just like the golden years should be.

One day it struck me like being hit on the head with a bat. I was spending twice the time in the laundry room. He was a late riser, I was an early riser; breakfast was served twice. No longer were we going out for dinner. He loved my cooking and liked to hang around the house.

Jack suffered asthma attacks and wanted me to sell the house so we could relocate to Florida. There I would buy us a condo. I turned him down. He went to live with his children in Florida. It was a short-lived romance.

This week I spent shopping for clothes I had always hesitated to buy because of the price. Now that's in the past. I have booked a cruise, and I'm off to the islands, spending my children's money.

These are truly my golden years, and I am going to enjoy them.

Being a widower is no simple matter. I had been in mourning for a year, never being swayed from my obligation in all that time. Now it was time to get out. My friend George, who is an old hand at this, would brief me and show me the ins and outs of the second time around.

I bought a new wardrobe. The old suit and old shirts would not do. The hair had to be tinted. Young was the order of the day. A new life deserves a new look. George was my guide. He introduced me to Trolly's, a local dance hall for seniors. We checked our coats and sat down near the checkroom to get first crack at what's coming in. The parade of potential partners started. They were fat, thin, tall, short. They all looked good to me. The women outnumbered the men, which made each man feel like a Casanova. I did plenty of talking and lots of dancing, always keeping to the rules George taught me. Don't talk about your money or your pension. If you date a girl, meet her inside the dance hall beyond the coat check so she pays her own way.

That took care of Saturday evenings. During the day, it was the Senior Citizen Center for a cheap meal and dancing. It was a great life, the golden years were truly gold.

When the center sponsored a weekend in the country, many of the girls asked me if I was going. I said I would meet them there. That way I wouldn't pay for them and they wouldn't hang on to me, killing my chances of meeting someone else. George and I shared a room. We had an arrangement that if one of us was using it and was not to be disturbed, he would leave a rubber band on the doorknob.

The first evening I met a pretty lady. Brought her up to the room. There was the rubber band on the knob. George got there first. Down we went for more coffee. An hour later the room was empty. My big moment had arrived. My luck. Of all the women I met I chose one who had the beliefs of a nun. Sex was the last thing on her mind. What a waste.

Back to the center. There I met a nice lady. Saw her several times and eventually moved in with her. It worked well. No more cooking, cleaning, or laundry. She did it all. A housekeeper and lover all in one. Life was great. I was saving my pension checks. We lived on our Social Security.

The winter was getting colder and the nights longer, which didn't do my asthma any good. I suggested she sell her house and buy a condo in Florida. That idea did not go over well, and now I'm on a plane to Florida. I will stay with my children, start all over. Now I have experience.

George taught me well. It won't be long before I land a well-heeled shark with her own house and settle down with that golden sun keeping me warm during the remaining golden years.

CHANGES

Glen S. Schreiner

Nothing stays the same, even if it still looks pretty much the same after it changes.

A group of us members of the Social Security set were playing cards the other day when someone remembered the first deck of cards he had ever seen. He had found them. Lost or thrown away by another person. He thought they were so pretty and wondered if they could be used as Christmas tree decorations.

His father set him straight. These, he was told, were the Devil's cards, designed to trap the unwary into gambling away their birthright. So for forty years, he didn't dare pick up a deck of cards. Yet here he was doubling my four-spade bid with the non-chalance of a tree shedding its autumn leaves.

His story reminded me of a particular washday when I was a sophomore in high school. It was the first week after school let out. We had all gotten up early and milked thirty-five cows by hand. I never appreciated brothers more than at milking time. After breakfast I filled three black kettles with cistern water and built a fire under them. Then I lined up three tubs on the wash bench and put bluing in one. Mom had her hands full sorting dirty clothes for a family of ten.

She was emptying pockets when she called me, by my first, middle, and last names, in a voice of shock and horror. I hurried inside and found her kneeling by my bed. She was deep in prayer, and in her hand was that unknown object I'd found in a bar ditch on the way home from school.

The packet was labeled "Trojan." To my mind that meant a wooden horse, but all I found were two odd-looking balloons. I blew one up but didn't like the shape, so I threw it away. I put the other one in my pocket and promptly forgot it.

Now here was Mom, tears streaming down her face, praying for the redemption of my soul. She told me to kneel beside her and beg God to forgive me. And I did. I prayed that He would forgive me for whatever that wooden horse had done to my life. I didn't know what else to pray for.

Attitudes about the evil of cards have certainly changed. Whole families get hours of enjoyment from playing cards and don't feel sinful doing it. And if a modern youth found the same thing I did, his mother would offer him a full explanation. She would give him a chance to tell her how he happened to have it, and use the episode as a lesson in living. Wouldn't she?

PARTY

Norman Sage

Today I am seventy years old. I am amazed by the simple fact, but will not remark on it further than to express mild alarm; and to remind myself that however hard you try to forget, it is easier to contemplate the past than the future—there is bound to be more back there than there is up ahead; and to remember that life slides by on the fluid crest of time, as they say. That's about as philosophical as I plan to get about it, although I can't help totting up this statistic: it has been one year, nine months, and thirteen days, at just about this hour.

Because I feel, in some obscure way, that the day should be noted, I am giving a party. It is to be catered by some young ladies who do that sort of thing, and they are going to do it all, from drinks and snacks to a sit-down dinner. It will cost me a bundle.

I will go to the office this morning as usual—it is now nearly five-thirty—and I will discuss and probably argue about proofs and editing and jackets and other things more or less interesting, and then I'll come home to bathe and dress and wait for my guests to arrive. I must remember to plump up the cushions on the sofa.

There will be fifteen for dinner, and I have just realized that they all have names that are in vogue now. Jan, Debbie, Kathy, and Em will bring their current husbands or friends, Josh, Uriah, Bones, and Bobby Lee. What happened to Tom, Dick, and Harry? As they arrive I will greet them with a peck on the cheek for the women and a firm handclasp for the men. And I will be astonished—again—at their youth. These are the people I work with, and for the most part they are pleasant to have around. They pose a little, and some of them drink and smoke too much, but they're good people and they like me, I think. In any event, they enjoy a good meal and a few drinks, and my parties are thought of kindly.

They will indulge me in my offerings of music for the occasion, all on tape, for I will allow no one to touch the records themselves. They will half listen, or not listen at all, because they will be busy laying bare their hearts to each other. But I will listen: "It's the Talk of the Town," "Ain't Misbehavin'," "Body and Soul," "Lover, Come Back to Me," "Opus 3/4," "Sugar"—I've even worked in a chunk of the last great movement of Dvorak's Fifth, just to see if anyone shifts gears noticeably.

I will look at them all and smile and lust after some of the younger women, of course. I'll tell you something about seventy: it isn't necessarily dead. I will look particularly at Debbie, who is very beautiful if not terribly bright. Once she saw a bird at my out-door feeder and asked what kind it was. When I told her it was just a little old junco, she wondered how I could tell it was on dope. But she is lovely to look at, and it seems to me that if one has the *idea* of a perfect late love it should be possible, that if the imagination is capable of establishing the circumstances, the active mind should have the power to bring them into being. Nothing, I have been told, is impossible. If you think I don't know better, you're a dime short.

So I will look at them and marvel at their vigor and wonder when I lost the moments that were there and those I felt would someday come and didn't; and I will envy them their youth but not their insouciance. I will imagine some of them unclothed, but I will not touch—I'm very trustworthy—and I will do my best to ignore their young men, in perfectly friendly ways, of course.

When the greetings have been made and the drinks passed around and the music played—which they have listened to only out of the corners of their ears—and when we have observed the formalities of dinner, I will steal out of the house to walk around the shores of our little lake, to hear the sweet evening sounds of spring and remember seventy fleeting years; and I will wonder how I came to this dreadful state. I see the world now much as I have always seen it—bearing in mind the facts of four wars, a depression, unimaginable voyages to the moon, an assassinated president and a deposed one, and a planet ill at ease with itself in the knowledge of awesome and imminent destruction. I will hear the night cry of a catbird and the lonely call of a hound across the water. And I will remember the rise and fall of a woman's breast as she breathes her last harsh breaths—that other part of me, sore missed.

I will think, My God! The promised time has come and gone; but I will tell myself that there is yet time. I will say to myself, Let your breath come without willing it to do so, and do not write sorrow on the bosom of the earth. The earth has plenty without your small part.

Then I will go back to my guests and they will not know I have been gone, for they notice only themselves. And *seventy* is quite beyond their comprehension.

CHOOSE LIFE

Nathan Horowitz

He sighed, shifted his position, and closed his eyes. Nu, so it hurts. What can you expect? Eighty-two years, parts wear out. It's a long, long time, Solomon. Thank God, he thought, there is a limit. Time has to run out. The heart, his engine. Cardiac arrest ... quadruple bypass ... joint replacement.... It's enough.

His legs were outstretched, his feet rested on the footstool. Doctor's orders, reduce the edema, the swelling of his ankles. A burden, I'm a burden to everybody. What's the use of further existence?

Daniel, his son, squeezed out time from a busy day and rushed in periodically to see him, to ease the burden of the long, eternal, never-ending day in the choking depression of the nursing home. Ladies in their eighties and nineties—Fannie Bloom was one hundred and two. Walkers, canes, wheelchairs. Geriatric disabilities.

Iber bottel—senility. Not a coherent male to engage in even a casual conversation. The same in every nursing home. Women live longer than men.

His face hardened when this was told to him.

"Really! Then why have I survived my Dora?"

Dora! His beautiful, adored Dora! The hurt was relentless. The insidious cancer. Five horrendous years and its final triumph on that devastating, unerasable early morning. Dora. The tears started welling. He had to get out of his room. The loneliness and longing was a smothering blanket.

In the hallway, as he sat undecided in his wheelchair, Elsie of the squinting eyes said to him, "Why don't you try walking?" The nurse shushed her and steered her away.

Why don't I walk? Good question. Ask God, he muttered to himself. Never gained a dishonest cent, moderately observant, provided for my family, saw the boys through college—doctorates yet. Why this? I'm used up. So end it, dear Lord, end it!

The Friday night service in the home was a sore trial for him. Patients from the infirmary were wheeled in. Two men from the Alzheimer's ward tottered to their seats. Volunteers from the outside world conducted the beautiful Erev Shabbos poetry: "Lekho dodi. ... Come, my beloved. ... Welcome Bride Sabbath."

He closed his eyes and immersed himself in the beloved old melodies. A palsied hand was on his arm. Louie, shaking Louie, could not handle his siddur. Momentarily startled, Solomon turned the page and pointed to the place. Louie managed a contorted smile of thanks.

Solomon stared intently at the poor soul. My God! I'm still of some use to somebody! Words he used to sing echoed in his ears. "Ov'havetem Chaim besosone memyvay hayeshua. And you will draw life with joy from the wells of hope."

He grasped Louie's shaking hand. "Thank you," he said.

Louie stared vacantly at him.

MY FATHER, MY CHILD

Elizabeth Castner

As I helped him dress this morning, he stared straight ahead. Where was he? In another world, another place, another time?

"Almost finished," I tell him.

"Almost finished, Anna?" he asks.

"Yes, Pa, but I'm not Anna," I say. "I'm Liz, your daughter. Who is Anna?"

"Anna is ..." He looks doubtful, and says it again. "Anna is ..." Then he sighs and clamps his mouth shut tight. He has forgotten Anna. Anna, my mother, his wife of forty-five years.

Before breakfast, I watch him remove the sheet from the calendar that tells the day, date, month, and year, hoping that he will remember it for a little while.

He walks, aided by his old carved oak cane, into the kitchen. "Good morning, Spot. Good morning ... uh ... uh, puss," he greets the dog and cat.

Hooray, good for him, I think. He has remembered one name, and that it is morning time.

"Wait, Pa, I'll help you," I say as his cane catches in the chair leg. Luckily he doesn't fall. I clip a large piece of plastic to his shirt. I tell him it is a cover, but it's really a big bib. He sits patiently with hands folded in front of him, staring straight ahead. Thinking ... of what?

Every morning it's the same menu. Prune and orange juice mixed. Cornflakes with bran, banana, and milk. Coffee, of course. You'd think it was eggs Benedict, fruit nectar, and champagne. But then, he always did like to eat. Nothing wrong with his appetite, thank goodness.

After breakfast I remind him he is to go to the bathroom. I help him up and lead him to the toilet. He stands there—he doesn't know what he is supposed to do. I tell him, but already it is too late. I see the dark stain spreading on his trousers. I'm angry and exasperated. He says, "Don't be mad at me," but I am.

Later in the day he goes out for his very short stroll, only to the third house up the street. I remind him how far he can go, and ask him again, "Who are you, what's your name?" He looks me straight in the eye and says, "You know who I am." I nod. I watch him walk off, a big man, straight and proud. He will be back shortly, bent, frightened, and confused.

I turn and glance at my flower beds and decide to pull a few weeds while waiting. This is my therapy. I'm engrossed and forget the time. Suddenly I realize Pa is nowhere to be seen. I get in the car and drive up and down the streets. I don't see him anywhere. I hope he is wearing his ID bracelet.

I go back to the house and call the sheriff's department. In five minutes' time a young deputy is at the door. He takes all the information. Then, trying to comfort me, he says, "Don't worry, ma'am, this happens a lot. There's always crazy old folks wandering off."

"That's my *father*," I tell him. My father, my child.

Two hours later the deputy is back, with my father seated beside him in the patrol car. Pa is chatting away, telling the polite deputy of long ago when he too was in police work. He looks at me and smiles. He doesn't realize the anguish he has caused me. I scold and he pouts. He doesn't know. He doesn't know I was afraid for him.

In the evening I put him to bed. "Have a good night, see you in the morning," I say, as always.

"You too," he answers.

As I leave the room I hear him call, "Thanks for everything, Anna." And then he starts humming loudly. Over and over, a tune only he knows.

TO MY SON, DYING OF AIDS

Jody Farrell

I hold you, my son,
in your last bed,
matching my breath to yours,
as if in that pacing
I could breathe for you.

Your window frames a distant blue.
Small vines and jasmine flowers
net the glass.
Sunlight weaves the sheets to lace.

My arms enfold you, my son.
Under my hands I feel your heart's slow pulse
dropping through my fingers
like the small stones of a rosary.

Hail, Mary. Full of Grace …
So she held her own son once.

I hold you, my son,
in your last bed
until white stars replace
the jasmine flowers
and it is night.

THE GRANDSON

Doris Sullivan

It was an ordinary night, a welcome
Friday with no social obligations, a good time to begin the
weekend's rest. I watched as Roy, my husband of thirty-eight
years, built a cheerful fire against the January cold, then settled
into his chair beside it. I reached for a book, ignoring again the
Christmas wreath that still hung above the mantel. I smiled at the
memory of Carolyn, my lovely young daughter-in-law, wrestling
with the live cedar branches a few weeks earlier to make us a
"real" Christmas wreath.

Bill was lucky to find her, I thought, my heart swelling with
pride for my twenty-two-year-old son. How fortunate we were in
our children: Ann with a four-year-old daughter, living with her

husband in Atlanta, and Bill with Carolyn, already a vital part of our family.

There are moments that alter the course of our lives, moments that change us from optimist to pessimist, from believer to nonbeliever. My moment came at 9:00 p.m. on that cold January night.

"Dead," said the sheriff of our Louisiana parish. "Bill and Carolyn both. Hit by a drunk driver."

The funeral, the consoling words of friends—nothing moved past my ears to comfort my heart. I had decided. I would never love again.

I faked my recovery from grief, responding with expected words to those who sought to reach me. When my daughter announced that she was pregnant again, I feigned joy, but in reality I saw her pregnancy as a threat to the life of my remaining child.

The baby was due in December, near the birthday of my son. We waited as a family, knowing now that we had no special immunity against tragedy. Imagine our joy at the birth of a healthy boy, named Will for the uncle he would never know.

But I continued in my private hell, for I could not connect with this baby. I held him, fed him, rocked him, and sang him the lullabies my son had loved, but my heart refused to accept him as one of my own.

One spring day we were alone, the little guy and I, and as I watched him kick playfully in the sunlight streaming through the glass to the center of the king-sized bed, I realized that I was scared to death. Afraid of a three-month-old, I mused as I left him and went to check the laundry.

That's when I heard the thump. I rushed into the bedroom. His mouth was open, but like me, he was unable to cry. Clutching him in my arms, I ran outside into the cold spring air. I held him against my face, his first real tears mixed with my own, and we sobbed together, he angry and frightened, me thankful that I had found with him a capacity to love again.

MY DINING ROOM TABLE

Cecelia O'Meara

We had bought a condominium, and our beautiful old mahogany table was too big for the space they laughably called the dining room. The table was special to me, and I hated the thought of giving it up, but I finally accepted the fact that the dining room wasn't going to expand and the table wasn't going to shrink. It had to go.

My husband assumed the responsibility of selling it, and I disliked the buyer as soon as he described her as very young and very sweet. I liked her even less when he told me he'd lowered our asking price a little because that was all she could afford. I didn't like the girl, and I didn't want her to have my table. I wanted it to go to someone older who would appreciate it. To anyone who'd listen, I ranted, "She probably doesn't know the difference between mahogany and plywood. She's just an airhead looking for a table, any table. Probably her check will bounce." To put it mildly, I was unhappy about the transaction.

She promised to call me before coming to pick the table up. A few days later, when I came around the corner with the back of my car full of groceries and saw a pickup truck at the curb and strangers on the lawn, I was furious. I had planned to be cool, serene, and in command when I met her, not hot, disheveled, and hauling in groceries. My only happy thought was that she had not kept her word about calling—that proved I was right in labeling her immature.

She was friendly and gracious as she introduced me to her tiny daughter, her husband, and her brother-in-law. They cheerfully insisted on helping me carry in the groceries. They were being so nice, and I was finding it hard to be civil.

While the men concerned themselves with how best to move the table without scratching it, I put on my warmest smile and most condescending air and proceeded to tell the young lady how valuable the table was and how fortunate she was to get it. I poured on the charm, but my message was obvious. I was looking down my nose at her. She heard me out, then quietly told me how long they had been saving for a dining room table. Not just any table, but something durable and beautiful they could have for their life-time, a focal point for gatherings of family and friends, a source of happy memories their daughter could carry with her when she left them to establish her own home. She said she knew our table was what she had dreamed of owning as soon as she saw it and that she would love it as I had.

As she talked, I realized that she could see right through me. She knew I was hurting because I was giving up something that had been a part of my life for many years. She was being kind and sensitive and overlooking the fact that I was acting like a snob. It was almost funny. I had planned to play the role of mature, grand lady, but at the moment she was far more mature and grand than I.

My hostility disappeared. It really was time for the table to move along. It wasn't used to the quiet atmosphere that had become our life. It needed activity and energy. It needed voices, laughter, elbows, cookie crumbs and milk, coffee cups and wine-glasses—things we could no longer provide.

I watched the table go out the front door, and my eyes filled with tears. I let the tears fall and listened to the sounds from the past: my mother laughing as she tried to blow out the candles on her last birthday cake, our son singing softly and playing his guitar while I drank my after-dinner coffee, our daughter trying to explain to her father why she wanted to move to an apartment, holidays, birthdays, and wine by candlelight with loved and loving friends. Early or late, whatever our schedule, we gathered around the table for dinner. We discussed religion, politics and sex, civil rights and the Vietnam War, curfews, where to go to college, wed-ding plans. We had laughter, tears, big fights, and little arguments. That table shared it all.

I grew up around a dining room table, and I had wanted the same experience for my children. My sweet young buyer wanted it for her daughter, and I loved her for it.

The table was placed lovingly in the back of the pickup truck. I watched them drive away, then walked through an empty dining room into the kitchen to start dinner.

BE IT EVER SO HUMBLE

Lola C. Little

It creaked and groaned, as if alive, gave one final shudder, and reluctantly fell to the ground. This old weathered and warped pile of boards and beams had once been our home. Could it possibly be aware of the panoply of life that had unfolded within its walls? Could it possibly remember the young couple moving into it, the new babies born in the bedroom, the noisy laughter and noisy tears of the children, the quiet laughter and quiet tears of the parents? Could it know that for all those years it had been our shelter from the harshness of the world?

The house was small. A back porch with a wringer washer, the kitchen with the black Monarch stove, a pantry with open shelves filled with home-canned fruits and vegetables, the small bedroom where our parents dreamed, loved, gave life to their children. Then there was the parlor, which in our simple life we called "the other room." It was the forerunner of modern family rooms, catching the overflow from the kitchen, the heart and hub of our house.

The wood-burning stove was positioned so that a small body could lie snug and warm behind it. Each spring this desirable spot had to be relinquished during lambing season, when woolly early arrivals needed to catch their breath after their entry into the cold, wet world of the Palouse Hills. There was a long wooden table where we all had designated places for meals. Dad sat at the head, Mom to his right, and the hired man at the end, with the kids sprinkled between. In the evenings, with the kerosene lamps lit, the cleared table became the gathering place for reading, talking, homework, card playing, and making shadows on the walls.

And oh, to remember the smells that radiated from that room! Loaves of freshly baked bread with crusts that slid over the edges of the black pans; doughnuts as big as inner tubes, frying and sizzling in the grease; pies heaped high with meringue; home-cured hams and bacon; thick spicy ketchup simmering on the stove, and big fluffy dumplings bubbling and bumping around in the soup pot. Each season was welcomed with traditional foods.

Steep stairs led to a loft, open on the left for the boys, closed on the right for the girls' privacy. With two beds, one small chest, one clothes rod, and five girls, the "boudoir" could hardly be classified as private! It was a drafty old house, and when the winter blizzards blew across the hills, we vied for the middle position in bed and jockeyed for a foothold on the sack of heated prune seeds that went up the cold stairs with us at night.

The front of the house was graced with a ceremonial porch where we greeted the Watkins man on his seasonal country calls or bought a bug-eyed salmon from the fish man during Lent. Most important, the porch served as the site for the Sunday inspection, the weekly roundup of the tribe, to be counted, sorted, and given a final spit-and-rub before we loaded up and headed out for the seven-mile trip to church.

Another building, not connected to our house, but definitely connected to our lives, hugged a hillside much too far away on cold, frosty nights. This important edifice was the typically sturdy, practical "two-holer," surrounded by closely planted and well-nourished hollyhocks.

The little building on the hillside was long gone, and so were the hollyhocks. Soon the old house would be gone too, hauled away as if it never stood, never mattered. Everything would be new now except the memories. We would take them with us.

I Do What I Must

Betty Schambacher

The moving van has gone. Loaded with the accumulation of a lifetime, it has started on the journey of a thousand miles to the northwest town where my son and daughter live and where a rented apartment waits for me. My new home. Home? A word as good as any.

I walk along the driveway of my house—not our house anymore, just mine—and look down the familiar street lined with jacaranda trees that carpet the lawns with lavender blossoms in late spring. Chances are I will not see this street again. There will be no reason to return. No one is here.

The side door opens, and my son appears to empty a pail of water into the row of juniper bushes that marks the property line. He has finished cleaning the kitchen floor, a final job before we lock the house for the last time and leave the key for the real estate agent.

The car is packed with cartons holding an assortment of canned and dried foods, with a box of keepsakes and valuables I could not relinquish to the movers, with suitcases and extra sweaters.

I start to speak to my son, but he has gone back inside. I suspect he is inventing more tasks to delay our departure. He has come to help me move, but he does not want to leave. Although he has not lived in this house since he went away to college, it is where he was born. To him it is the place that means home. To me it is the place that holds pain.

I go up the porch steps under the arch of scarlet bougainvillea Lee planted so long ago. My son's father. My husband, Lee. They tell me that when a year has gone by I will have come to terms with his death. Fifty years stripped of their power to devastate in twelve months? I do not believe it.

The pain, always busy, produces a vicious stab when I step inside the entry hall. The blue ceramic tiles Lee put down are shining; the built-in bookshelves he made are clean and empty, their books, usually dusty, none of them new, gone with the van.

In the empty living room the bare walls are etched with the outlines of Lee's paintings, each inspired by some photo we'd taken a thousand years ago. The painting over the mantel renewed memories of Capri, where one midnight, full of song and love and wine, we had danced for the sheer joy of dancing in the garden courtyard of our pensione.

Across the room, captured in oils, malevolent storm clouds massed above a lonely highway in Wyoming. It was the year we drove across the country in our first new car, Lee's Wildcat. How he had loved it—a kid with a new toy.

On the wall above the piano, a Cotswold village scene reminded us of the ancient hotel maid who bumbled into our room while Lee was pulling on his underwear. At her offended look we had laughed until we cried, unable to maintain even a shred of dignity while she stood there.

So many memories packed in crates and moving along a freeway somewhere in southern California.

Through the big window I see my son checking out the patio his father built. New ferns are in the planter that once held a fountain Lee made. He could not be content unless he had a project under way. He called it progress. One of his favorite words. Progress.

Pain abruptly grips me by the throat, and I run for the bathroom to retch into the toilet. My son pauses by the door and calls out to me. I tell him I'm fine. He is also full of pain, and I cannot add to it, nor even help myself by sharing my own.

There is no way out of any of it. People offer words meant to comfort, but the pain cannot hear and stays close to me. It is invincible. Months, years perhaps, stretch ahead without Lee. Unthinkable, but I think of it. I am lost.

My son calls again; it is time to go. I come out of the bathroom and collect my coat and my purse. There is nothing more to be done. The house is empty.

My son waits in the car, the motor running. Two of the neighbors stand in their yards waving and calling out words I do not grasp, although I nod and smile and wave back. I notice the thorns on the bougainvillea. Dangerous thorns. The vine must be pruned, but that's someone else's problem. I close the door of my house.

People survive, and perhaps I too am a survivor. Right now I am not sure.

I do what I must do. I close the door on my life.

FOREVER YOURS

Ernest Esposito

Do you know how it feels to be dead and yet not dead? Alive and yet not alive? On July 15, 1990, at 10:00 a.m., my wife died of cancer, and I died along with her. Do you know how it feels to die? There's an ache in your stomach, constantly eating away at your soul, and a sense of not being where you're at, not knowing or caring either. Just a feeling of nothingness. You even have thoughts of taking the little life you have left in you and killing it. "Suicide" is the word for it? I call it "going home." Going home to your loved one. But my friend, a Catholic priest, says taking your own life is an unforgivable sin against the will of God, so there would be no going home for me, only eternal misery without Him or her. So I exist and pray every night that our Lord will watch over her and me. I ask him every day please not to let our love die, for it is a beautiful love, surely made in heaven.

Do you ever get up in the morning and find yourself opening the venetian blinds to let the light in, for no other reason than to see the smile on her face when she wakes up?

Do you know why you find crawling in traffic on the highway at five miles an hour so good, though you hate it, because you can hold her hand?

Do you know what it's like to battle and fight all night long but always kiss before you go to sleep, and upon awakening say, "That was yesterday"?

We lived, we loved, and she was sick, and she was gone from me, without any way of my going with her or being with her except to sit and stare at her picture and play tapes of her voice, over and over again. It's all I have of my life, her image and her voice. I have no desire to live, and yet I'm afraid of dying.

What to do with what's left I just don't know. I just don't really know.

I WILL NOT QUIT

Treva Zoellner

William B. Zoellner, out of MGM's home office in New York, the principal speaker at the Theater Owner's Convention in Oklahoma City, a man who had experienced the world. I, a young woman from a small town in Oklahoma, who grew up under the watchful eye of a chaperon. Bill and I met. I ran. He chased me. One year, one month, and sixteen days later we were married.

A Hollywood wedding in Manhattan! The Christians and Jews Friendship Club, MGM, RKO, Columbia, and other film companies honored us with lavish wedding showers and lovely parties. Life was filled with excitement. I felt that all of it had been part of me forever!

We lived in Connecticut on the bank of a river, at the foot of a mountain where deer wandered among the white birch trees. Bill gave me the world from great airplanes and ships of the sea. We saw Paris, London, Rome, classical theater in Vienna. We represented MGM at the Berlin Film Festival. We dove into the ocean's depths off the shores of Bermuda and made films at the Taj Mahal. We laughed and cried and shared with people in many lands, but our hearts always leaned happily toward home.

The children we wanted so badly never came. I counseled exceptional children. On warm summer nights twenty or twenty-five of them, ages ten to fourteen, would find their way with sleeping bags to our long terrace and fall asleep under the night sky, lulled by the river below. Our Doberman, Woody (Treva's King of Brentwood), kept lookout as he lay at the end of the terrace pretending to sleep, a squirrel or two cuddled in the arch of his neck or a robin perched on his hip.

Our live-in help would go away for the weekend if we weren't entertaining some of the theater folk who found respite in the quiet of our home. When we were alone, Bill would make a special brunch and serve it with French champagne. We had fun together, we laughed together. I was Mrs. William B. Zoellner.

When I walked into the bedroom that day, Bill was on the phone: "Bernard, I'm bleeding." He was rushed to the hospital. Doctors and nurses ran helter-skelter. Massive blood loss ... everything collapsed except heart and lungs ... brain damage. "He is gone as we knew him," they were saying. "He won't be back." My world shook, eternity flashed before me. "Oh, God," I sobbed softly.

I took Bill home from the hospital three months later. He struggled to comprehend his mental and physical deficiencies. In the meantime, my mother and father had died. Soon Woody would also die, from stress.

Nine years later, my tears continued to flow. I saw two or three doctors a week, and I had been in the hospital three times that year—psychosomatic problems turned physical. I thought I would soon die, and then who would care for Bill?

One of my doctors sent me to a yoga class. The instructor led us through stretching, bending, and twisting exercises. We learned how to relax and breathe as we had when we were born. The instructor said, "You must learn to use the strength, the power within you—God's strength within you. He gave you a mind, He gave you a will. Use them. Choose positive, creative thoughts. Find and accomplish your ideals." I heard her. My tears stopped.

Bill did not know me. Every day he would say, "Come, let's look for Mrs. Zoellner," or "I want to find my wife." My three brothers insisted that I come home to Oklahoma with Bill for family support. Our money had to be reinvested. I put everything in Oklahoma real estate. Seven years later the Oklahoma economy failed. I lost everything in 1986. All three of my brothers had died in the previous eighteen months. I had no money. I sent the caregivers away. People said, "Treva, you can't do it alone." I said, "You watch me. I will not fail. I will not quit."

When Bill slept, I would lie beside him with my arm around him. One day he smiled broadly, joyfully at me and said, "Oh, Little"—my pet name—"you have come home!" No greater blessing—his mind had returned. We shared a magic afternoon. We held hands and smiled at each other a lot. Bill grew quiet. Then he stretched out his right arm and reached to the left. He was laughing happily. "They are here. They have come for me," he said, and lay back on his pillow and closed his eyes. He released his breath. His pain had stopped forever.

The great oak grew from the little acorn out of the darkness of the ground. It bowed down to the mighty winds and harsh storms, then stood taller and stronger for its experience, to spread its leafy branches and shelter the weary. I, like the great oak, grew through the storms. O Lord, let me give love and help the hurting with a smile, an encouraging word, these two willing hands.

I'm Not Alone, Jack

Anne Browner

I turned in my sleep and reached out to your side of the bed. My hand moved across the empty pillow, but my slumbering mind sensed the presence of your head. I brushed your cheek with my lips; you hadn't shaved, who cares. The rhythm of your soft snoring soothed me. I put my arms around you, drew my body close to yours. Suddenly you took my hand. Still in darkness, I saw your smile and felt a tender tingle as your eager lips touched mine.

Then I heard the noise. The morning paper had hit the door. I opened my eyes and spoke, but you weren't there. You weren't there anymore.

But are you here? I have seen you in the drawers I emptied, in the closet when I took out your clothes, and there's your comb and brush, your shaving cream. In the kitchen I found your favorite cup, the little knife you bought—"It's great for peeling oranges," you said. I see the big chair in the living room: you're sitting there beside me, and the TV set is on. Sometimes you nod your head in sleep, sometimes you reach out for me. All the furniture you made—I touch the pieces every day. Your skillful hands once touched them too.

I see you in the eyes of our children and in their pictures on the wall. I hear you in their spoken words and when they laugh or cry, and I know you in their anger when they raise their voices high.

Yes, you're here! You are in my dreams and my thoughts, in the ache of my lonely heart, and in every corner of our home. You are here with me, and I am not alone! I'm not alone, Jack.

THIRD WORLD

Ouina Sutter

In 1980 I reached the age of sixty-seven and almost reached the abyss of depression and self-pity. My son very forcefully and skillfully pushed me to enroll in some courses where I might learn to be of use to others. I began to teach non-readers to read and liked it. A year later we had an influx of Asian refugees from Vietnam, Cambodia, and Thailand who not only could not read English but could not speak or understand it. At the time there were no ESL (English as a Second Language) programs in our county, and again my son found me a short course specializing in this type of teaching. When I finished I offered my services to a nearby school, and they were absolutely delighted. The program was an immediate success. Unbelievable as it may seem, many students were brought to grade level in four to six months, with the others not far behind. I had found my niche. I worked five days a week full-time with the children, and evenings and weekends with their families. My love for them was no less than their love for me.

In appreciation, the governor of my state presented me with a plaque honoring me as Volunteer of the Year in my section of the state. Shortly after the ceremony I met with a recruiter for the United States Peace Corps, who urged me to apply. Me, now age seventy-one? Go to a foreign country to work? Could I do it? Wasn't I too old? I didn't know, but I would try.

Within months I found myself in Latin America learning a new language and a new culture. I found myself working with people in the campos and jungles of a Third World country. I lived with them in their poorly constructed houses and became a member of their community. I ate with them, played with them, cried with them, taught in their schools, exchanged ideas and customs. Soon they were teaching me as I was teaching them. Once again I fell in love, this time with a whole countryside of adults and children. It was not long before I realized that they were giving me much more than I was giving them.

My friends at home couldn't understand why I would "sacrifice" so much to live in shanties in a country where food was in short supply, medical care miles away, city life and entertainment as we know it almost nonexistent, transportation poor. Why? I'll tell you why! I was their friend, I was their confidant, I was their light at the end of the tunnel, I was their hope. I ate their rice and beans, I took their cold shivering showers without complaint, I traveled their rutted roads by foot, ancient bus, cart, and horse. I visited their homes and taught their children the new language they so eagerly wanted to learn. When I was ill they used their herbs and massage techniques to make me well. Their churches took care of my spiritual needs. From the tiniest child to the oldest adult, they gave me their honest love and trust. Any wonder I wanted to stay with them forever?

After almost five years, my tour with Peace Corps was completed and I had to come home. And so, at the age of seventy-seven, here I am.

Will I return? You bet your life. I left my heart there.

CANCEL THAT CREMATION

Esther Nelson

When you get old, the most difficult thing to deal with is your own body. It no longer fits you, and neither does anything else. It's bad enough to be uncomfortable in your clothes, but at least you can take them off. When your skin no longer fits, what can you do?

Our bodies constantly betray us, often in very significant and obvious ways. Somehow most of us surmount these or accept the devices that help us live with them. It is not the big heart attack but the smaller disasters that do us in—the tremors, the salivating, the dropping of food, all the unmanageable little things you try to cover up. Nothing really works, because the elastic is gone and your skin no longer hugs your bones.

In Portugal there are many bones. They are carefully preserved because the people believe that God must have the skeleton on which to drape the new and glorious body. When one of the old churches had to be rebuilt, a lot of bones got mixed up, so they dug deep pits with manhole-type covers. In they all went, higgledy-piggledy, trusting that God would be able to sort them out and those dead could be resurrected in the flesh.

I have chosen to believe that. My order is in for a sleek new body. I will glisten like a wet seal. It will fit tight, and not even the corners of my mouth will droop. Does it come with wings? They didn't tell me!

NOTES ON THE CONTRIBUTORS

HELEN DARCY ABBOTT, 75, is an artist and writer. Recently widowed after 47 years of marriage, she has eight children and many grandchildren. She loves books, classical music, travel, and camping, and lives in the California Sierras.

WILSON G. ALONSO was born in Barcelona in 1920, came to the United States in 1937, and has been working ever since. Educated in Europe and Egypt, he served in the U.S. Army from 1942 to 1945, married in 1946, and has three children and three grandchildren. He lives in North Palm Beach, Florida.

LAURA ARBEIT, 72, studied acting with Stella Adler and Lee Strasberg and had a 30-year career in the theater. Encouraged by her husband, Carl, and her daughter, Jill, she wrote a mystery novel. She lives in Boca Raton and is working on a book of memoirs for her grandsons, Steven and David.

Born in 1915, CELIA C. ASHTON was married for 34 years. She has five children, five grandchildren, and an M.S.W. from Fresno State. She worked as a psychotherapist for 40 years and is now enjoying a new lifestyle in a beautiful retirement community in California.

BESSIE DUTY ASPAN, 75, was born in southwest Mississippi and now lives in Houston. She is retired and loves to write, read, attend church, garden, and visit with family and friends. Her son, Michael, and his wife, D-Ann, have two daughters, Ari and Holly.

SALLY BALER writes and directs musical shows for the Jewish Federation of Palm Beach County. A former dancer and newspaperwoman, she is from the Boston area and has been a Florida resident for five years.

BETTY TARBELL BARTEN, 73, is a retired R.N. from East Aurora, New York. She writes and researches health topics, biographies, and genealogy. She loves to write nostalgic bits drawn from raising four children and spoiling nine grandchildren.

JAMES DRANE BARWICK, 69, is living quietly and happily ever after with his wife, Doris Langford, in Jackson, Mississippi.

SARI BLACHARSKI lives in New Jersey.

ERIKA BRODSKY, née Thuna, was born in Vienna in 1924. She lives in Pompano Beach, Florida, and has three daughters, seven grandchildren, one twin brother, and a wonderful husband.

ANNE BROWNER, 79, lives in Deerfield Beach, Florida, has two daughters and four grandchildren, and has been a member of Writer's Workshop for the past 16 years. She and her husband, Jack, had been married for 52 years when he died in 1990.

Born on the Mississippi River shore, nudged by Eads Bridge and "Westward Ho!," MILDRED BUNK has experienced history's most fabulous era.

BLANCHE CAFFIERE lives with her husband, Cyril, on Vashon Island, near Seattle. She has two children and six grandchildren. Now retired after 35 years as a teacher and/or school librarian, she volunteers, writes, and has self-published a book, *Much Laughter, a Few Tears*.

At 73, MICHAEL CARACAPPA is retired and still going strong. He has many interests and doesn't know where they'll take him, but wherever, he's *going*. He lives in New York City.

CHARLOTTE CARPENTER, 74, has lived on a farm all her life and has been married to a farmer for 52 years. They have five children, eight grandchildren, and three great-grandchildren. With the talent God gave her, she has been able to write hundreds of poems and articles, many of them published.

Since 1987, ELIZABETH CASTNER, 65, has been a member of the Long Term Care Ombudsman Council, an advocacy group for residents of nursing homes and other LTC facilities. Her philosophy is "Live and help live" (I. Singer), and she is *delighted* to have reached Medicare age. She lives in Tallahassee.

ROBERT CHRISTIN lives in Virginia.

JOHN COLEMAN has written many stories about his 10 years in the coal mines of Scotland as a boy. He enjoys visiting local nursing homes to sing the old-time songs and read the poetry he writes, his first love.

MYRTLE COOPER, 85, holds a B.A. and an M.A. and is a retired research librarian. A member of the DAR, PEO, and Kappa Kappa Gamma sorority, she lives in Billings, Montana.

Born in 1924, H. RUTH COPPINGER is widowed and has two children and three grandsons. A retired clinical social worker, marriage and family counselor, and psychotherapist, she lives in Seminole, Florida. Her hobbies include singing with Sweet Adelines International, gardening, and writing.

HELEN COVELL, 86, spent a year with the American Red Cross during World War II and has been in the fashion business most of her life.

Born on a farm in New York State, she now lives at The Fountains, a retirement center in Tucson.

ELIZABETH BORNCAMP COWLES was born in Boston in 1903 and now lives in Santa Barbara. Writing has been her interest since she was 15, and she has been encouraged by her instructors in adult education courses and University of California extension classes. She has two daughters.

BERNICE MINNIE SAPIRSTEIN DAVIS divides her time between Ohio and her island home on the west coast of Florida. Her lifelong interest is horticulture, and during the six months she spends in Florida, she cultivates citrus trees in large terra cotta pots. Her record is 56 lemons on one tree.

ED DENZLER, 70, is retired and lives in Pearland, Texas. He can occasionally be found in the pulpit on Sundays or consulting on an engineering problem on weekdays, but always on the golf course when the weather is fair. Not necessarily good, just fair.

LOLA B. DEVAUGHN was born in 1911 in Mantachie, Mississippi, where she still lives today. She attended college in the summers and on Saturdays to earn a B.A. in elementary education and an M.S. in special education. She and her husband have one son, George, three grandsons, and one great-grandson.

Born in Greenwood, South Carolina, MARIE ELIZABETH DODSON graduated from Queens College in Charlotte, North Carolina, with an A.B. in English literature. She has two sons and a daughter, and lives with her husband in Annapolis.

EMERSON EMORY, M.D., was born in Dallas, Texas, the son of Corry B. and Louise Emory. He attended public school, went to Prairie View College, and graduated from Lincoln University of Pennsylvania and Meharry Medical College.

ERNEST ESPOSITO lives in Brooklyn. He believes that God's greatest gift to us is our love for each other, and hopes that this gift of love will be treasured in our hearts and shared with all.

JODY FARRELL, 69, lives in the small coastal town of Inverness in northern California. The mother of seven grown children, she is actively involved in her community and is currently at work on a book of poems about her son's death from AIDS in 1989.

FRANCES FELDMAN has four grandchildren and four great-grandchildren. She lives with her daughter in Baltimore, loves animals, and has a small Yorkie to keep her company.

Born in Manhattan in 1914, MAE FERRIS has been living in Los Angeles since 1955. Her obsessions are gardening, reading, hard crossword puzzles, and easy piano pieces.

A retired pharmacist, SAM FISHMAN, 80, writes poetry and short stories. He has been married to his wife, Mildred, for 52 years. They live in Marlboro, New Jersey, and have two children, Larry and Janet, and five grandchildren, Mara, Lisa, David, Daniel, and Sara.

DOROTHY FRIEDMAN lives in West Hollywood, California. Now in her seventies, she is working on two books, one about her grandfather, a rabbi, and the other about a motorcycle trip she took with her younger son two years ago.

After the liberation of the Nazi camps, FRIEDA FRIEDMAN went to Sweden, where she met her husband, Salomon, and had two children, Rachel and Max. Now 75, she lives near her daughter in Mobile, Alabama, and thinks about the past a great deal.

In her first life, MATILDA FRIEDMAN taught special education for 30 years. Now she divides her time between New Jersey and upstate New York, where she writes poetry and works in her garden.

BRONIA GALMITZ GALLON has lived in four countries on three continents, learning to say "peace" in six languages. Her entire family was obliterated by the Nazis. She shares her hopes for universal peace with her son and daughter, who grew up to become her closest friends.

After a career of almost 40 years in Jewish communal work and Jewish tourism, VICTOR B. GELLER began to think of what he would leave to his grandchildren. The result was an autobiography, which he hopes will link them to a past they never knew. He lives in Forest Hills, New York.

DORIS B. GILL is the author of two self-help books, *My House to Yours* and *My Houseful of Hints*. A resident of Rossmoor, a retirement community in Walnut Creek, California, she writes articles for magazines and newspapers and is working on a second screenplay.

Veni, vidi, vici is the least common denominator of HERMAN G. GLICK's 77 years of mortality. He came from Ohio. He saw the Burma Road. He conquered the doldrums of domesticity. He lives in Merrick, New York.

Liberated by the Russian army in May 1945, ANNA GRUN married and emigrated to the United States. A retired R.N., she has two sons and six grandchildren.

ABNER PHOEBUS GRUNAUER was born in 1901 and died on

February 26, 1992. A reporter, writer, pundit, and scholar of international affairs, he was a great fun guy to live with, according to his wife, Phyllis. He was a lover of New York City, the Yankees, humanity, and her—most likely in that order, she says.

CAROLE HALL was born in England and lived for some years in Jamaica before moving to "the best of all possible worlds," the U.S.A., where she had a 25-year career in the hotel field. She lives in Vallejo, California.

LEE HAMES, 74, is married and has two children and two grandchildren. A navigator on a B-17 in World War II, he was shot down on his thirteenth mission and spent two years as a POW in Germany. He retired 10 years ago and moved to rural Wisconsin, where he enjoys reading, writing, and weaving.

LYNN HAMILTON, 70, is a writer, teacher of music and writing, mother of four, and grandmother of two. She lives in Novato, California, and runs her own businesses, Our Music Friends and Wordwatchers.

LINDA M. HARDIN has lived in West Palm Beach since her arrival in the United States in 1946. A former newspaper columnist, retired schoolteacher, and restaurant manager, she is widowed and has two children, Michele and Ralph. She writes freelance and as a hobby.

Born in New York, LYDIA HARTSOCK spent 10 years in Latvia, her father's native land. She now lives in Ashton, Maryland. A retired teacher of German and Russian, she translates a number of languages. Her hobbies are writing short stories, learning to paint watercolors, music, and gardening.

JACKYE HAVENHILL retired after more than 30 years of teaching and now lives with her husband on a farm in Denton, Texas. Her days are filled with gardening, horseback riding, enjoying her two daughters and five grandchildren, and writing.

SHIRLEE KRESH HECKER grew up in Brooklyn during the Depression, the youngest child of a loving Jewish family. She began writing stories so her grandchildren would learn about a time that has passed and customs that have been lost through the years. She and her husband live in Delray Beach, Florida.

ROSINA HEMSHORN is an over-the-hill retired farmer's wife who has always wanted to write about her life on the farm so her grandchildren would know about the hardships of the Depression. She lives in Woodburn, Oregon.

Born and raised on a Texas sharecropper's farm during the Depression, MABEL B. HERRING put herself through law school and worked for a major corporation until she retired in 1988. She lives in the San Fernando Valley and likes to read, write, and visit with her three children and five grandchildren.

NATHAN HOROWITZ, 85, was born on New York's Lower East Side and now lives at the Robison Jewish Home in Portland, Oregon, where his hobbies center around reading and writing. His sons have careers in academic history and journalism.

NANCY HOUGHTALING, of Bedford, Pennsylvania, left her native state in 1941 and returned happily in retirement with her husband in 1988. In the interim she taught in many states and in Germany, enjoying every year. She has four terrific daughters and five great grandchildren.

SISTER IRENE HOULE, Congregation of St. Agnes, Fond du Lac, Wisconsin, is 82. She worked in health services and had a second career as a teacher of high school English. Now retired, she enjoys keyboard, knitting, and freelance writing about her origins in Michigan's Copper Country.

A retired physician, **JUDITA HRUZA** lives in New Jesey.

DONALD L. HURON is the father of a fine son and daughter and has two exceptional granddaughters. None of this would have been possible without the active participation of Merita, his wise and lovely wife of 52 years.

Born in 1894, **HERBERT JAEDIKER** was art director of United Artists Motion Picture Corporation and designed the original Mickey Mouse watch. He played chess in Central Park and painted. He died on December 7, 1992, still lovable and good-humored, and is missed by his daughter, Ernestine Norsgaard.

MYRTLE E. JESKA, 69, lives in Hopkins, Minnesota. Writing has always been her passion. She has written a book about the Depression hardships of her immigrant family, who settled on a farm in Minnesota.

ELAINE JOHNSON lives in Brooklyn.

EDWARD L. JUSTIN was born in New York City in 1912. A graduate of New York University and the NYU School of Law, he served in the U.S. Army from 1942 to 1945. He now lives in San Diego.

Since retiring in 1981, **BEATRICE KALVER** has been attending writing workshops and has had a number of stories published in literary magazines, one of which even paid her! So in her old age she has started a new career.

PATTY KAYSER, née Tighe, was born in Brooklyn and now lives in Ormond Beach, Florida. She is compiling memoirs of family adventures in Turkey (1948–56), where her husband of 45 years, Bill, was a Pan Am maintenance supervisor, and where her three children were born.

Born in Japan, KATSUKO KETCHUM came to the United States in 1956. She has two daughters. Retired from the University of Rochester, where she worked in the administration, she has done freelance Japanese-English translations.

MIRA RYCZKE KIMMELMAN was born in the Free City of Danzig in 1923. A Holocaust survivor, she came to the U.S. in 1948 with her late husband, Max. She has two sons and two grandchildren, teaches in the Oak Ridge (Tennessee) Hebrew School, writes and lectures on the Holocaust, and is active in Hadassah.

NAT I. KORNHABER has been writing since age 12. One of his stories was published in his junior high school magazine, and another was anthologized in 1934. And now *Legacies*!

JANET D. LAKE and her husband of 50 years have a son, a daughter, and six grandchildren. After 15 years as a navy wife, she became a columnist for her town paper and was the first woman elected to the Board of Selectmen. She now lives in South Carolina and writes an occasional column for the *Myrtle Beach Sun News*.

DOROTHY WEINER LAVINE lives in Atlanta, where she was born. Her husband was killed in action during World War II. Now retired from her job as executive secretary to the president of Rich's, Inc., the South's largest department store, she enjoys friends, travel, music, and writing.

SHELDON LEIBOWITZ has just finished two motion picture screenplays, a comedy and an action-adventure story, and is the inventor of a television game show, *Hieroglyphics*, which has aired on Florida cable TV. He lives in Coconut Creek and does volunteer work for the American Cancer Society.

Born in Warsaw, MASHA LEON arrived in the United States via Vilno, Kovno, Moscow, Vladivostok, Japan, and Canada. She and her husband, Joseph, run a publishing firm. Mother of three daughters, grandmother of four, she also writes a weekly social column for the national English edition of the *Forward*.

SID LEVIN is a widower with three children, five grandchildren, and innumerable neighborhood children who claim him as a substitute grandparent. Since retiring, he has embarked on a joyful writing career and has completed a number of short stories and a novel.

BEN LEVINE is a painter, a sculptor, and a writer of essays, short stories, poetry, and a play that was produced Off-Broadway. He was also a member of the New Dramatists Committee.

ARLENE LEWIS retired from elementary school teaching in 1990 to devote herself to traveling and writing, particularly autobiographical anecdotes, to give her two sons, daughter, grandson, and four granddaughters a greater understanding of their ancestors. She and her husband, Marvin, live in Lynbrook, New York.

JOE LIEBERMAN, 68, lives in Tarrytown, New York. A retired teacher, he writes short stories and has begun a novel. His work has been published in *Short Story International*, *Story Art*, and *After Sixty*.

LOLA C. LITTLE and her husband, Sam, live in Port Angeles, Washington.

MARIAN MCHALE learned to read at six and became an ardent rider of books' magic carpet, which rescued her from abusive parents. She married, had four best-beloved children, taught school, and worked in a juvenile hall, where she hopes she made a difference in some lives.

DONALD K. MCKEE, professor emeritus of political science at Upsala College in East Orange, New Jersey, is the author of *The Strategies of Politics*. He served in Europe during World War II and was a national representative of the Textile Workers Union of America (CIO) for eight years.

Born in Georgia in 1921, EULA LEE MADDOX has two outstanding sons. She worked for the U.S. Signal Corps and for a lawbook publishing company, which she successfully sued for sex discrimination in a landmark case. Now retired, she enjoys writing, gardening, and digging up her family history.

PHYLLIS MAJOR, 74, has four sons and lives in Palm Desert, California. One marriage. One man. Fifty-one years.

ANTHONY MARINACCIO is married and has three children and three grandchildren. A retiree, he is from Larchmont, New York, and spends most of his leisure time reading novels and exercising.

LETHA S. MARSHALL retired in 1987 to the near-perfect seacoast climate of Oxnard, California, to swim in the sea and to write nonfiction.

HENRIETTA MAYER, 81, has two children and four grandchildren. She lived in Vienna from 1942 to 1949 and now lives in Santa Monica.

MARTHA GENE KEZER MERIDETH was born in 1921 in Okemah, Oklahoma, and has been married to Kenneth William Merideth for 51 years. They have two children, six grandchildren, and three great-grandchildren. A retired L.P.N., she is active in the Okemah Methodist Church, the DAR, and other civic organizations.

Born in 1920, LORE METZGER came to the U.S. after *Kristalnacht*, married her former rabbi, and taught Hebrew school for 47 years. She is active in several women's organizations and has been honored by the National Federation of Temple Sisterhood. Recently widowed, she lives in Monroe, New York, and has one son.

An unretired scientist, consulting ecologist, writer, videographer, and ice skater, EDWARD MILLER lives in the sticks of Michigan with his poet wife of 46 years, Hilde, and their watchcats, Max and Maxine. He has written three books, unpublished, and has enough ideas to keep writing for the next 75 years.

IRMA MOSS is a teacher (early childhood) and has two daughters. She wrote and produced plays for the New York City school system, writes a weekly "Kids Kolum" for *Gold Coast*, and has had her poetry anthologized.

Born, bred, and buttered in Boston, IRENE K. MURDOCK now lives in Sarasota, Florida. A retired executive with a degree in human services administration, she is proudly liberal in theology and politics.

WILLIAM J. NAGEL's father was killed in World War I, and his teenage mother died giving birth to him shortly thereafter. A retired Marine lieutenant colonel with 30 years of service, he has also been a self-employed cartographer, architectural engineer, and commercial artist. His wife sleeps in his arms every night.

ESTHER W. NELSON, 82, lives in Spokane. Her hobbies are reading, writing, and piano playing.

EDNA C. NORRELL began writing seven years ago, at age 65. She has four children, five grandchildren, and six great-grandchildren. Her hobbies are writing, music, walking, and traveling.

OSCAR OGMAN, 72, has two sons and five grandchildren. A widower who remarried two years ago, he is as happy as a lark. He lives in Brooklyn.

CECELIA GAVIN O'MEARA, 73, lives in Sacramento. A widow, she is retired and works as a volunteer and advocate for the frail elderly.

GEORGE M. OMI is married and has four children and three grandchildren. He lives in Mill Valley, California, and is president of Omi Lang Associates, a landscape architecture firm in San Francisco. His hobbies include tennis, skiing, writing, and bonsai.

BILL PEARSON, 68, grew up in Fillmore, California. During World War II he served in the U.S. Air Force in New Guinea and the Philippines.

A retired urban planner, he lives with his wife, Carol, in Las Cruces, New Mexico. They have two sons and a grandson.

BERNICE MOSBEY PEEBLES, 77, comes from upstate New York and has lived in New York City since 1955. A retired elementary school principal, she is now an educational consultant at the New York City Board of Education. She freely confesses her addiction to Scrabble.

A former director of a nursery school, MILDRED PENSAK is active in her local senior center in Queens, New York. She loves to write.

WALTER PIERCE, 68, is fortunate enough to have a fantastic wife who can tolerate a retiree who has decided to take up writing as a hobby.

WARREN PLATT was born in 1911 in a log cabin in the high mountains of southern Wyoming. In 1919 he moved to Medicine Bow. After he retired from Boeing in 1976, he and his wife, Betty, moved to Issaquah, Washington, where he discovered the joy of writing (stories and a science fiction novel).

CHARLES POLACHECK, 79, lives in Los Angeles with his wife, Jean. A retired television producer, he has three sons and three grandchildren who live in Austin.

NEIL QUINN lives in New York City.

JOANNE GOODYEAR RANDOLPH has been freelancing since 1982, when she was published in the "California Living" section of the *San Francisco Examiner-Chronicle*. She lives in Eugene, Oregon, with her husband of 40 years, Lee.

WILLIAM G. RAPACKA, 66, is a retired subcontractor and former laborer, teamster, ironworker, lather, prospector, and breeder of thorough-bred horses. Married for 41 years, he has two children and lives in south Florida. His hobbies are horse racing, coins, reading, and his granddaughter.

A former dancer, teacher of dance, and hospital administrative assistant, GERTRUDE REISS went back to college after her children finished their education. She has been writing since childhood.

LILLIAN GARFINKLE RHODES was born in Bayonne, New Jersey, a long time ago. She graduated from college a short time ago. She lives in Plantation, Florida, with her husband, Marty, and hopes to pass on to her children and grandchildren the legacy of laughter her father left to her.

FRANK RICHMAN, fingerprint technician, World War II veteran, and painting contractor, enjoys writing and is a volunteer teacher for a senior creative writing workshop. He lives in the Bronx.

DOUGLAS C. RIGG, 80, has been a seaman, prison warden, lawyer, and juvenile court judge. His story is respectfully dedicated to Hillary Rodham Clinton.

EVA-MARIA ROBINSON lives in Wichita, Kansas. At one time she wrote and sold stories to the romance market. Reading is her passion.

MYOR ROSEN, 76, was principal harpist with the New York Philharmonic under Leonard Bernstein and Zubin Mehta for 28 years. He is still active in his musical career and is working on his memoirs. He lives in Palm Beach Gardens, Florida.

BERTHA RUSS is retired and lives in Miami. A widow, she has one child, Joanna Russ, a well-known science fiction writer and professor of creative writing. Encouraged by her daughter, she has had some success with her poetry and short stories. She enjoys cards, especially bridge.

NAOMI RUSSO was a wife of 54 years, a mother of three, and an executive secretary at the Baltimore County Board of Education. From adolescence until her death in 1991, shortly after her seventy-eighth birthday, she dreamed of traveling the world and writing for publication. *Legacies* is indeed her legacy.

NORMAN SAGE worked at the University of Iowa Press. Now retired, he walks his dog, writes, and is a hobby printer.

Born in Riga, Latvia, in 1929, MIRIAM MARK SALPETER moved to Toronto in 1938 and to New York City in 1945. A professor of neurobiology at Cornell University, she is married and has two married daughters, Judy and Shelby, and three grandsons.

HANNAH SAMPSON, age negotiable, is a critic, essayist, columnist, college teacher, lecturer, consumer advocate, and mom. She is working on a book titled *How to Complain*.

BUSH SATTERFIELD has been in business as a motor fuel distributor in Conway, Arkansas, for the past 49 years. A former mayor of Conway, he was Governor Bill Clinton's legislative liaison during his first term. Married for 56 years, he has three daughters, a son, eight grandchildren, and three great-grandchildren.

BETTY SCHAMBACHER is making a new life in a small country town in Washington State. After too many years as a copy editor for a southern California newspaper, she now writes for herself, the sound of the running creek outside her window always in counterpoint to her typewriter.

Born in Dusseldorf in 1920, LOTTE SCHILLER got most of her oft-interrupted education in Palestine. In 1947 she and her architect husband,

Hans, moved to the U.S., where they raised three children and now enjoy their three grandchildren. Her extensive volunteer work has always centered on education.

FRANCES SCHMADEKE lives in California and writes for pleasure and therapy.

GLEN S. SCHREINER lives in The Woodlands, Texas.

ESTHER SCHUMAN lives in New York City.

NORBERT SEIF, 72, lives in a retirement community in south Florida. His newfound passion is writing poetry in sonnet form.

A retired veterinarian, ROBERT ODUM SHANNON, 65, lives in Covington, Georgia. He and his wife, Cora, have three children, Kay, Bob, and Ben, and one grandchild. He works on behalf of animal welfare, does a weekly column, "Animalines," for the local paper, and enjoys reading, sports, and writing.

ARN SHEIN's 25-year career as sports editor and columnist for the Gannett newspapers was ended by illness. Since 1984, he has written two books and has been widely published in major magazines and newspapers. He and his wife, Mary Lou, live in San Diego, as do their three married daughters and six grandsons.

MORRIS "MARTY" SILVERMAN is a lawyer and has three children, nine grandchildren, and four degrees. Drafted into the infantry during World War II, he was promoted to major and was later assigned to the War Crimes Commission at Nuremberg. He is now retired, runs a family charitable foundation, and is having a ball.

JUANITA H. SONGER, 70, lives in Ashland, Kentucky. She's a born substitute, into all sorts of things for a short time but no good on the long haul. She has a husband, a daughter, and son, and four cats.

MARCIA COHN SPIEGEL, 66, earned her master's from Hebrew Union College after the last of her five children entered junior high. Founder of the Creative Jewish Women's Alliance and the Alcohol/Drug Action Program of Jewish Family Service, she has co-authored three books. She has two grandchildren.

MARY JANE SPRAGUE has one husband, four children, and 12 grandchildren who have made life a joyful if sometimes bumpy ride. For 38 years she has called California home. She enjoys reading, writing, keeping in touch with her scattered family, and working on a community newspaper, which stimulates her creative juices.

A retired taxi driver, IRVING STERN is 71 and has been happily married for 46 years. His son is an obstetrician/gynecologist, and his daughter is an assistant principal in the New York City School system. He has five grandchildren and likes to work out, play shuffleboard, and travel.

RED STEVENSON was stolen by Gypsies when he was two years old. At age seven he was given, sold, or swapped to a family in the small rural Oklahoma town of Bixby, where he still lives, and where his company, Red S Aircraft Sales, is based.

CARRIE E. STEWART-HAYNES, 71, is overjoyed to see her children and grandchildren pursuing the family tradition: "Get that education!" She is organizing her late husband's writings on his 60 years as a model plane hobbyist and preparing her own writings of the past 25 years for publication.

EARLENE STONE taught elementary school for 24 years, survived the Depression, was a Wave during World War II, and married late. She has four daughters and five grandchildren. Retired now, she lives in Baton Rouge and plays around with creative stories for children.

SOPHIA STRONG first started writing at age 80. She is now finishing a book about her adventures working for the Red Cross in Okinawa in 1945 and then for U.S. Military Occupation in Japan. She taught art in the New York City schools for 25 years and also worked as a realtor and travel agent.

DORIS SULLIVAN has been teaching since 1947, when she received a degree from Northwestern State University in Natchitoches, Louisiana. She is presently a teacher of senior and sophomore English at Briarfield Academy in Lake Providence, Louisiana.

OUINA SUTTER inherited her sense of humor and her sense of responsibility from her Scotch father and German mother. Her life has given her a good education, three understanding husbands, and three great sons. She spent five years in the Peace Corps in her seventies. Now in her eighties, she continues her volunteer work.

WANDA L. SUTTON lives in Arizona.

For 20 years BETTY EDGEMOND SWORDS has been a cartoonist for *Redbook*, the *Saturday Evening Post*, *Ladies Home Journal*, and other publications, and has taught many college courses on "humor power." She and her retired geologist husband, Leonard, live in Denver, as do their two sons, Rick and Steve.

Born in Hungary, ELIZABETH SZOKE studied in Germany, Austria, and France before fleeing Hitler with her husband and six-year-old daughter. The family eventually settled in New York City, where she taught languages at Riverdale Country School. Since retiring, she has taught English to immigrants as a volunteer.

GERTRUDE M. TAYLOR taught as a reading specialist and a Fulbright scholar in England. A published freelance writer, she lives in a retirement community in the hills of northern New Jersey. She is active in volunteer work, her church, and Delta Kappa Gamma, an international honor society.

ELIZABETH THOMSON, word lover and freelance writer, lives in Tallahassee. After graduating from Florida State College for Women (now Florida State University) in 1927, she presented one-woman shows of Uncle Remus stories in the New York City area. She taught oral interpretation of literature at FSU for 42 years.

LOTTIE TISH, 74, lives in Tallahassee but is always ready to travel. A widow, she has four children, eight grandchildren, and two great-grandchildren. Last year she learned to swim and dance, and celebrated her birthday in a helicopter that landed on a glacier in Alaska.

POLLY TOOKER lives in the San Francisco area with her geologist husband of 47 years. Her home-based typing and editing service has spanned five decades. She attends writing and stitchery classes, volunteers in community projects, and brags to everyone within earshot about her three small grandchildren.

ESTHER TRIGGER lives in Walnut Creek, California. She has four children and eight grandchildren: Levi, Mia, Kaitlyn, Matt, Kenton, Cole, Carlee, and Shannon.

A retired teacher and social worker, INEZ UNRUH, 68, lives in Youngtown, Arizona. She has one daughter, one granddaughter, and one grandson. Her hobbies are writing and travel.

GILDA vanSAND, née Molina, was born in New York City 70 years ago. She worked as a censor during World War II, and in advertising, marketing, and bilingual education. Her husband is of Danish descent, and her two children could say the amenities in four languages before they were six.

DAVID WEIXEL was a film editor for NBC before retiring in 1981. He now enjoys sculpting in wood and stone. He and his wife have a married son and daughter and three lovely grandchildren, and they all live in Manhattan.

LEONARD M. WEYANT, 73, spent his youth on his father's farm in the Hudson Highlands, Fort Montgomery, New York. He is retired and lives in Punta Gorda, Florida.

A retired master teacher, ADAIR WIESS lives in the Florida Panhandle with her husband, Dick, amidst 12 acres of woodland shared with deer, raccoons, squirrels, birds, and a stray dog. She is the mother of three daughters and the author of more than 75 published stories and articles.

EVA BELL WILLIAMS, 81, is busy and active at the Southeast Center in Englewood, New Jersey. Her Cherokee grandfather is gone now, but she is still welcomed at the rabbi's as a member of the family on holidays and special occasions.

HENRY WILLIAMSON was discharged from the army a few months after the liberation of Dachau. He died on April 6, 1993, in a plane crash in Wyoming, his home state for 45 years, and is mourned by his wife of 52 years, his three children and three grandchildren, and a host of friends.

RUTH C. WINTLE, 71, lives in La Mesa, California. She has three living children, eight grandchildren, and four great-grandchildren. A retired R.N., she enjoys spending time with her grandchildren, sewing, and playing the organ. Her aspiration is to be the Grandma Moses of the literary field.

JOHN D. WOODWARD, 69, is retired from the U.S. Air Force. His hobbies are writing and U.S. Air Corps history. He lives in Largo, Florida, and has three sons, one grandson, and two granddaughters.

SYBIL WYNER lives in New Jersey.

MANUEL ZAPATA, 62, is a retired New York City high school teacher. He now devotes his time to writing poetry in Spanish and English, and likes to travel with his wife between their son and daughter.

TREVA ZOELLNER, 78, lives in Oklahoma City. For her mind, she studies languages. For her spirit, she tries to help other people along the way. Six days a week she watches her diet carefully; the seventh, she goes for broke. She sings in a choir and is writing a book about her life.

MOLLIE ZUCKER belongs to an international biking club, Nature Friends, that takes periodic two-week trips into the Sierras, their provisions carried in by mule. She also enjoys listening to music, reading, and folk dancing.